It's Easy To Bluff...
Playing Guitar

by Joe Bennett

London/N... ...agen/Madrid/Tokyo

Exclusive Distributors:
Music Sales Limited
8/9 Frith Street, London W1D 3JB, England.
Music Sales Corporation
257 Park Avenue South, New York, NY10010, USA.
Music Sales Pty Limited
120 Rothschild Avenue, Rosebery, NSW 2018, Australia.

Order No. AM973962
ISBN 0-7119-9349-1

Written by Joe Bennett.
Edited by Sorcha Armstrong.
Musical examples by Richard Barrett.
Music engraving by Digital Music Art.

Book design by Phil Gambrill.
Cover design by Michael Bell Design.
Illustrations by Andy Hammond.

Specialist guitar pictures supplied courtesy of Balafon Books
Text photographs courtesy of London Features International, Redferns,
The Kobal Collection and Pictorial Press.
Chord photographs by George Taylor.

Printed in the United Kingdom.

It's Easy To Bluff...
Playing Guitar

by Joe Bennett

Wise Publications
London/New York/Paris/Sydney/Copenhagen/Madrid/Tokyo

Contents

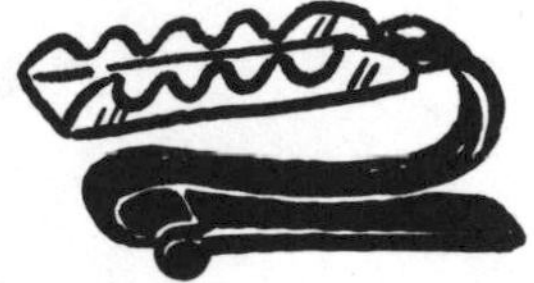

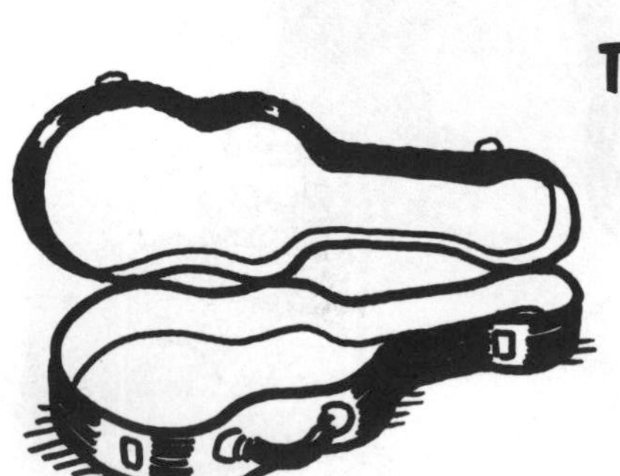

It's Easy To Bluff... Acoustic Guitar

It's Easy To Bluff...

Blues Guitar

John Lee Hooker: the original bluffer manages to get away with using 3 chords, a couple of string-bends and some serious frowning. **Take note!**

Introduction

Every guitarist loves the blues. It's easy to get to grips with, fun to play and (most importantly) it's a *great way to look cool.* Would Robert Johnson have sold his soul to the Devil in return for a pointy death-metal super-axe? Would Jake and Elwood have been icons for a generation if they'd been called the Jazz Fusion Brothers?

It's fairly easy to bluff your way at blues if you know a few simple tricks. For example, *don't* enjoy yourself (or if you do, don't be *seen* to enjoy yourself). This is serious, mystical music, and if you let your bluffer's facade crack for a second, people might find out that you're just playing two badly-fretted chords and some wildly inaccurate string bends.

Have an opinion, and stick to it whatever anyone says. **John Lee Hooker** only knows two scale shapes and doesn't play in time? That may be true, but he's the man, he's the dude, he was there at the start, you can hear his influence in every note **Hendrix** ever played...

Also, it's essential that you learn the language properly. Words like 'feel', 'tone', 'classic', 'authentic', 'man' and 'touch' can be combined in almost any order to make you a truly articulate blues bluffer.

Try This...

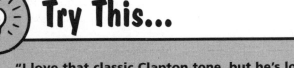

"I love that classic Clapton tone, but he's lost the touch. He used to have such an authentic feel, man".
Or how about...
"I loved Clapton's feel, but he's lost the authentic tone. He used to have such a classic touch, man."

This is 100% bluffer's gobbledegook, and best of all, anyone who disagrees "just doesn't understand the blues".

It's Easy To Bluff... Blues Guitar is a complete handbook for the bogus bluesman. Not only does it explain all the essential riffs, techniques, chords and scales you need to bluff through any gig from Louisiana to Luton, it also tells you what to wear, which albums to name-drop, and what gear to use if you're going to impress everyone in the bar afterwards (and if you were thinking of ordering a vodka and lime, put this book down now - there's no hope for you).

The Story of the Blues or 'Who to name-drop, and when'

Historians disagree amongst themselves about exactly when the blues began, but let them argue it out - anyone who's managed to get a full-time paid gig as a blues historian is a better bluffer than you or I anyway.

Early Influences

To appear knowledgeable about your blues background, you only need to drop a few names. One is that of **Robert Johnson**. Although he was by no means the first recording blues guitarist, he's almost certainly the earliest one whose licks we all steal. Bottleneck triplets? Robert was there first. Riffs changing with the chords? Bob again. From a bluffing point of view, he's a good history subject to choose because his convenient early death means you don't have too much studying to do.

The other essential names to slide subtly into conversation are those of the even earlier bluesmen (**Blind Blake**, **Blind Lemon Jefferson**, **Charley Patton**). It doesn't matter that you've never heard any music by these guys - none of the assembled company will have either, so you're on safe ground bluff-wise. If another bluffer tries to get in there with a Robert Johnson reference, just go one better with a phrase such as "yeah, Johnson was cool, but all his bottleneck licks are straight steals from Charley Patton."

The Electric players

After the early popular bluesmen - primarily Johnson and **Aaron 'T-bone' Walker** - a new wave of players arrived in the 1940s-50s. **Albert King**, **Muddy Waters**, **BB King** and **John Lee Hooker** were all electric players, so they're the earliest group of guitarists you can confidently cite as an 'influence' when you play that pentatonic lick you learned from Bon Jovi.

As the '50s and '60s progressed, the guitar sounds got dirtier and the players more flamboyant. **Albert Collins**, **Freddie King** and **Buddy Guy** held the torch for a decade or so, and although they're not as essential name-drop material as the previous generation, they did bridge the gap until...

...1965, when the British arrived. **John Mayall's Bluesbreakers**, **Cream**, and early **Fleetwood Mac** pioneered more powerful electric blues, aiding the blues/R&B/rock crossover that was complete by the time everyone started describing **Led Zeppelin** as a rock band.

Jimmy Page - "blues tone with a rock feel". Or should that be "rock tone with a blues feel"?

Here's another great conversation to bluff your way through. If someone describes **Jimmy Page** as a great rock guitarist, you can take the opposite stance - "man, every lick he ever played was pure blues - he just had a rock tone". You could equally defend the opposite viewpoint, of course, as long as you mix the words up a bit - "man, every lick he played was pure rock - he just had a blues feel".

Most guitarists are **Hendrix** fans to some extent, so there's little point in dropping Jimi into conversation unless you're sure of your ground. You could try some ambiguous references to his predecessors along the lines of "there's more **Muddy Waters** in his playing that most people think, you know?" but generally, steer clear of bluffsville when it comes to Hendrix.

Of the sixties greats, Clapton and Hendrix are the two about whom you need to know the most anecdotes, but it helps to have a smattering of **Peter Green** (grew really long fingernails, went a bit off the rails, comeback not as great as we hoped) and **Rory Gallagher** (wore a plaid shirt, hated effects, used Strat/AC30 combination until his death in 1995).

Rory Gallagher - "plaid shirt"

The New Generation

As the 1980s came along, many guitar players looked towards big hair and even bigger guitar sounds. A few players continued to turn out 'authentic' blues, but with an unprecedented degree of technical skill.

Robben Ford, **Stevie Ray Vaughan**, **Jeff Healey** and **Gary Moore** all produced polished, slick blues albums throughout the decade. Despite their contemporary status, it's fine for bluffing guitarists to name-drop these guys, as long as you obey the lineage rule; "man, SRV had that something - you can really hear his pain in those **Albert Collins** licks he adapted. Of course, Albert never left the house without the Lightnin' Hopkins songbook..."

Right now, we're in a bit of a blues drought. Many of the classic players are still around (**Clapton**, **Johnny Winter**, **BB King**, **Peter Green**) but there are few contemporary players bringing blues guitar playing to the mainstream record buyer. And if a great new player does come along and you've never heard of them, it's always safe to bluff your way through with this handy emergency bluffspeak phrasebook below.

Bluff Phrasebook

Use this handy table to compare any new player with any classic player. Simply mix and match the words shown here; depending on the number of guitarists you know, this can be used to create over 16 million credible blues phrases.

New Player			
	touch	is	genius
	pick technique	is pretty much	the best
	feel	isn't	classic
	sound	ain't	damn good
	style	sure is	hot
	album	sounds	derivative
	lineage	has gotta be	from God
	guitar playing	always was	the real thing

For example...

Clapton's - touch - sure is - the best

check out	the	Old Player	influence
feel	the classic		phrasing
listen out for	the stompin'		lick/s
you can really hear	that uncanny		spirit
you gotta feel	that unbelievable		legacy
did you get	the dude's		feel
I love	the obvious		echoes
do you buy	the amazing		style solo

you can really hear - the classic - **Muddy Waters** - legacy

The late **Jimi Hendrix**. Be careful what you say about him - you're likely to be outbluffed.

The Players

Bite-size biogs

Blues purists will consider it blasphemy to have a player's entire life summarised in one page, but in reality, you can bluff your way through with a surprisingly small amount of knowledge. In this chapter you'll find an instant guide to six top blues guitarists.

Remember that these aren't necessarily the most important or famous players - we haven't included **Gary Moore** or **Muddy Waters**, for example - but they are the names which crop up most frequently in blues gig-speak.

For each artist, I've included some basic **biographical information**, notes on **playing style**, plus (most importantly) which **techniques** you should steal in order to abet your bluffing career. Of course, you have to know the **gear** they used - remember that equipment trainspotters are everywhere and could pounce at any time.

To save you from having to wade through a truckload of albums, I've also picked out one **essential album** for you to mention (not necessarily the best-known - it can sometimes pay dividends to bluff your way by showing you listen to the obscure stuff). If you're actually asked to prove that you've heard the artist, you'd be stuck without the quick and easy '**finest moment**' reference.

Finally, because blues-speak can get pretty dogmatic, it's useful to have a few oven-ready opinions up your sleeve. For each player, I've included an 'instant opinion' (usually ambiguous enough to cover all situations) and an 'acceptable criticism'. If you're cool enough to intelligently criticise one of the greats, your status as a blackbelt blues bluffer is assured.

15 Robert Johnson

HISTORY AND BACKGROUND:

Born 8th May 1911, Hazlehurst Mississippi. Influenced by early blues pioneers such as **Blind Lemon Jefferson, Son House, Lonnie Johnson**. Went on to influence pretty much every electric blues and rock player, directly or indirectly, especially 1960s electric blues revolution (his songs were covered by **The Rolling Stones, Captain Beefheart**, and **Cream**). **Peter Green** recorded *The Robert Johnson Songbook* in 1998, an album which exclusively featured Johnson cover versions.

Recorded 32 songs in his lifetime (though there are rumours of a mythical extra 'undiscovered' track which is the blues bluffer's Holy Grail). Disappeared for some time and eventually re-emerged a much improved guitar player. Legend has it that he sold his soul to the Devil in return for his fretboard skills. Died 16th August 1938, almost certainly murdered. Conflicting stories abound that he was stabbed by a woman or a jealous husband, given poisoned whisky, or simply paid his debt to Beelzebub.

PLAYING STYLE:

Acoustic blues, fingerstyle and some bottleneck, using a variety of tunings, most related to open G (DGDGBD) with or without capo. Often plays licks in unison with the voice.

TECHNIQUES TO STEAL:

Use capos with open G tunings on guitars with high action. Try raising the first string to top G in open G (DGDGBG) with or without capo. Unison voice/guitar licks. Play triplets as downstrokes on the top two strings while moving the slide down one fret at a time for intros/outros. Use thumb for four-to-the-bar bass notes accompaniment and fingers for lead licks or chords on the top three strings.

GEAR:

Gibson L1 Acoustic Guitar, bottleneck, voice.

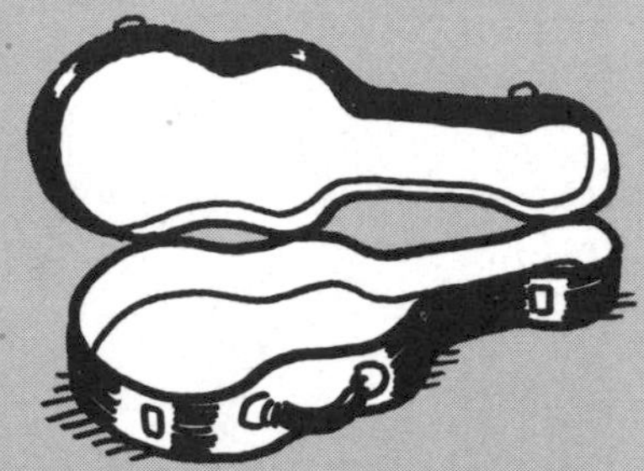

BLUFFER'S ALBUM:

Entire collected works are usually available on single CD compilations. Anything with 'rarities' or 'unreleased recordings' in the title is obviously more impressive to other bluffers.

FINEST MOMENT:

Biggest hit in his lifetime was 'Terraplane Blues' but the main accompaniment riff and lead work on 'Crossroads Blues' is arguably his most influential track.

INSTANT OPINION:

"He just had such an amazing sense of timing, y'know? The way he messes with bar-lengths to suit what was in his heart - no-one's bettered that, before or since."

ACCEPTABLE CRITICISM:

The *only* criticism allowed is that he died too young. Anything else... well, you might as well accuse the Pope of not washing his whites properly.

John Lee Hooker

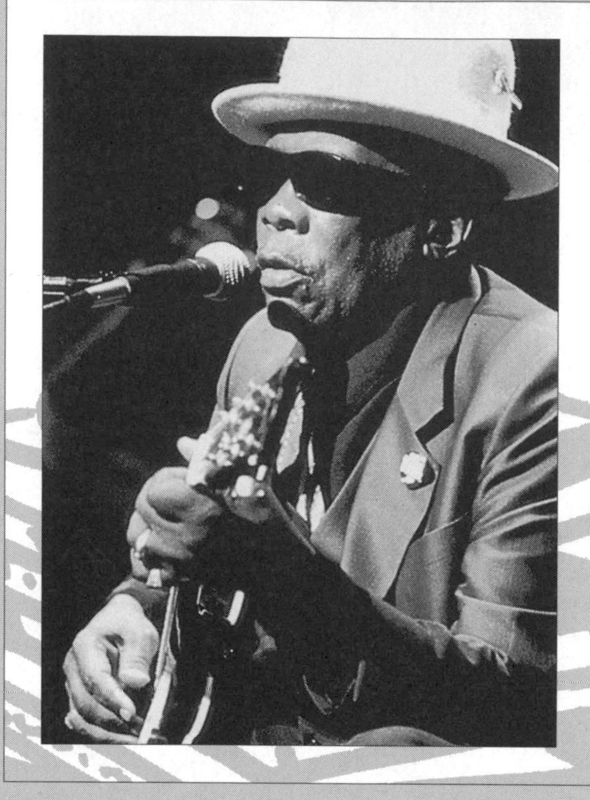

HISTORY AND BACKGROUND:

According to his passport, he was born 22nd August 1917 (although he says that he was actually born in 1920, and lied about his age in order to get an army uniform to attract girls). Even though he started recording fairly late (1949), his solo career has now clocked up over 50 years. Early user of electric guitar as accompaniment. Recorded a series of classic electric blues/R&B tracks 1948-59 under various names; Johnny Lee, Johnny Williams, The Boogie Man, Texas Slim, Delta John, and Birmingham Sam and his Magic Guitar (note: add these to your list of players to name-drop). Has been 'rediscovered' at various times, most famously in 1980 when he appeared in *The Blues Brothers*, and then again in 1989 when he recorded *The Healer* with musical guests including **Carlos Santana** and **Bonnie Raitt**. Talks exclusively in unremittingly meaningless bluff-speak. Sample quotes; **"When Adam and Eve first saw each other, that's when the blues started"... "The kind of guitar I want to play is mean, mean, mean licks"... "Blues is no colour; blues is a human being. The blues, you can't see, you hear the blues"...**

PLAYING STYLE:

Responsible for the shuffle electric blues style known as 'Boogie' - basically Delta blues with a stronger pulse. Plays in the key of E a *lot*. Plenty of bass string accompaniment, with riff-based sections between vocal phrases. Throws in bars of 3/4, 5/4, 7/4 etc with gay abandon in order to make the music fit the lyrics.

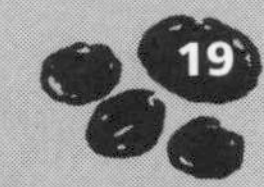

TECHNIQUES TO STEAL:

Double-stop sliding licks in E. Standard E-A-G blues backing (see page 30). Keeping time by stamping your foot. Making up the lyrics as you go along. Mumbling.

GEAR:

Semi-solid f-hole guitars, often (but not exclusively) Gibson ES-335s. Reportedly 'unfussy' about amp choice.

BLUFFER'S ALBUM:

Hooker 'N Heat (1971) was a collaboration (the first of many) with Canned Heat, who have worked with 'The Hook' several times since. Best choice, though, is any compilation of his 1950s stuff.

FINEST MOMENT:

First recording 'Boogie Chillun' (1948) is most significant because it influenced so many, though 'I'm in the Mood' and 'Dimples' also feature classic Hook-isms.

INSTANT OPINION:

"There was some great stuff on *The Healer*, but why did they have to add all that big 1980s production to The Hook's sound?"

ACCEPTABLE CRITICISM:

1997 album *Don't Look Back* was repetitive and uninspired compared to previous work. But **Van Morrison** produced it, so it's OK to blame Van rather than The Hook himself.

BB King

HISTORY AND BACKGROUND:

Born Riley B King in Mississippi, Sept 16, 1925. (The 'BB' was adopted in the 1950s and stands for 'Blues Boy'). Influenced by classic bluesmen **Blind Lemon Jefferson** and **T-Bone Walker**, and jazzers **Charlie Christian** and **Django Reinhardt**. After several years spent busking in Memphis, he was asked to play on **Sonny Boy Williamson**'s KWEM radio show. In true bluff-referential style his first hit was a classic blues cover - BB's version of **Lowell Fusion**'s 'Three O'Clock Blues' topped the R&B charts at the time. Since then, he's been constantly recording as a solo artist, plus a predictable level of classic collaborations - **Buddy Guy**, **Albert Collins**, **John Lee Hooker**, **Eric Clapton** etc. He's almost certainly responsible for inventing blues/rock vibrato technique. Possibly the most influential electric blues player of all time.

PLAYING STYLE:

The man is smooth, very smooth. His entire lead style is based on bends and vib, and he rarely plays rhythm - he once told **U2**'s Edge **"I'm not too good with chords"**. Can play a complete gig with the guitar miles out of tune, using super-accurate bends to get each string exactly up to pitch.

TECHNIQUES TO STEAL:

Play a three-note lick like it was the last thing you were ever going to play. BB always 'says more with less'. Stay within absolutely safe minor pentatonic box shapes, but play them slowly, deliberately, and accurately. Don't go any lower than the 10th fret, staying beyond the 12th most of the time. Oh, and wince with a combination of joy and pain when you bend a high note.

GEAR:

Since 1958, he's played Gibson ES335s, with which he's become synonymous. He always names his guitars 'Lucille' after a girl who was the unwitting cause of a bar fight in 1949.

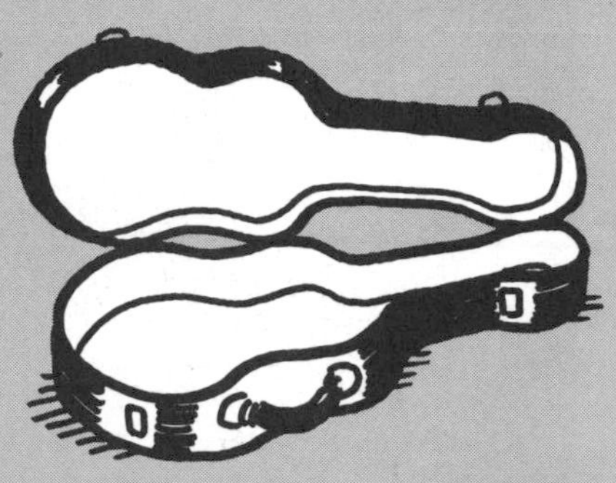

BLUFFER'S ALBUM:

He's at his best when he's playing a gig, so any live album will do. Mention *Blues Is King '67* and *Live at the Regal '65*.

FINEST MOMENT:

Arguable, but if you bring up his 1969 hit 'The Thrill is Gone' you should be fine – BB is massive amongst guitarists, but you'll rarely find one who can name more than three tracks he's recorded.

INSTANT OPINION:

"He's no Stevie Ray speed-wise, but he can sure make Lucille sing what's in his heart."

ACCEPTABLE CRITICISM:

Don't even think about it.

Jimi Hendrix

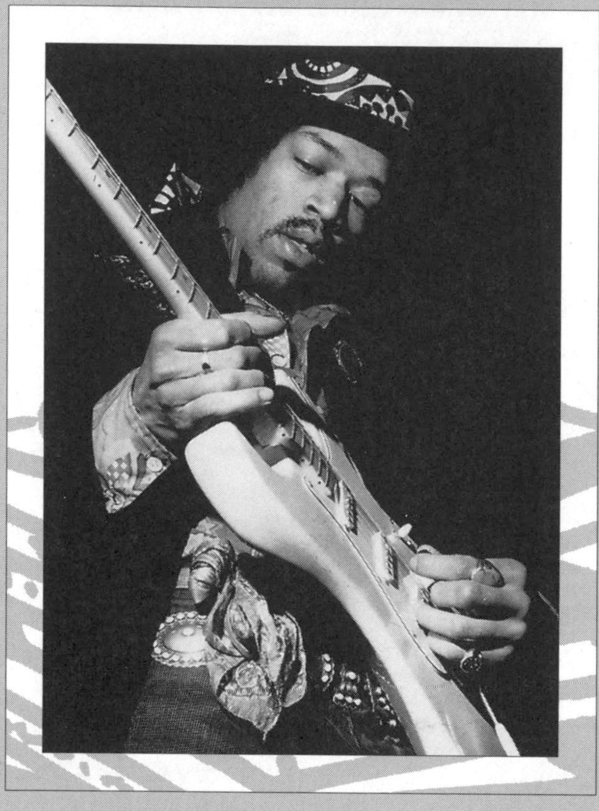

HISTORY AND BACKGROUND: Born 27th November 1942. Allegedly had his name changed by his father from Johnny Allen Hendrix to James Marshall Hendrix. Primarily perceived as a rock player, but his background, technique and note choices are typical blues. Influenced by **BB King** and **Muddy Waters**, among others. Worked with various soul/R&B acts, including **Little Richard**, **Curtis Knight**, **Ike Turner**, until he was 'discovered' by Animals' bassist **Chas Chandler**, who brought him over to the UK.

The 'Jimi Hendrix Experience' was formed in 1966 with bass player **Noel Redding** and drummer **Mitch Mitchell**. Early hits eventually led to discovery by US audiences. Notable live gigs included Monterey Pop Festival, Woodstock and the Isle of Wight Festival (the latter two occurred after Redding left in 1969). Died in his sleep, choking on his own vomit, on 18th September 1970.

PLAYING STYLE: Pyrotechnic is the word. Outrageous swooping bends, whammy bar dives, controlled (and uncontrolled) feedback, all played Very Loud Indeed. His more laid-back material features subtle grace notes using hammer-ons, and distortion dynamics controlled by plectrum picking. Made great use of the minor pentatonic scale, but solos and riffs also featured major pentatonic, Mixolydian and natural minor scales. Some techniques (e.g. thumb used to fret bass strings) relied on the fact that he had very large hands.

TECHNIQUES TO STEAL: Any of the crowd-pleasing flash techniques (e.g. playing guitar behind your head, setting guitar alight, lewd behaviour with whammy bar etc) are viewed as sacrilegious by most aficionados, so use these with care. However, any technical tricks are up for grabs - try playing trills while moving the whammy bar; moving the wah-wah while playing rapid lead licks; muted 'unpitched' chords used as a percussive effect...). Just don't admit that it's Jimi you're stealing from!

GEAR: Usually played a right-handed Strat strung left-handed and hung upside-down, through Marshall amps. Also used a variety of stompboxes, modified by English FX guru Roger Mayer. (Name drop opportunity here!)

BLUFFER'S ALBUM: Start with the 1967 Experience album *Axis: Bold As Love*, but eventually you've really got to buy them all (stay away from early-60s archive re-releases though - Jimi was rarely more than a rhythm-playing session man on these recordings).

FINEST MOMENT: Musically, it's probably his cover of Dylan's 'All Along The Watchtower' (exceptional control of bends, consummate tone, beautiful phrasing). However, bluffers would do well to acquaint themselves with his legendary 'Star Spangled Banner' live recording, which uses the guitar to emulate rockets firing, bombs dropping etc. It sounds utterly awful, but of course you must never be seen to admit this.

INSTANT OPINION:
"God came to earth and walked among us for a few short years".

ACCEPTABLE CRITICISM: Possibly, just possibly, you might tentatively suggest that the guitar could just maybe have been slightly out of tune during 'The Star Spangled Banner'?... (HOW DARE YOU MOCK THE MASTER - GET BACK UNDER WHATEVER STONE YOU CRAWLED OUT FROM, YOU REVOLTING PIECE OF WORTHLESS SLIME etc).

!!?#

Eric Clapton

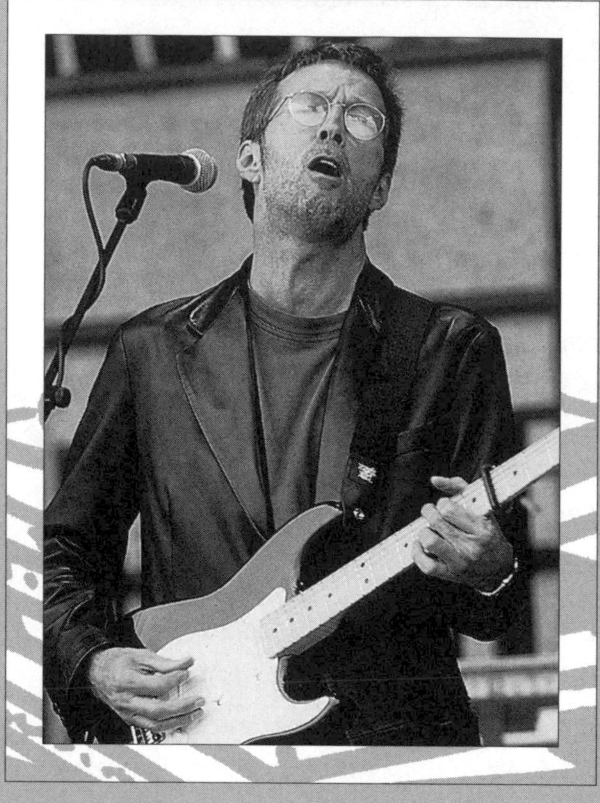

HISTORY AND BACKGROUND: Born 30th March 1945, Surrey, England. Perhaps the Godfather of all blues bluffers. Influenced (naturally) by **Muddy Waters** and **Robert Johnson**, and was hugely influential himself, not least because of the amount of black blues music that he took to a white rock audience. Joined the **Yardbirds** in 1963, but left quickly, his reason being that their debut single wasn't 'pure blues'. As a result ended up with blues purist **John Mayall**, then left after 15 months to form **Cream** with **Ginger Baker** (drums) and **Jack Bruce** (bass). This was the first blues 'power trio', pre-dating **Hendrix** by more than a year. Outrageous blues-rock guitar antics followed for four albums and numerous US and UK gigs, until the group split in 1968. Formed a succession of 'anonymous' bands, allegedly in an attempt to hide from the guitar-hero label (**Blind Faith**, **Delaney** and **Bonnie**, **Derek & The Dominoes**) although the public always seemed to find out that Eric was behind these within a matter of weeks. Became a solo artist in 1970 and has concentrated on more mellow material ever since.

PLAYING STYLE: They don't call him 'slowhand' for nothing. Since Cream he's calmed down considerably, relying on tone and phrasing to make his long, sustained bent notes carry a platinum-selling tune. He's no mean fingerstyle player either, as demonstrated on the 1992 'MTV Unplugged' album.

TECHNIQUES TO STEAL: Hey, why not play slowly? Slow bends, slow vibrato, slow tempos. The only rapid thing about our Eric is his CD sales. It's also worth trying out playing solos using the neck pickup with just a little overdrive - the resulting 'Woman Tone' is Clapton's blues trademark.

GEAR: Used a Les Paul with the Bluesbreakers, then an SG and 335 with Cream, but arrived in Stratsville in 1970 and has stayed there ever since. First Strat, known as 'Blackie', was retired after 20 years of use; he now plays his own Fender signature model. Used a small Marshall 45 watt combo in Bluesbreaker years; full-tilt Marshall stacks with Cream; now mostly favours Soldano amps.

BLUFFER'S ALBUM: Without a doubt, the album to gain maximum cred with is *John Mayall's Bluesbreakers Featuring Eric Clapton*, known to purists as The Beano album because Eric is shown on the front cover reading the comic. But anyone interested in blues-rock crossover should check out Cream's *Fresh Cream* and *Disraeli Gears*. Some of his solo material is wonderful, but less fashionable than these earlier recordings.

FINEST MOMENT: The solo from the 12-bar-derived epic 'Sunshine Of Your Love' - the first phrase is the main melody from 1950s crooner standard 'Blue Moon', but played with blues timing so it's almost unrecognisable.

INSTANT OPINION: "He's at his best live - never plays a solo the same two nights running."

ACCEPTABLE CRITICISM:
Bizarrely, the more success Eric has, and the more sensitive his playing becomes, the more the critics (and the blues trainspotters) want to criticise him. However, you can't beat them, so you might as well join them - pretend that anything post-1970 is 'commercial sell-out' and that his playing's gone downhill since he left the Bluesbreakers.

Stevie Ray Vaughan

HISTORY AND BACKGROUND: Born 3rd October 1954. Younger brother of Jimmie Vaughan, guitarist/vocalist with **The Fabulous Thunderbirds**. Influenced by electric blues players including **BB King**, **Lonnie Mack**, and **Albert Collins**. Formed band 'Double Trouble' in 1981 (the band were named after an **Otis Rush** song) and their demo album *Texas Flood* (recorded in only 3 days) so impressed the record company that it was released without any of the tracks being re-recorded. Three other studio albums followed over the next six years, plus one live recording, each demonstrating the band's obsessive attention to quality control. Luminaries such as **Clapton**, **John Lee Hooker**, and **BB King** admired Stevie Ray's skill and artistry during his lifetime, and he even guested on **David Bowie**'s recording 'Let's Dance' in 1983. The blues world mourned when he was killed in a helicopter crash on August 27th, 1990.

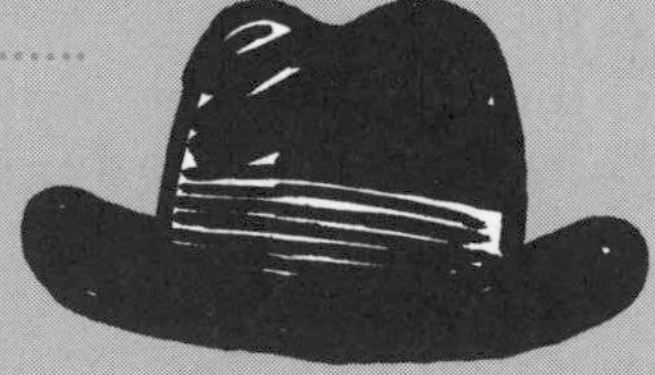

PLAYING STYLE: Extremely fluid up-tempo electric blues, mainly in open-string keys (mainly E, A and B, but de-tuning the whole guitar a semitone). Even his slower tracks featured astonishingly rapid improvising in places. His playing features trills, slides, bends and 'rakes' (skimming across one or more strings before picking the note), and gives more than a cursory nod to Hendrix.

TECHNIQUES TO STEAL: In a word - legato. Use hammer-ons and pull-offs like you're on a commission for every one you play. You might like to throw in some wide vibrato and plenty of 'static' bends (bend up one string, then hold the bend while you play a different note on the next string). Also, try switching pickups every 16 bars or so during a solo.

GEAR: Various Strats, including a famous early '60s model nicknamed 'Lenny', with which he recorded the instrumental of the same name. Started mainly using Fender Vibroverb amps, though in later years began to favour Dumble heads and even Marshalls.

BLUFFER'S ALBUM: You might want to start with the band's debut *Texas Flood*. As there are only four albums, you should really have all of them, and besides, it's bluffing suicide if all you have is an SRV greatest hits compilation.

FINEST MOMENT: In true blues referential style, some of his greatest playing occurs on the band's instrumental cover version of Hendrix's 'Little Wing', but the open-string licks in 'Pride And Joy' are exemplary.

INSTANT OPINION (stolen from John Lee Hooker): **"He was one of the greatest musicians who ever lived, and it was a great loss to the world, to the blues, and to me."**

ACCEPTABLE CRITICISM: Poor choice of inter-gig transport.

Emergency backup bluffs

Here are some bluffing basics on a further four players, just in case you need additional reference to prove your depth of knowledge.

1. Kenny-Wayne Shepherd

Included because he's the newest guitarist on the scene – mentioning KWS can guarantee instant cred with younger blues dudes. Strat player, and the youngest Fender endorsee to have his own guitar designed for him.

Debut album 'Ledbetter Heights' launched onto a largely desolate US blues market. **SRV** inspired Kenny to play blues, but like many a good bluffer, he sensibly now cites the obligatory **Muddy Waters**, **Albert Collins**, **Howlin' Wolf** etc. as influences.

2. Freddie King

Influential Texan electric blues player - bridges gap between **Howlin' Wolf/Muddy Waters** era of the 40s/50s and electric blues explosion of mid-60s. Gibson semi-solid player - used ES-335s, ES-345s and ES-355s. Used plastic thumbpick and steel fingerpick to pick out melodies.

Early user of distorted tone. Some players may know his 1970s recordings, on which **Clapton** guested. Brave bluffers should fearlessly compare these unfavourably with his '50s and '60s material, including the singles 'Hideaway' and 'Lonesome Whistle Blues'.

3. Blind Lemon Jefferson

Blues pioneer - essential to know if you're going to outbluff a **Robert Johnson** fan. Made his first blues recording 1925 – i.e. earlier than almost anyone else – and died four years later. Played acoustic fingerstyle, using alternating thumb technique, creating mix of gospel, blues and country.

Had a chauffeur who drove him everywhere because he was genuinely blind (that's Blind Lemon who was genuinely blind, not the chauffeur). Hits included 'Pneumonia Blues', 'Black Snake Blues' and 'Matchbox Blues' (covered by **Carl Perkins** whose version was, in turn, covered by The Beatles).

Mysteriously, no guitarist ever seems to own any Blind Lemon Jefferson recordings, so you can usually talk knowledgeably about tone, feel and technique without fear of contradiction.

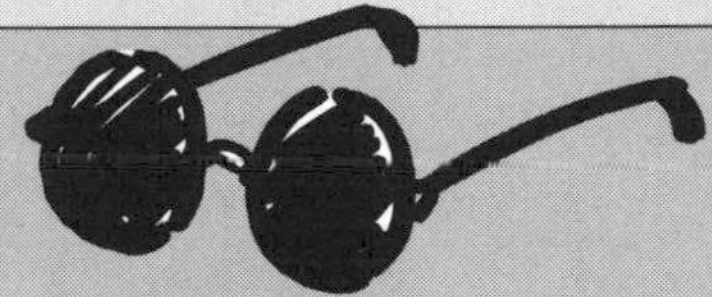

4. Peter Green

The most arcane of the UK blues-rock players. Started well, even showing signs of embryonic bluffing skills by name-checking **Freddie** and **BB King** as influences.

Joined **John Mayall**'s Bluesbreakers in 1966, replacing the departed **Clapton**. Left Bluesbreakers (leaving a space for a young **Mick Taylor**, later of **Rolling Stones** fame) to form **Fleetwood Mac**, recording classic singles such as 'Oh Well' and 'Albatross'. Disappeared due to drug and mental health problems for a decade or so, resurfacing briefly in the early 1980s to produce relatively unsuccessful albums, then re-appeared in 1996 to record 'The Peter Green Splinter Group Album'.

Mainly a Strat player, but has been seen with Gibsons too. Known for excellent intonation, consummate vibrato and intuitive phrase construction (or, put in bluffer terms, 'amazing feel', 'God-given touch', and 'the talent to make that piece of wood sing'.)

It's Easy To Bluff... Music and TAB Guide

Most guitar players can't read music. There. We've said it. So you can stop feeling guilty about it and get on with the serious business of pretending that you can. On these two pages you'll find tab and treble clef notation for all of the techniques featured in this book, along with tips on how to play them.

HOW TO READ TREBLE CLEF: The note on the bottom line of the treble clef is middle E – that is, it's the E which is found on the 2nd fret of the D string. The top line is F (1st fret, high E string).

Guitar notes that are lower or higher than this range are notated using 'leger lines' – these are extra stave lines drawn in above or below the main clef.

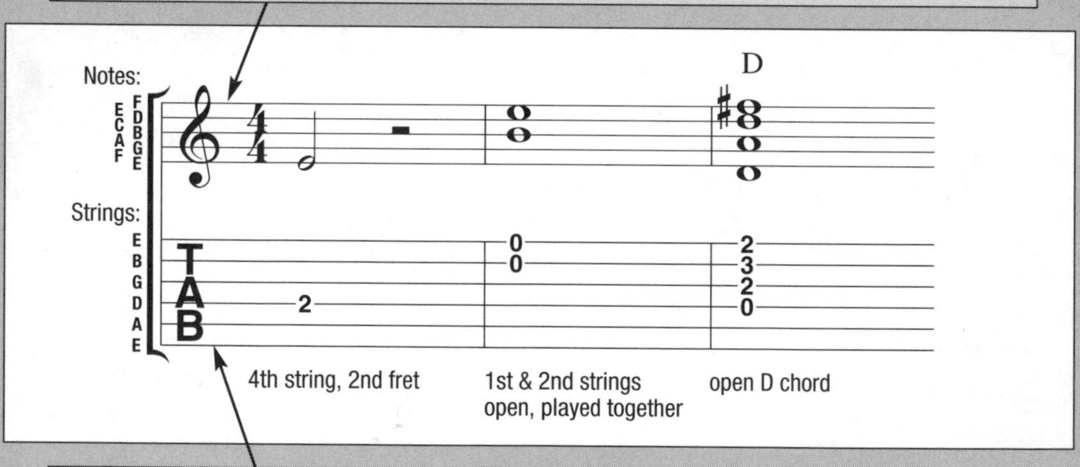

HOW TO READ TAB: The six lines represent the strings – the thickest (lowest) string is at the bottom. The number shows the fret.

HOW TO READ CHORD PARTS: The chord names are written above, and sometimes the musical rhythm of the part is notated underneath.

If no rhythm is given, or you see several even 'slashes' in a bar, then normally you should make up your own rhythm pattern. If you see two chords in a bar, it's normally assumed that they're played for two beats each.

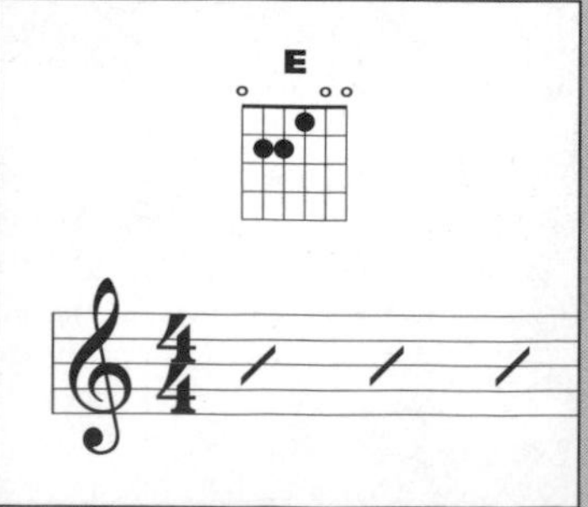

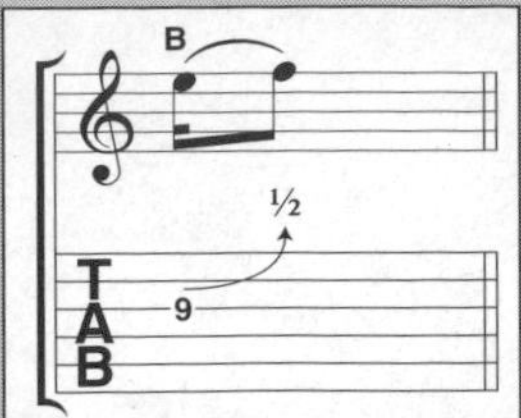

SEMITONE BEND (OR HALF-STEP BEND): Play the note with the picking hand then bend it up a semitone (so it reaches the pitch of the note on the next fret).

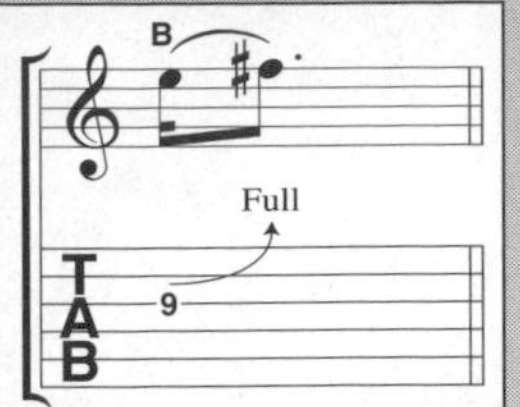

WHOLE TONE BEND: Duh! Just bend it further!

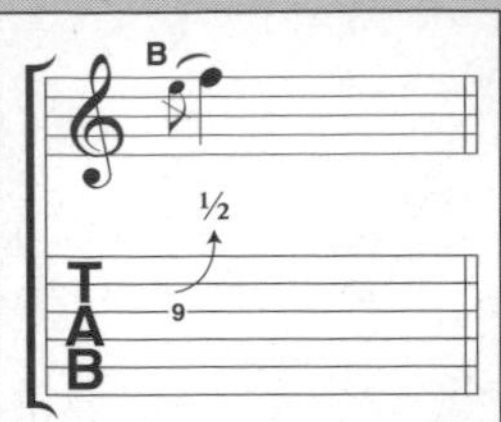

GRACE NOTE BEND: The only difference with these is that you start bending as soon as you've picked the note. You should hardly hear the first note.

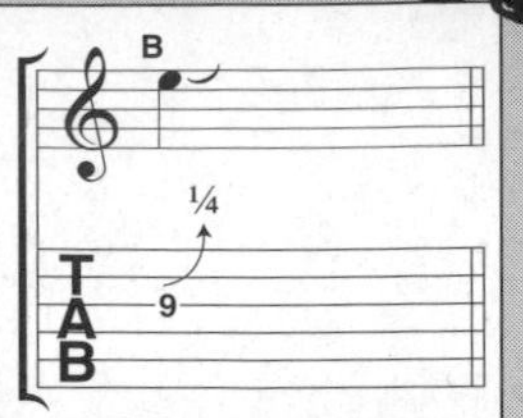

QUARTER-TONE BEND: Just bend the string a little – don't go as far as a semitone. Quarter-tone is used to mean any bend that's less than a semitone.

BEND AND RELEASE: Play the note, bend it up, let it back down again.

PRE-BEND: Bend the note up before you play it.

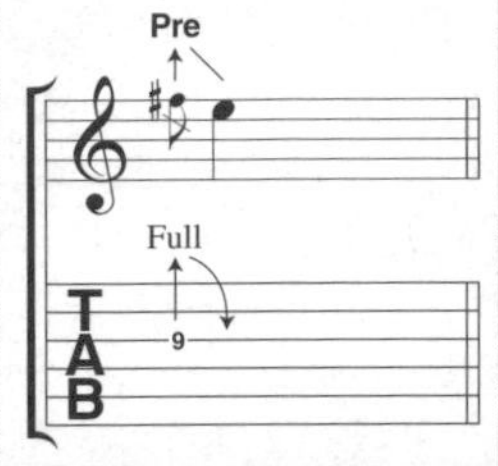

PRE-BEND AND RELEASE: Bend the note up, then play it, then release the bend while the note rings on.

VIBRATO: Move the string up and down by rapidly bending and releasing it by a small amount.

HAMMER-ON: Pick one note, then sound the higher note by fretting it without re-picking. Hammer-ons are always ascending in pitch.

PULL-OFF: Get both fingers into the positions shown in the tab, then pick the higher note. Whilst it rings on, pull the finger off the string to sound the lower note.

SLIDE/GLISS: While the note is sounding, slide the fretting finger up or down to the position shown in the tab.

SLIDE/GLISS AND RESTRIKE: As before, but this time repick the second note after you've finishing sliding.

TAPPING: Fret the note using the picking hand by tapping onto the position shown. Usually followed by a pull-off.

PALM MUTING: Rest the picking hand on the strings very near to the bridge. This partially mutes the notes – the technique is used a lot in blues and rock rhythm playing.

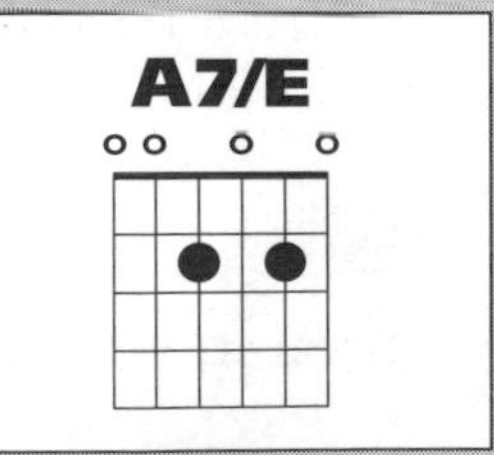

SLASH CHORDS: Many players get confused when they see chord notation like this for the first time. Do not fear – it's simple. The letter name before the slash is the chord you play. The one after the slash is the bass note. Bluffing tip - if you find it too difficult to play a particular bass note at the same time as the chord, try ignoring it and just playing the chord, then get a bassist or keyboard player to supply the bottom end.

Willie Dixon's 'Little Red Rooster' was covered by blues disciples the **Rolling Stones** in 1964.

Rhythm patterns or 'Flash don't make cash'

If you have to bluff your way through a whole blues gig, you'll need to convince everyone in the band that you know your 'blues chops', so it's vital that you can play some basic accompaniment styles. In this section you'll find seven rhythm and picking patterns, in progressive order of difficulty, that blues guitarists use when accompanying vocalists or other soloists.

Rhythm Tips

- Most electric blues players use a pick rather than fingers for rhythm work. And if you're playing in 4/4 time, you should generally favour downstrokes rather than upstrokes.
- **Avoid piling on too much distortion because the chords will lose definition...**
- ...but don't have the sound too clean either. Most blues strum-merchants try to recreate the sound of a *slightly* overdriven amp (mainly so they can use bluff-friendly words like 'bite', 'crunch', 'edge' and 'meat').
- **Straight major chords can almost always be improved by replacing them with 7th chords...**
- ...and try replacing straight minor chords with minor 7ths. Instant jazz-blues!
- **If you're playing an acoustic, ditch that £1000-plus Taylor or vintage Martin that plays like a dream. Get a cheap piece of Korean-made nastiness with two-year-old strings and a balsa wood body. In many cases, you'll find that acoustic Delta blues actually sounds more authentic on cheap guitars.**
- If you're using a cheap electric guitar with an action like an egg-slicer, simply tune it to an open G chord (DGDGBD) and get yourself a bottleneck. A high action is actually an advantage for slide players.
- **Don't strum all of the strings, all of the time. Blues accompaniment is often extremely sparse, and usually concentrates on the bass strings of the instrument.**
- Strat players - don't set the treble on the amplifier too high, and avoid the bridge pickup at all costs. You don't want your accompaniment to slice through a mix as, say, a funk player might. Most of the time, you should be after a more middly tone.
- **Try playing slightly 'behind the beat' (i.e. make sure some of the strums occur a fraction of a second 'late'). This will help to give your playing a naturally laid-back feel, and also help to combat the natural tendency of most inexperienced guitarists to speed up throughout a song.**

No Sweat Rooster

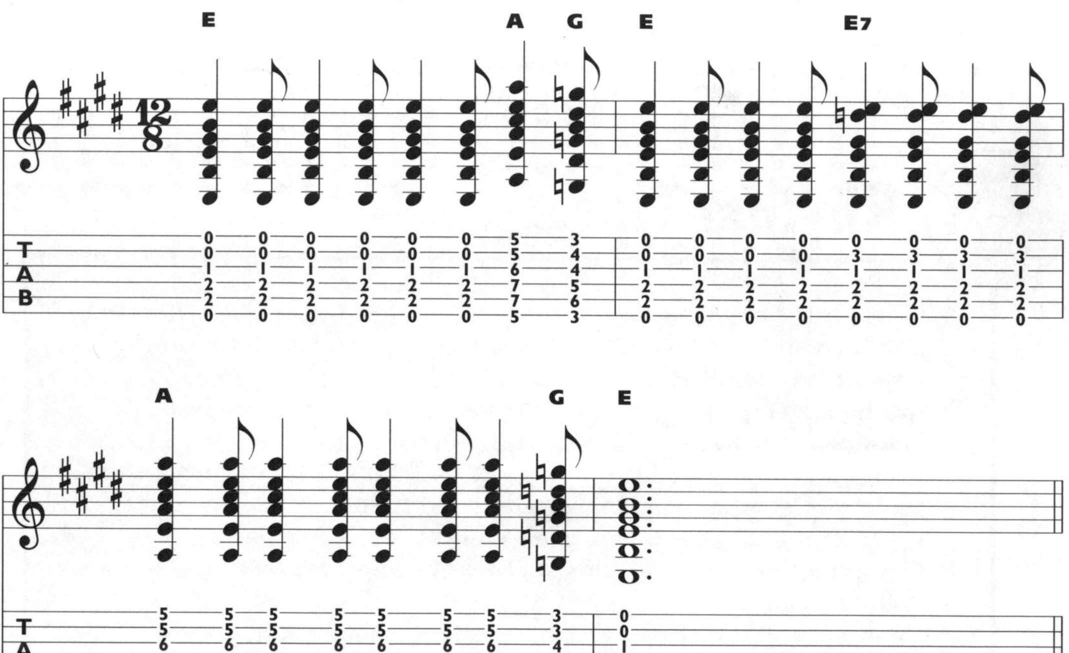

This moody 'Little Red Rooster' style figure should be played at a relaxed tempo. In any case, it would be difficult to play quickly without compromising the feel and/or your image as a laid back blues player.

In an emergency, you could make life easier by covering the changes using open strings for the first/last beat of each chord. **Don't let anyone catch you sweating!**

Time To Bluff

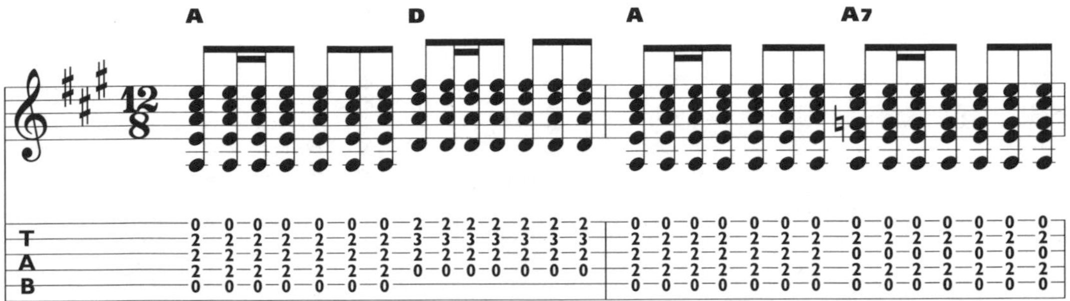

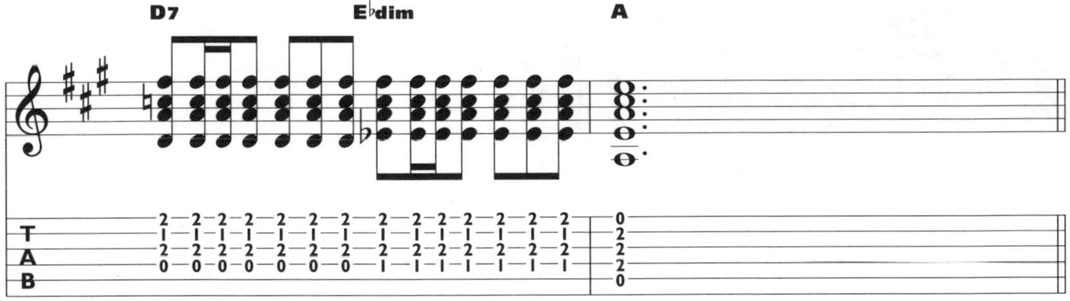

A bluffer's dream! All that strumming makes it easy to keep track of the beat and camouflages chord changes beautifully. To make life easier still, try lifting each chord off on the last quaver beat, giving you longer to find the next chord while the open strings ring. And no matter how good it sounds, remember to look a little bit bored.

Bluffing From Birth

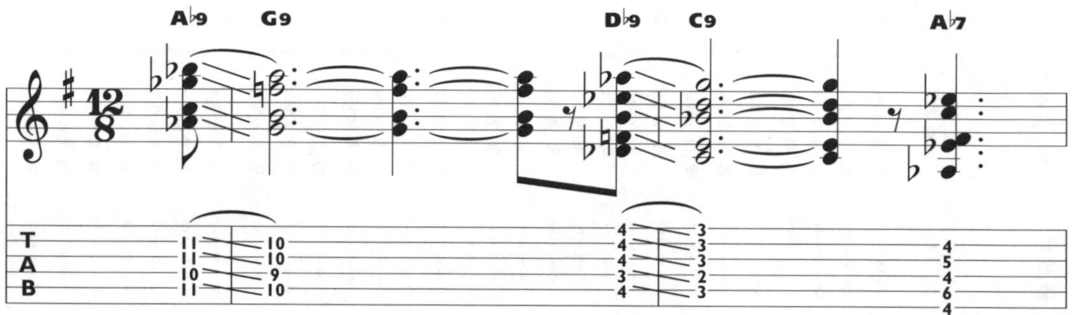

Spice up an otherwise static rhythm pattern with a dose of chromaticism. **It could turn your standard blues licks into a religious experience!**

This simple movement of chords a semitone at a time will convince all but the most hardened bluffer that you have been playing the blues in smoky bars since before they were born.

Smokestack Shuffle

This groove is reminiscent of **Hubert Sumlin**'s 'Smokestack Lightnin' and it features everything that's cool about an unaccompanied blues riff; lazy shuffle beat, muted rhythm accents and a hint of pentatonic scale.

This makes it an ideal candidate for carelessly reeling off as if it were second nature while tuning up - if you work on it at home first!

Freddie In A Felt Hat

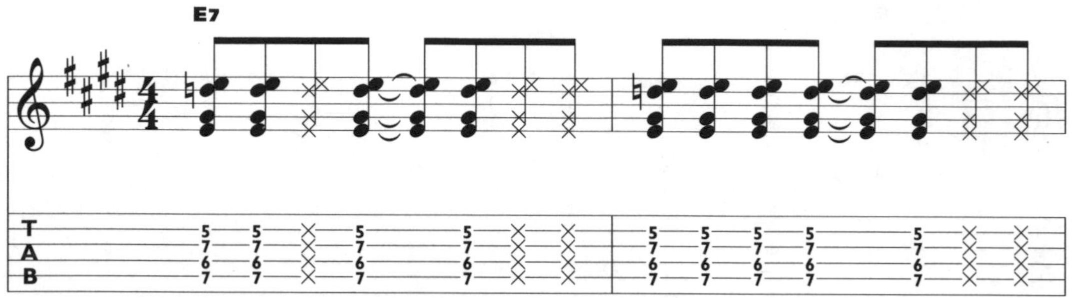

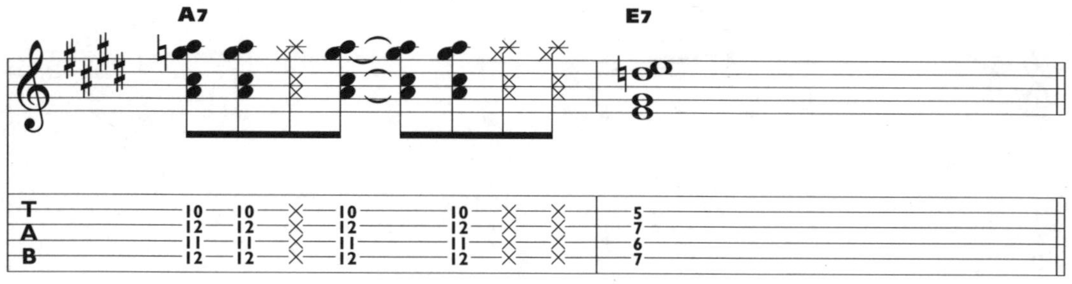

This relaxed accompaniment style was very popular in the '60s when it was used by artists like **Freddie King** and **The Rolling Stones**.

Don't blow your cred by getting too busy with the strumming. It's okay for your hat to fall over your eyes, but you don't want to risk it falling on the floor...

Spirit Of Jangle

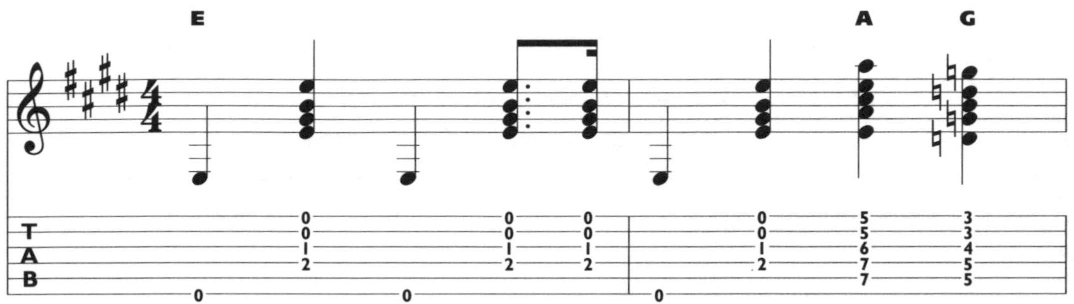

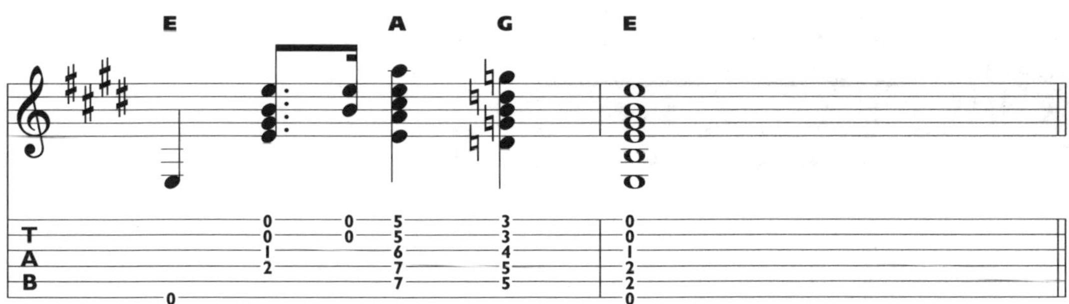

For a brighter, more 'jangly' type of blues rhythm, this strumming style is ideal. Try mixing it with some of the other more subdued patterns to give your rhythm playing more dynamic variation.

Remember, if your rhythm playing is good, people don't seem to mind you taking longer solos.

Moore Of Rory

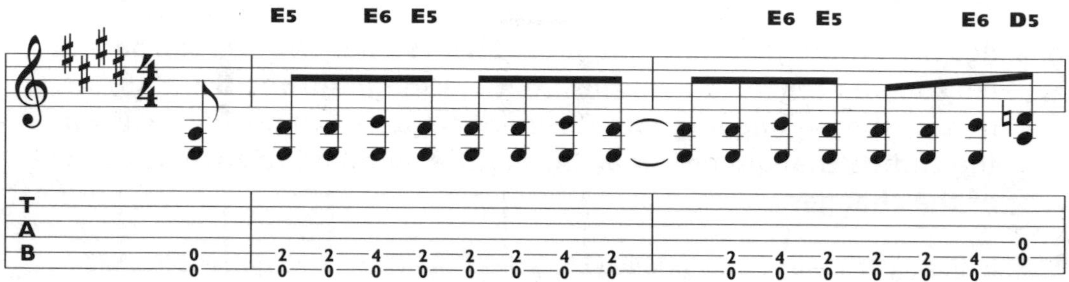

This hard-edged blues riff wouldn't sound out of place under a searing **Rory Gallagher** solo. Give it a swing feel and it also conjures up images of **Gary Moore**.

When a song's rhythm part is as upfront as this, you should keep the accompaniment exactly as written, **then go wild on the solo!**

Blues Riffs or 'Play it over and over until it sounds good'

Blues, perhaps more than any other form of guitar music, relies heavily on the riff. A riff is almost always one, two or four bars in length, and repeats at various points throughout the track. It can be transposed (moving into different fingerboard positions when the chords change) or it may be slightly modified to take account of the changes.

In this section, we've also included blues 'licks'. A lick is a lead guitar part that you learn beforehand, and then include as part of an so-called 'improvised' solo. It follows that licks are, of course, vital to a bluffer's defensive equipment, because they can be inserted in a lead part without anyone knowing that you prepared them before the gig.

The difference between a **riff** and a **lick** is basically that you may only use a **lick** once (pretending it's a great phrase you just thought up) but you can use a **riff** over and over, demonstrating how you can make one simple idea into a whole musical experience by the power of your touch, feel and tone (man.)

In this section you'll find 18 riffs of varying levels of difficulty, together with tips and suggestions about when - and when not - to use them. If you're a complete beginner on guitar, don't be afraid to concentrate purely on the easy examples - other players will admire your sense of cool restraint.

Quarter Commitment

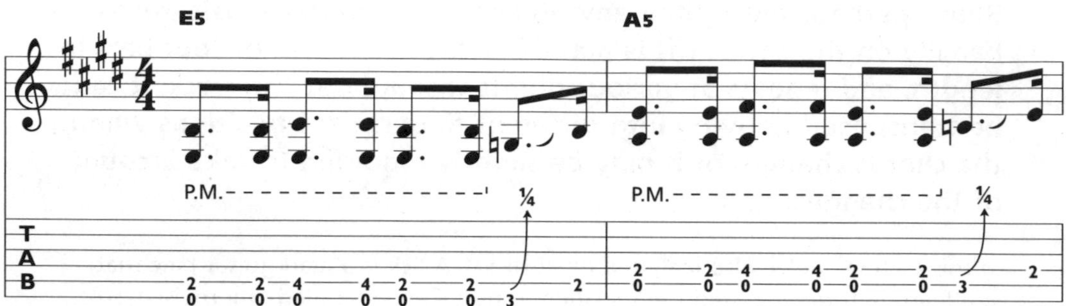

This Bring It On Home-style playing works best with the neck pickup selected and the tone on about half. The partial palm muting means almost no hand movement is visible, which looks much more impressive to a blues audience. Don't underestimate the importance of those quarter tone bends either. **They play an essential part in the bluffer's art of refusing to commit to major or minor!**

Any Time Now

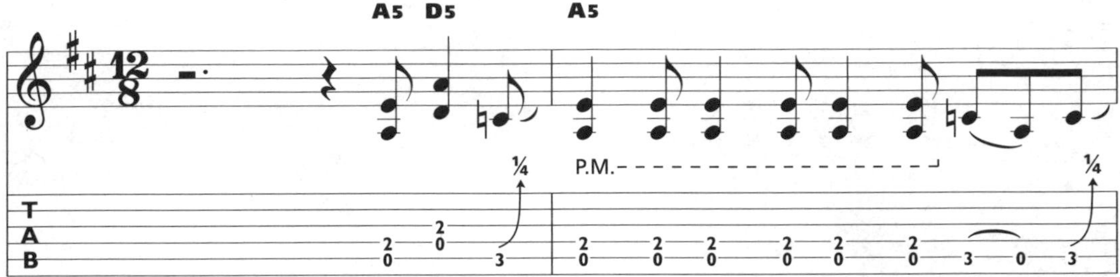

Settle into a menacing pulse with this solid accompaniment riff, which just hints at the fact that you could launch into a wailing solo at any moment! The quarter tone bends and pull-offs will gain further credibility if you don't try to make them too perfect.

Warning

The occasional sharp note or string rattle is expected of you, so don't blow your cover by being too rehearsed.

Many of **Jimmy Page**'s classic rock riffs with Led Zeppelin were based on blues ideas - he just played them a little louder than most people...

Passport To Bluffsville

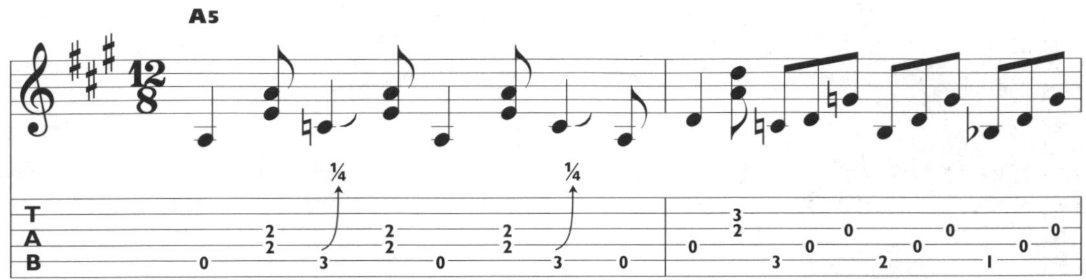

There's no way anyone will ever doubt your blues credentials if you slip this turnaround idea in at the conclusion of a solo. If you replace the E7 in the fourth bar with an A7, **you have the perfect ending too!**

I'm Still Here, Man

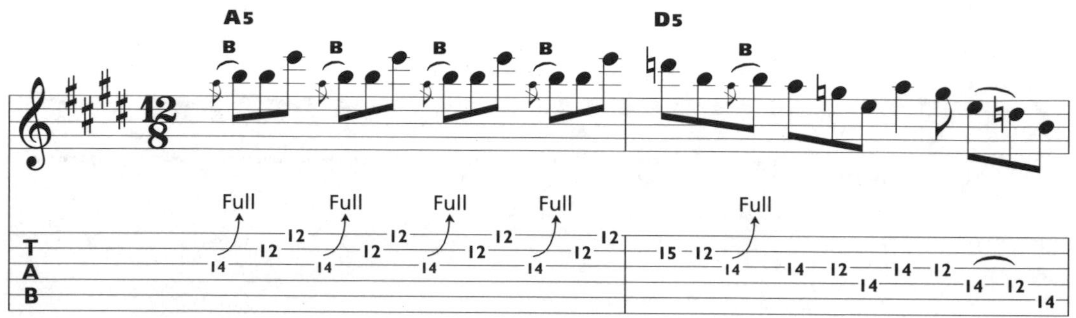

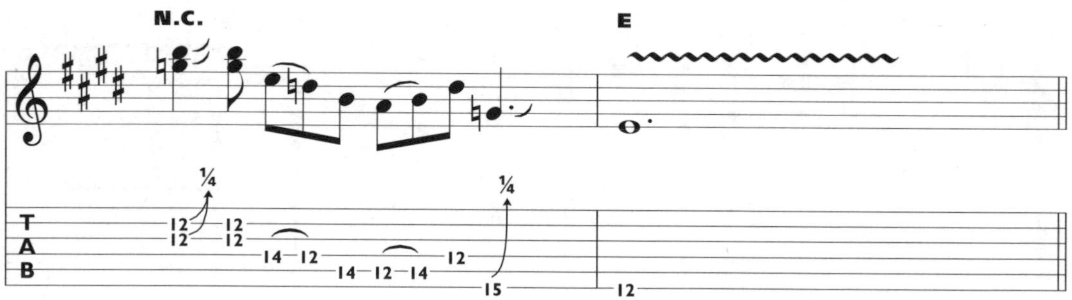

When you feel it's time to make your presence felt a little more; i.e., **after a flashy sax/harmonica break**, employ this repetitive device at the beginning of your solo, to show you won't be left in the dust.

Don't let any concern about this show in your face - perhaps frown and nod a little as you let it fly.

Bluffaway

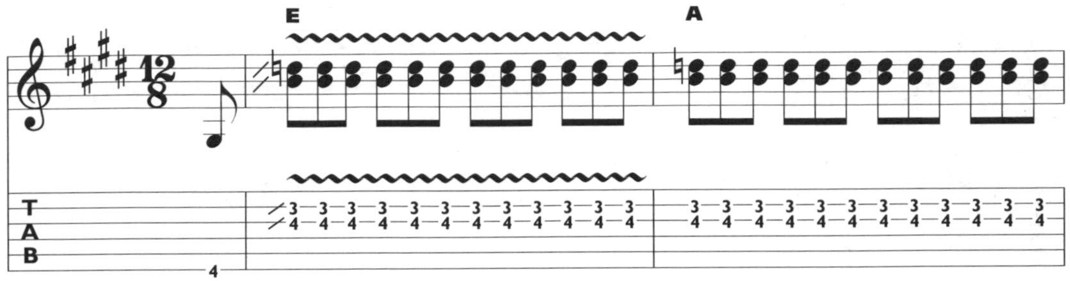

This riff works really well unaccompanied, making it ideal as an intro or as part of a solo, while the band just play chord accents. It should be played with a little vibrato and lot of attitude!

If asked, you should say that your slightly overdriven tone is influenced by **Eric Clapton**'s Les Paul/ Marshall sound on 'Hideaway' from the *Bluesbreakers* album (which you have on vinyl of course).

Albert's Sweet Kansas Home

Once again, here is an ideal intro/solo phrase, with a hint of '50s Rock'n'Roll in those double stops. This would really cut a dash with a razor-sharp **Albert Collins** style tone.

Though it's quite aggressive, you'll find it ideal for reeling off casually, while the band put all their effort into those chord stabs!

Cool Stops

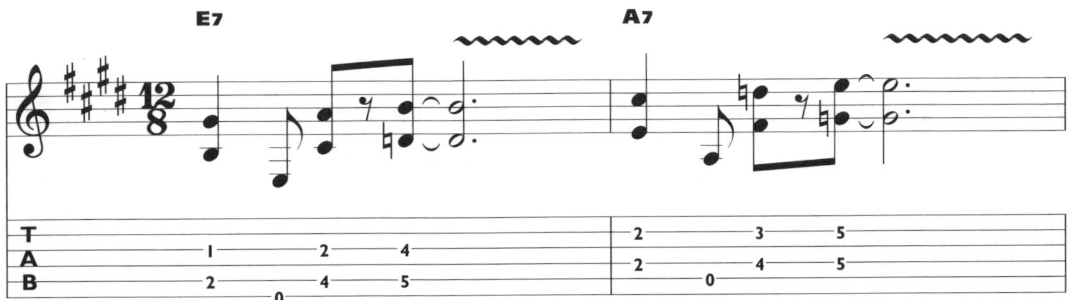

Using this figure creatively, it should be fairly easy to put together a great laid back blues backing that sounds full and interesting, without ever using a complete chord.

Perhaps a couple of choruses would benefit from being played in the busier style demonstrated in bar 3, then reverting to the sparser part, to add dynamics and generally be more impressive.

Almost A Solo

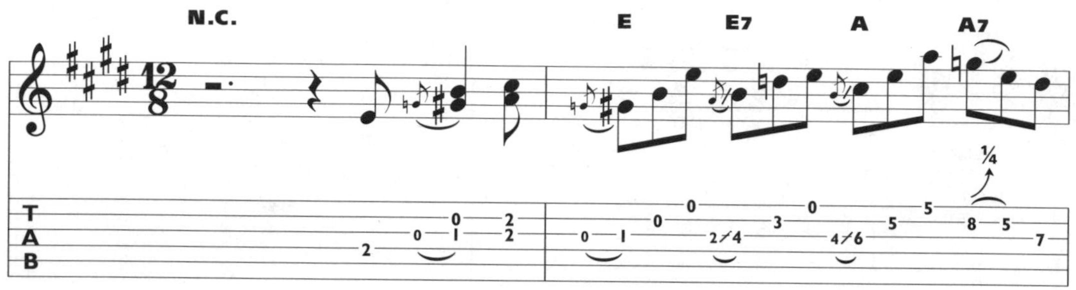

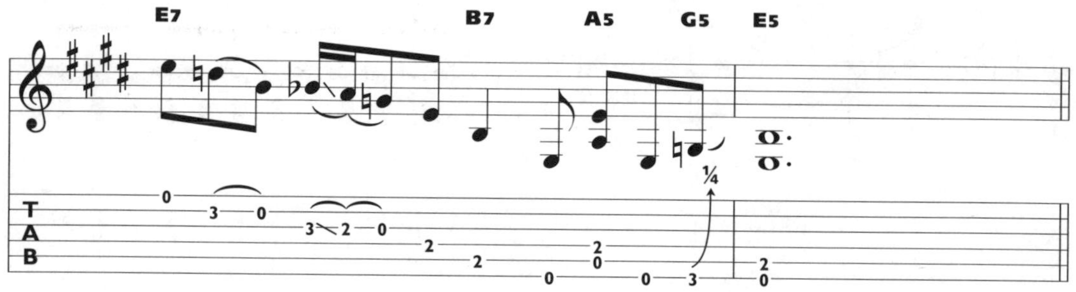

This figure is easier to play than it sounds, making it ideal for when you need to pull something special out of the bag, while maintaining the correct blues demeanour. The quarter tone bend in bar 2 breaks the usual precedent by pulling the string down to facilitate an easier pull-off. The shift back down to open position keeps this riff out of 'solo' territory.

Acoustic Delta

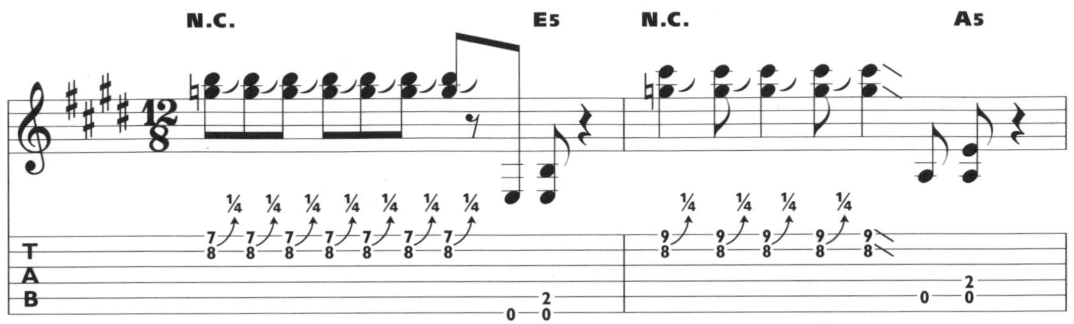

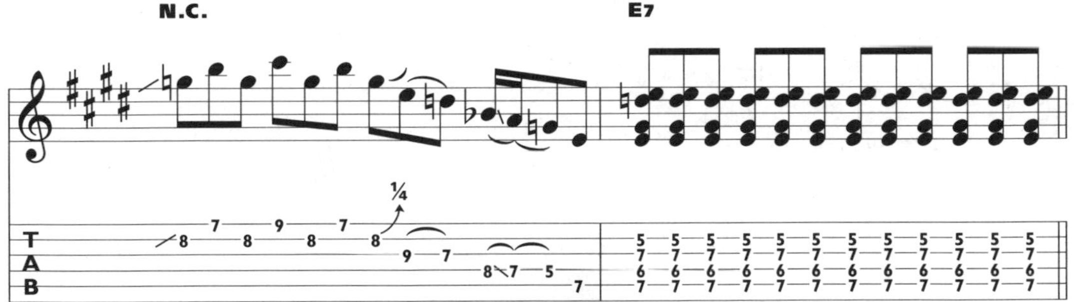

Play this one when you're trying out acoustic guitars in the music shop.

It makes a real feature of the ever-present quarter-tone bend. Try not to bend the first string or some of the effect is lost. Of course, the chord stabs might not seem so necessary with a bass player and drummer to lend a hand, but they do add punch and make it look as if you are leading the band.

Fast And Cool

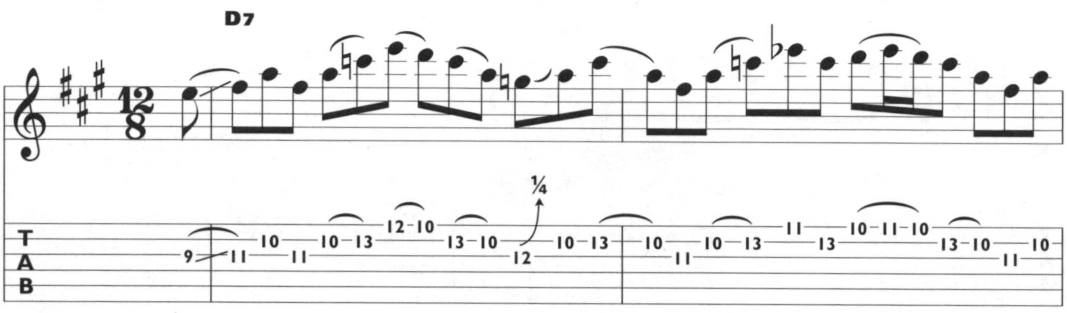

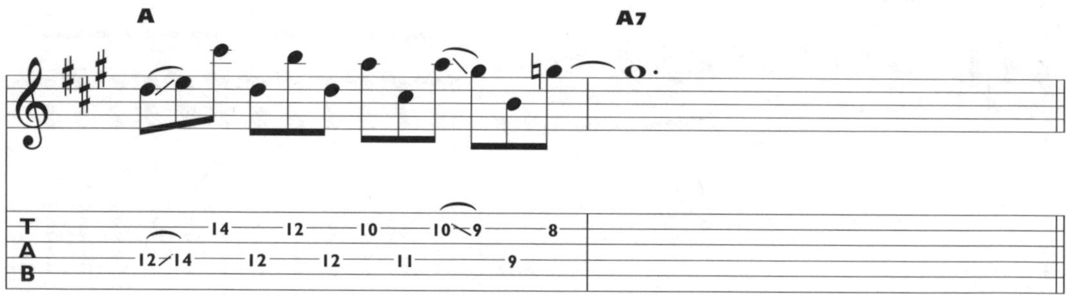

Although it's not all that fast, this is an undeniably fiddly-sounding solo lick, and is moveable to a variety of keys around the fretboard. The intervals in bar 3 will probably be easier to articulate at speed using pick and fingers. Because there is quite a lot happening in a short space of time, this is recommended for more up-tempo numbers (it also makes any fluffed notes less noticeable).

Fast And Hot But Still Cool

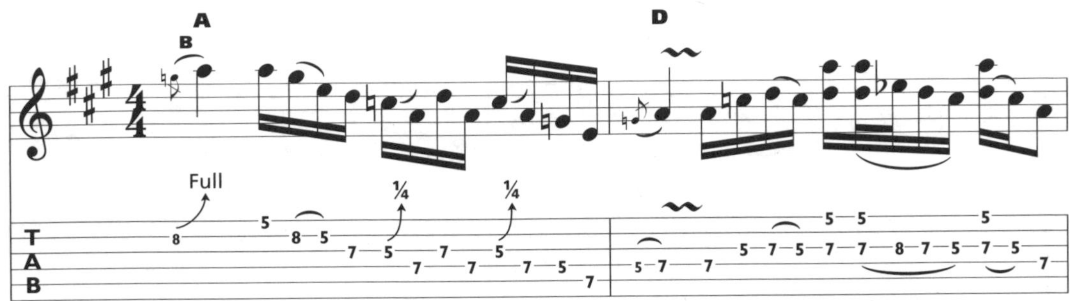

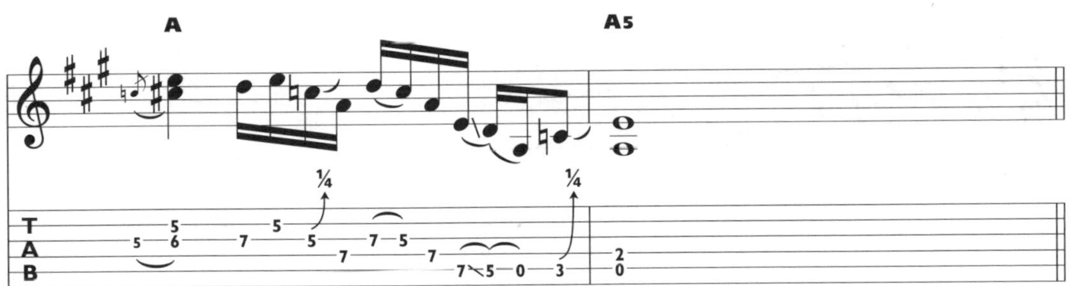

Crotchet arco on the downbeat, followed by semiquaver groups featuring diads - or, put another way, long notes and short notes in the same riff! The phrase mixes traditional double-stops with a **'Clapton-esque'** single note approach.

Needless to say, you will of course mention that the roots of this mixture can be traced back to **Robert Johnson** and **Charley Patton**.

Rehearsed Improv

Hendrix Tip

This concentrated example of **Hendrix-style** double stops doesn't need to be played with pick and fingers technique.

It sounds better using a hard picking attack with a relatively clean tone. Don't try to be too tidy with your execution - rehearse it over and over again until it sounds spontaneous.

Bottle Bluffing

Taking a few traditional influences on board, this phrase begins with the classic quarter tone bend sequence that shows your blues pedigree from the start.

During the second bar, the slides are voiced to subtly imitate the sound of a bottleneck (a trick used by **Jeff Beck**) without all the hassle of actually using one. It winds up with a cool slide/pull-off sequence down the E blues scale.

Taste-Free Zone

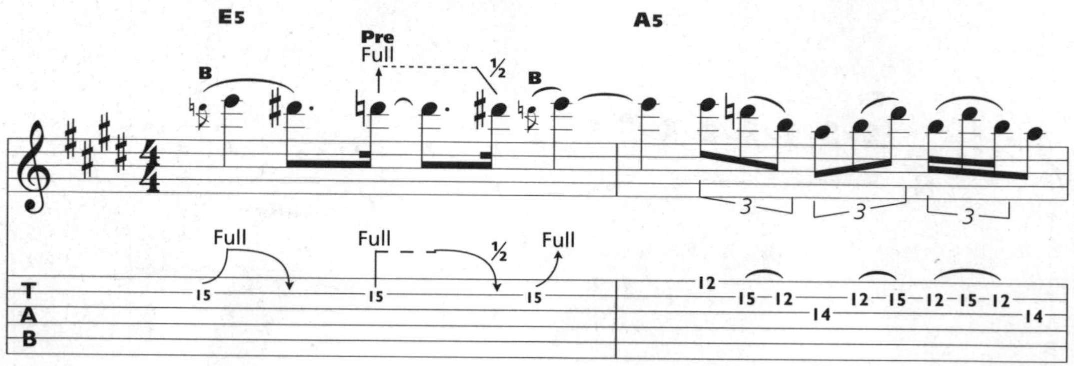

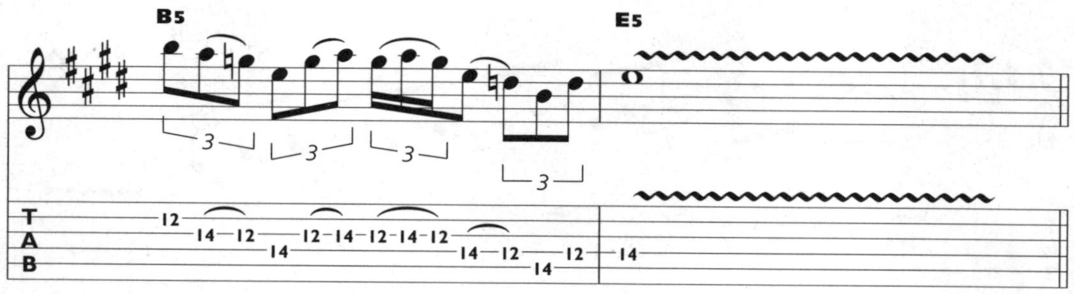

Select the bridge pickup, turn up the distortion and throw your head backwards for this **Gary Moore**-style pentatonic blast. Show how soulful you can be in the first bar, then cut to the chase with the embellished triplet lines in bar 2 and 3. When you feel confident enough, make them as fancy/widdly as you like.

Warning

You can only afford to show off like this once or twice per gig.

Gary Moore achieved technical mastery of many great playing techniques, including his trademark throw-your-head-back-and-screw-up-your-face string bending method.

The Trill Has Gone

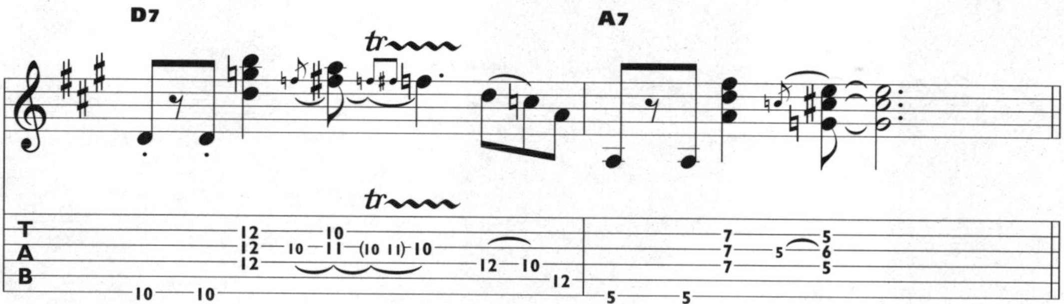

This is a multi-purpose lead/rhythm lick, with a distinctive bluesy major/minor feel. The trills should be relaxed and lazy, rather than fast and super-accurate. If you find yourself unsure of the direction an improvised solo is taking, reel it back in with this traditional-sounding but versatile idea.

To change key, simply move the whole shape around the fretboard.

Take Me Back Home

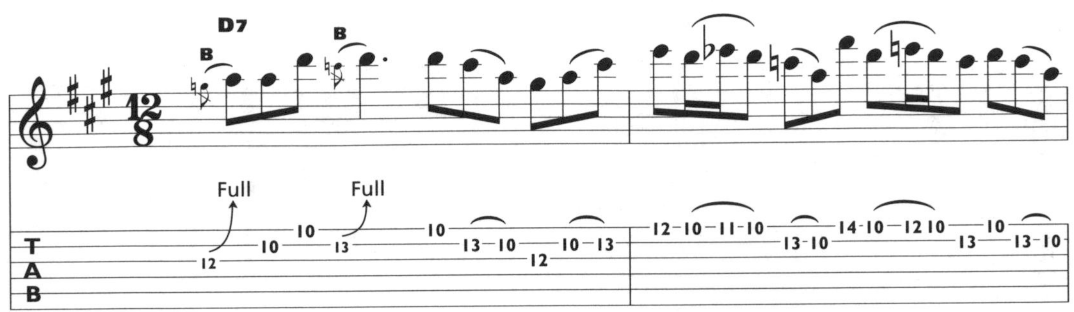

Most of the examples in this section will work over the '1' chord - i.e. if you're in the key of A, this will be a chord of A.

This one, however, is to be used over the '4' (i.e. the first time in a 12-bar that the chords change). To play this lick in a minor key, just move all the F♯s down a fret to F natural and the final C♯ down to C.

Mississippi Time

Here's an 'authentic' **Robert Johnson** intro/outro, using a descending D7 chord shape over the open fifth string - notated with the stems pointing downward down to signify that this part is played with your picking hand thumb.

There is a little rhythmic syncopation in the 3rd bar, so keep your foot tapping to avoid losing the thread. Hopefully the audience will think you've got a big Delta influence in your sound, and won't suspect for a second that you've got a problem with timekeeping.

Diminished Response

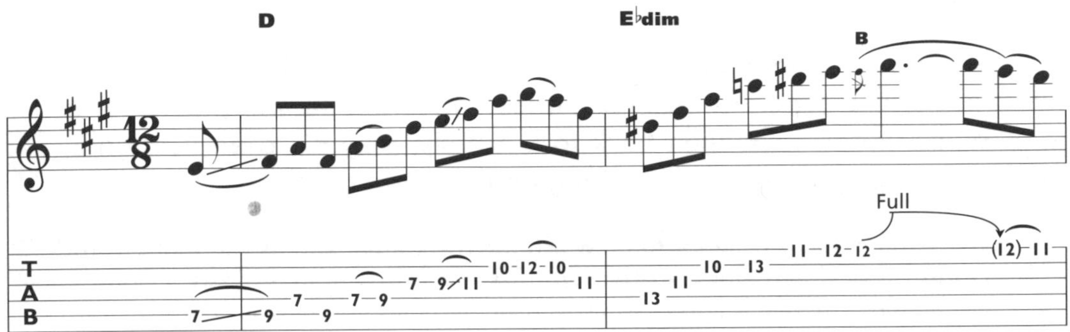

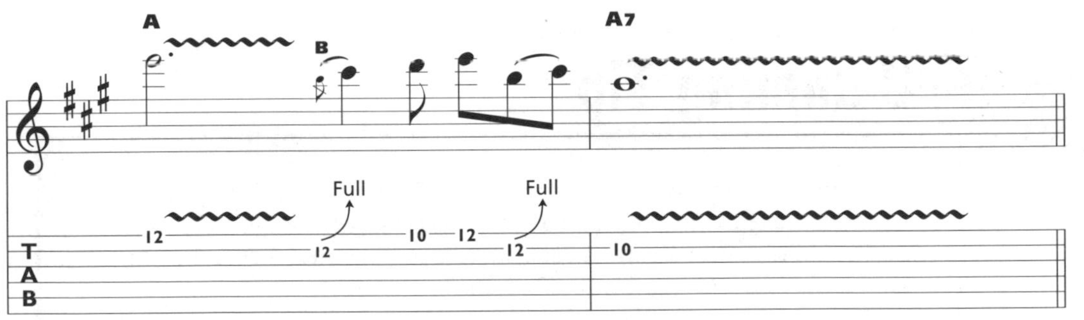

If you were wondering what to play over a diminished chord - as featured in a few of the examples - there are two ways to approach this. **Firstly**, you could ignore it - there is no need to play anything other than the blues or pentatonic scale. **Secondly**, you can try the diminished arpeggio shape featured at the beginning of bar two. Start with the root note (in this case E♭) and this will translate anywhere on the neck.

Chord Sequences or 'What, you mean there's more than one?'

There's a common misconception that the 12-bar is the only 'authentic' type of blues (you know the one I mean - play E for a while, move to A, then back to E. Finally, play B7, then A, then E, before playing the whole thing again. And again).

While there are many great tunes which use this format and its variations (**Blind Lemon**'s 'Matchbox Blues', **Robert Johnson**'s 'Crossroads Blues', **SRV**'s 'Pride & Joy' to name but three) it's also possible to play the blues using many chord changes (anything by **Steely Dan**) or none at all (**John Lee Hooker**).

Jamming Tip

When you're jamming along to a chord sequence at a gig, never, repeat NEVER, look at anyone in the band. If you make eye contact with another musician you'll lose that far-away look that keeps the audience believing that your playing is the result of a direct hotline to God.

Also, you mustn't be seen to look at another guitar player's hand to find out what chord they're playing (assume it's an E and you'll be right about 60% of the time, which is a better rate of accuracy than most jazz players, for example). If in doubt, keep your eyes closed. Just remember to open them every 32 bars or so to check that people aren't heading for the exits...

In this section you'll find several versions of the 'standard' 12-bar plus a few different sequences that crop up from time to time. All the chords are shown as fretboxes, and each example includes tips on how it can be used.

Standard 12-Bar In E

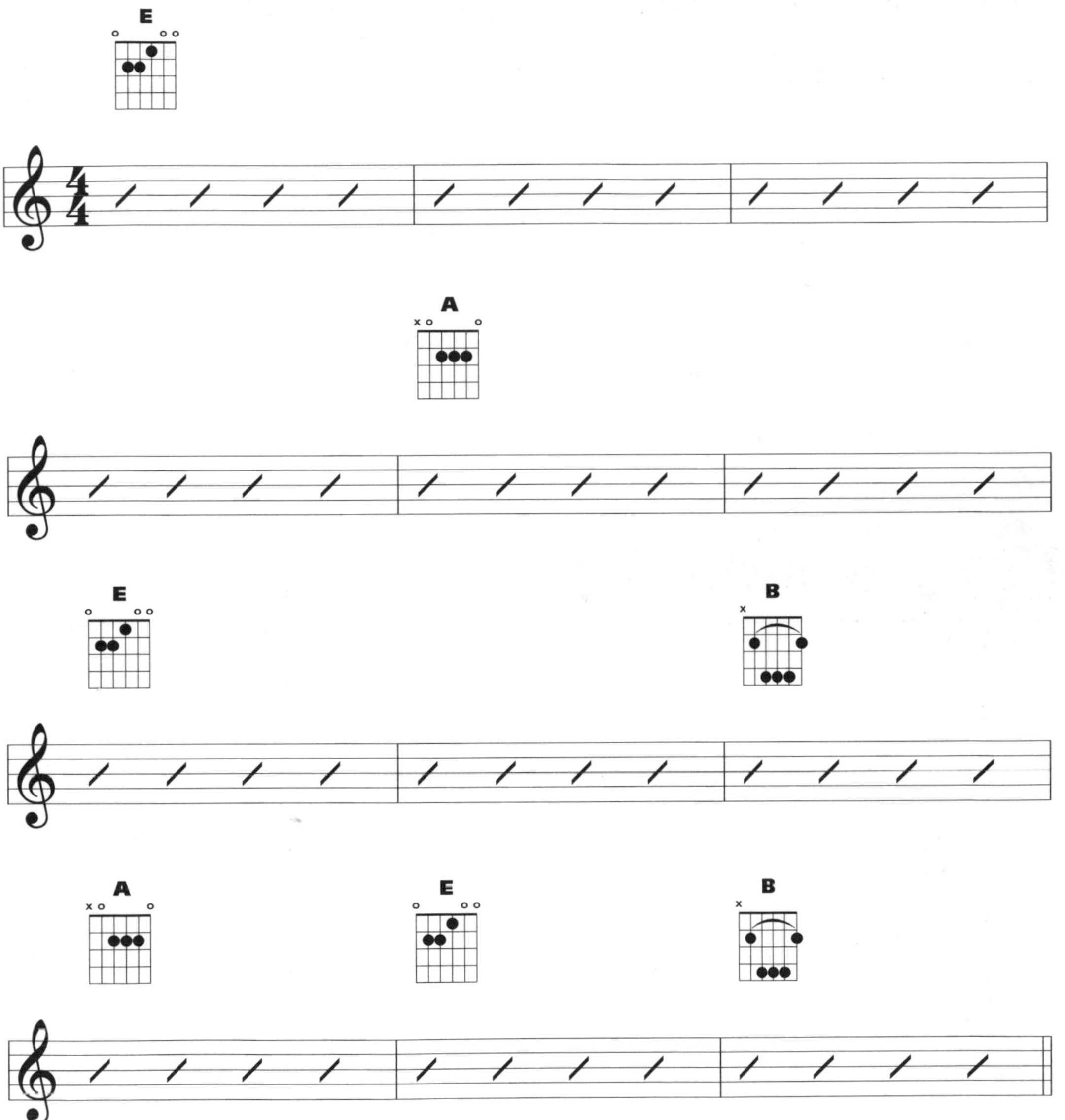

The best place to start has to be the standard **12 bar blues** pattern. Though this is shown as a four to the bar arrangement, it translates easily into any rhythmic feel. Try experimenting with a few of the rhythm patterns and/or dynamics and you will soon recognise the basic structure of many a blues standard.

Adding Changes

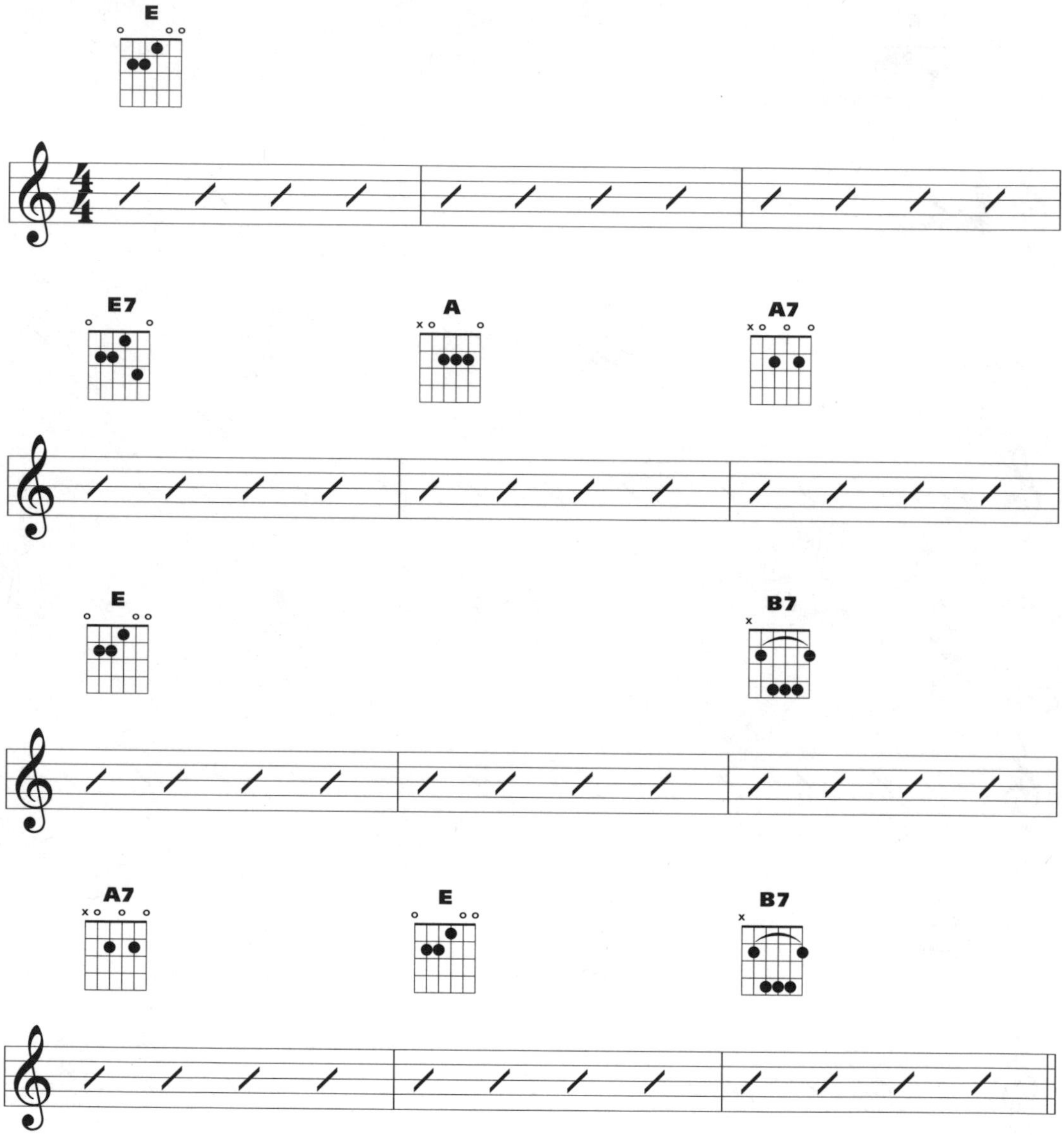

E

E7 A A7

E B7

A7 E B7

Take the standard 12 bar pattern and embellish it with a few extra chords to make the backing more interesting for the listener. Beware of taking this idea too far though - it's all too easy to cross the line into jazz, in which case you might have to put on a different style of hat mid-solo - **tricky**!

Peter Green 12-Bar

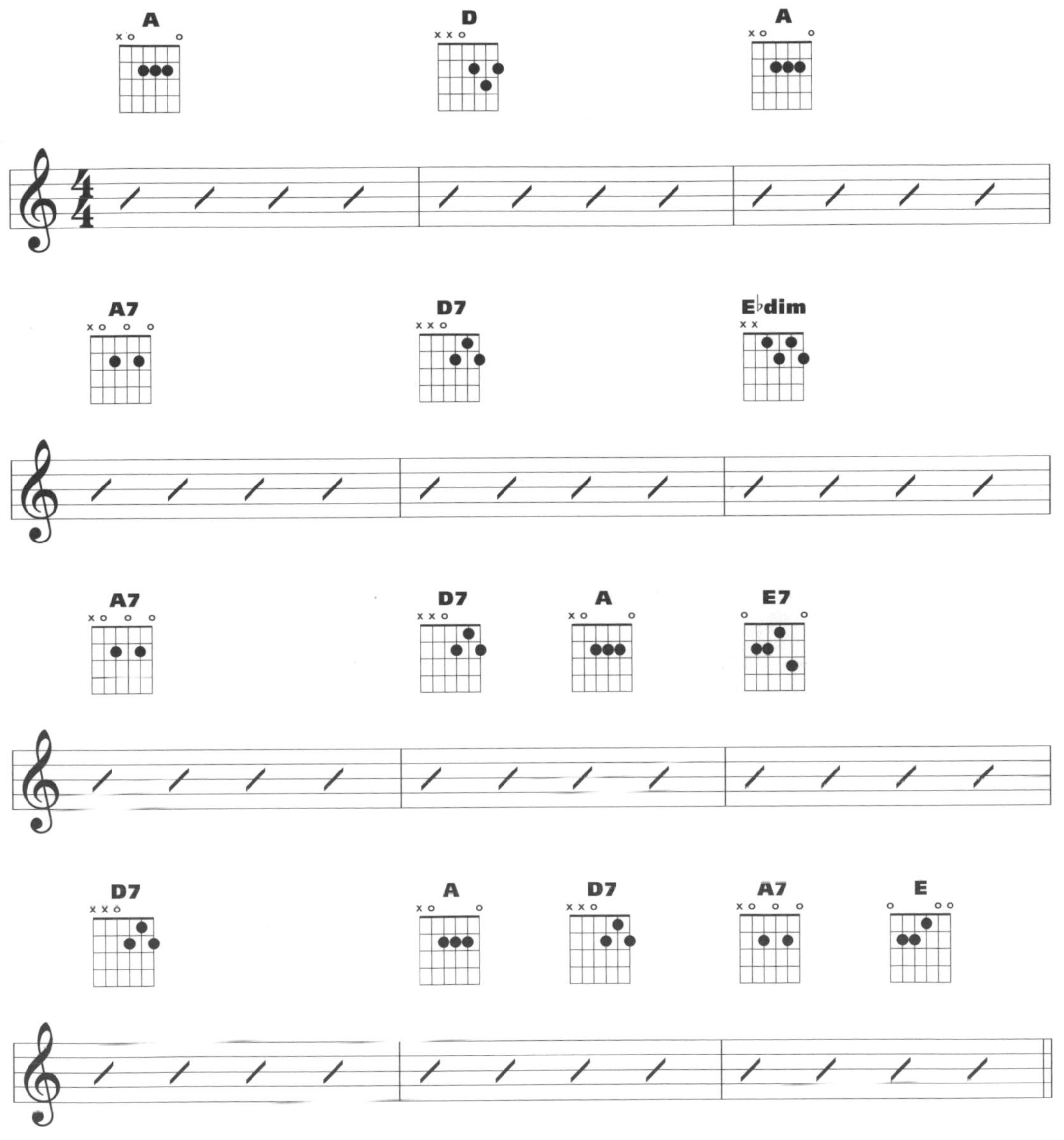

Here's another variation on the 12-bar, featuring a diminished chord voicing, as heard in **Peter Green/Fleetwood Mac**'s 'Need Your Love So Bad'. These chords can give a dramatic feel to an otherwise straight 'major' progression. The turnaround in the final two bars utilises the popular I IV I V figure (chords one, four, one and five, so if you're in A, that'll be A, D, A and E). Use Roman numerals to refer to chord numbers wherever possible - it confuses people and enhances your bluffing status.

Smart-Ass 12-Bar

E5 G5 A5 E5 G5 A5 E5 G5 A5

E5 G5 G♯5 A5 C5 D5 A5 B5 D5

E5 G5 A5 E5 A5 B♭5 B5 E5 G5

A5 G5 F♯5 E5 G5 A5 E5 B5 D5

With a laid back shuffle rhythm, this sequence still follows the basic 12-bar pattern, but takes a riff-based approach to the chords. You'll find that it can be played in a variety of different ways, with many of the chords being interchangeable. It's great for impressing fellow band members with your extensive chord knowledge - **but try not to look smug!**

Slow Minor 12-Bar

Though it's less common, a good minor blues progression is an **essential part of the blues bluffer's arsenal**. It also lends itself to wailing pentatonic solos like nothing else! This sequence works equally well at an incredibly slow pace, or taken up to a foot stomping shuffle. It uses a minor version of the same turnaround as the 'Peter Green 12-bar' on page 71.

BB's Ninth 12-Bar

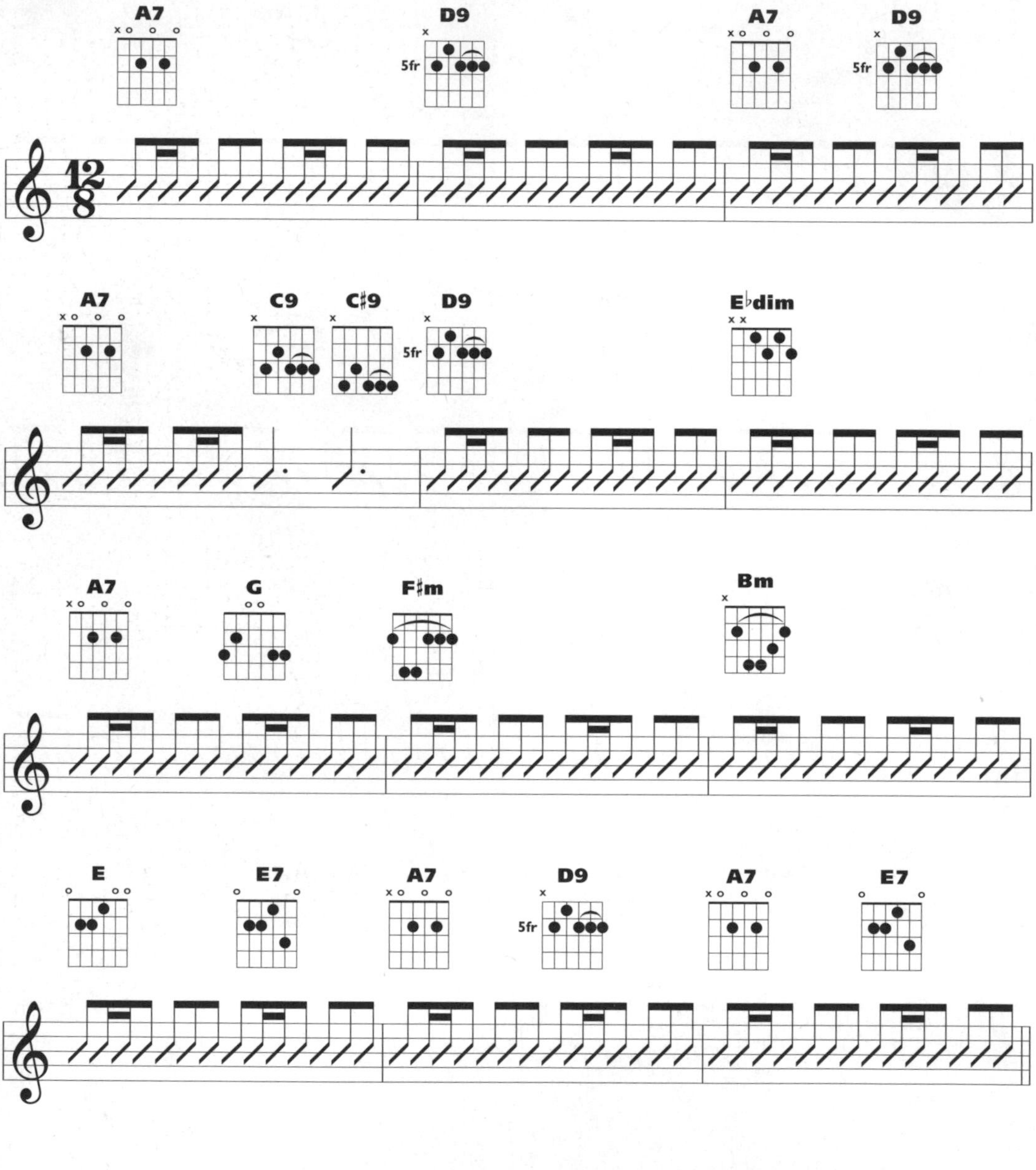

A7 D9 A7 D9

A7 C9 C♯9 D9 E♭dim

A7 G F♯m Bm

E E7 A7 D9 A7 E7

Though often associated with jazz, the 9th chord shown in this example has featured heavily in the music of **BB King** as far back as anyone can remember. It's fully interchangeable with a 7th chord, so can help you to avoid playing identical rhythm parts in every chorus. Being a small, easily moveable shape also makes it ideal for chromatic 'step' ideas, as shown in bar 4.

Bluesman **Jeff Healey** plays the guitar laid flat on his lap and knows all his scale shapes by touch alone.

Scales or 'What, you mean I have to use more than two fingers to play this lick?'

Yeah, yeah, I know. If you've got this far, you're probably good enough to bluff your way out of learning any theory, yes? I can hear cries of; "If you gonna play the blues, you gotta feel it, man, you don't need no book-larnin' music theory, my gran-pappy done' gone' tol' me if I feel the blues I just go with that feelin'..."

This is fine most of the time (and has worked for the likes of **John Lee**, **Blind Lemon**, **Willie Dixon** etc), but unfortunately, in the last 30-40 years electric blues players have simply become better. Don't blame the guitar teachers, blame the players. From **Peter Green**, **Hendrix** and **Eric Clapton** in the 1960s to **SRV**, **Robben Ford** and **Gary Moore** in the 1980s, the blues virtuoso is here to stay. And now and again you'll need to prove that you know what you're doing with scales.

In this section are eight scales which should give you a good overview of the different note choices that you can make in a solo, all shown in the key of E or A. Most guitar players already know the blues/minor pentatonic scale or one of its variants, but it's included here for those who are new to lead playing.

Good Idea!

Remember, once you can play the scale itself, you don't have to use the whole thing in your solo - sometimes as few as two or three notes can make a great lead lick over the chord backing.

These examples are by no means exhaustive - the blues scale of E, for example, can be played in at least 7 different positions (including sitting on your front porch with a bottle of beer) - but they will make you look good. Any blues guitarist who sees you play all eight of these shapes in one gig will think you a true blues master.

All scale fretboxes are shown upright, with the headstock at the top, and the strings ascending in pitch from left to right: i.e. **the lowest E string is on the left.**

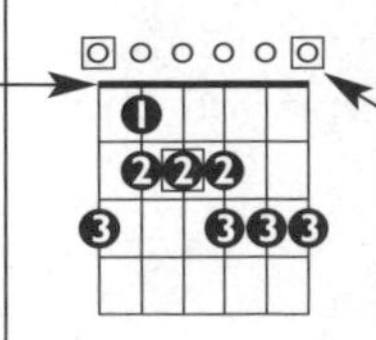

A box around a note or open string simply means that note is a 'root' note. E.g. **in A major any boxed out notes will be A.**

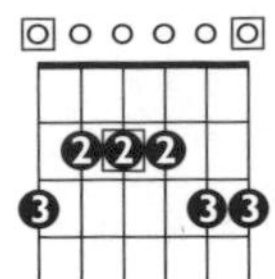

Em Pentatonic Scale

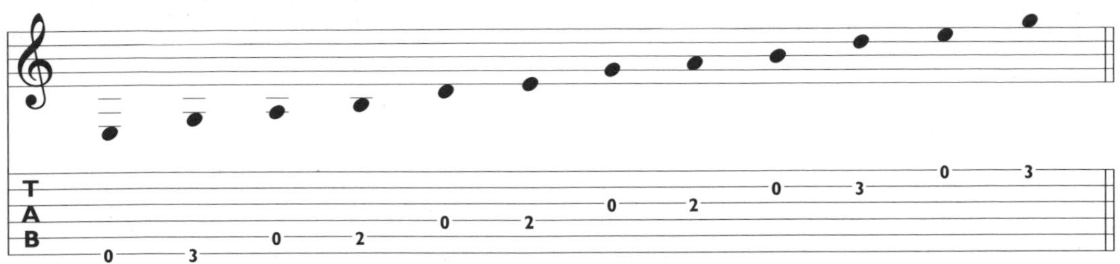

Without question the most essential scale shape bar none! The minor pentatonic scale is the basis of countless solos, riffs and even songs. Prominent users include players as diverse as John Lee Hooker, Jimmy Page and Albert King. This is the open E version - the most popular shape, in the most popular key.

E Blues Scale

Staying with the same idea, this is the Blues scale, also in the key of E. As you can see, it's basically the same as the minor pentatonic with an added note in two places. This is known as the flat fifth (♭5). This one note gives that classic mean 'n' moody blues vibe - even if you simply play up and down the scale.

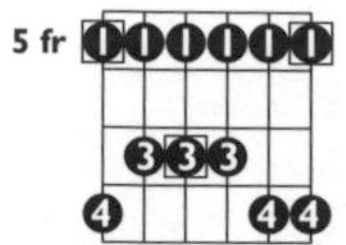

Am Pentatonic Scale

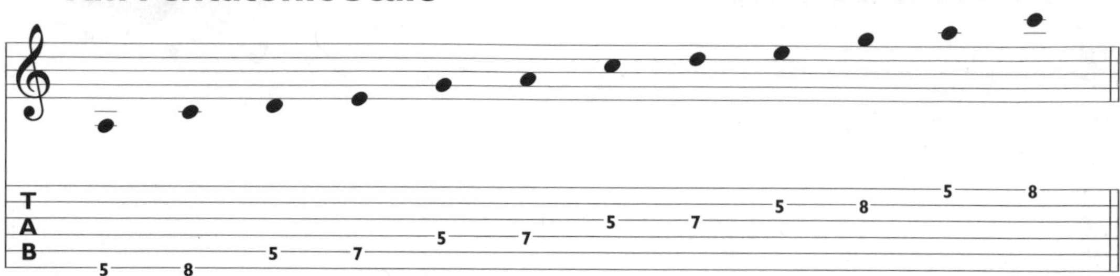

To demonstrate how easy the minor pentatonic scale is to use, take a look at this version in the key of A. If you use your first finger for all the notes on the fifth fret, the pattern is easily recognisable as a fretted version of the E minor pentatonic. Simply add a whole tone bend at the 7th fret of the third string when running through this, and you're playing a solo!

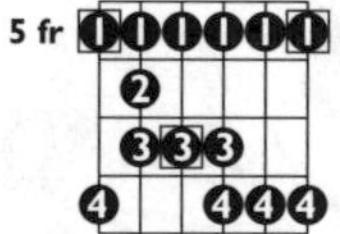

A Blues Scale

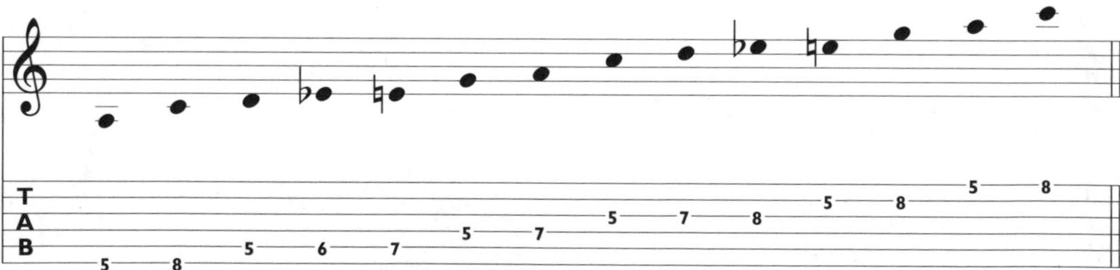

Here is the Blues scale again, this time in the key of A. The ♭5 note in this key is E♭. Try bending the third string as described in the previous example, then try bending it just a semitone (one fret's worth) for real blues authenticity.

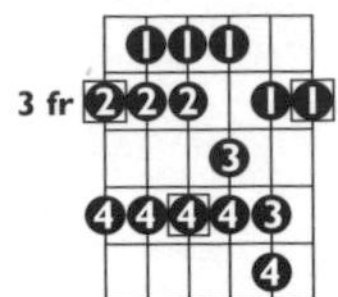

G Mixolydian Mode

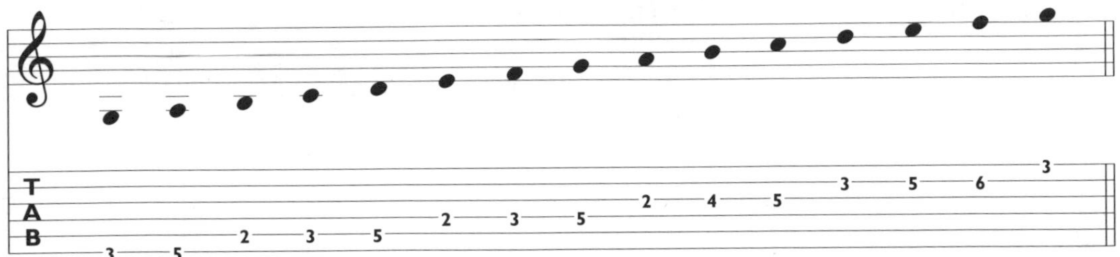

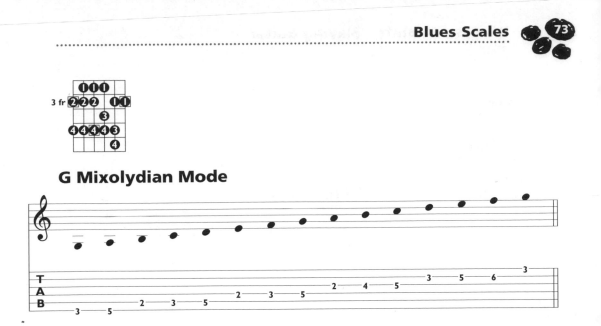

This scale is known as the G Mixolydian mode, or if that sounds a bit scary, G major with the 7th note flattened. This means the seventh note of the scale - normally F♯ - is lowered to F natural, making this version of the scale much more usable than the standard major pattern in a blues context. Try nailing that F note over a G7 chord, to draw admiring glances from other guitarists.

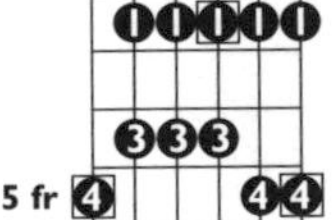

A Major Pentatonic

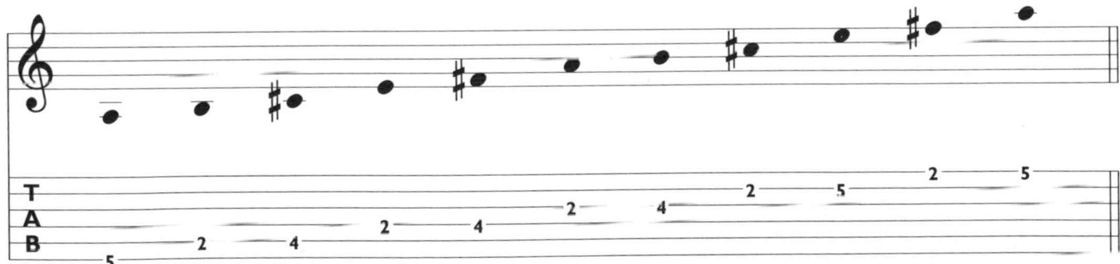

Playing blues licks in a major key can be a hazardous business. A minor pentatonic would almost fit over an A major based blues, but there would be some questionable moments; e.g., a C natural coinciding with the C♯ contained in an A major chord! To avoid these problems, try this A major pentatonic scale. All your favourite bending licks etc will fit beautifully, without you having to avoid any notes in the pattern.

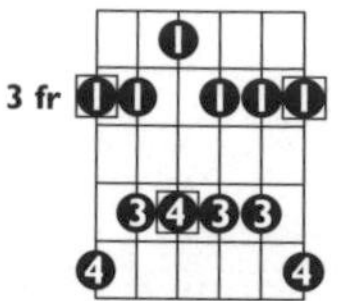

Am Pentatonic with Major 6th

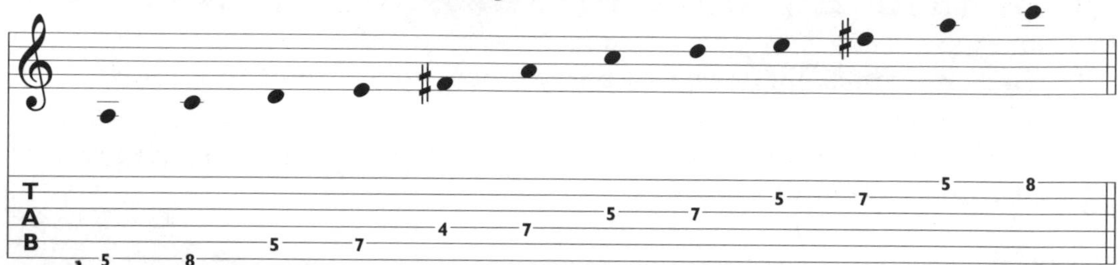

This variation of the A minor pentatonic is used and much loved by **BB King** and **Robben Ford**. It features an F♯ where there would usually be a G, and can be used to give a dramatic 'outside' almost jazzy effect. It works especially well if you are playing over bass and drums only, as there's no instrument defining the major/minor chord backing, meaning that any old bluffing around using this shape will sound credible.

Em Pentatonic Scale

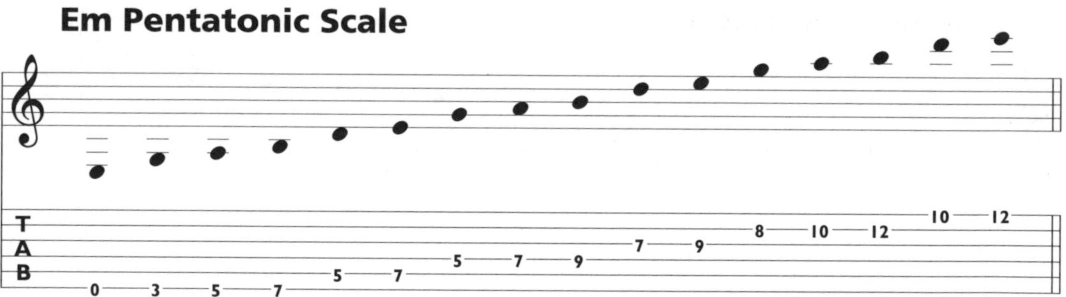

If you only ever learn one scale shape, make it this one! Spanning three whole octaves, from the open sixth string to the twelfth fret of the first, it incorporates elements of all the minor pentatonic scale positions along the fretboard. Though it works best as featured, in the key of E, parts of it can be transposed into any key.

Music Shop Classic or 'How do I fit everything in this book into 24 bars of showing off?'

Here is a specially designed party piece, guaranteed to impress next time you're in a guitar shop. Arranged in answering phrases like many a classic blues track, the feel is reminiscent of John Lee Hooker's 'Boom Boom'.

It begins with some open position pull-offs, and this main riff is kept strongly in evidence for the first 12 bars, which also contains elements of **Hubert Sumlin**, **Robert Johnson** and **Freddie King**. Around the halfway mark, a few more modern influences creep in, like **Eric Clapton**, **Gary Moore**, **SRV** and **Kenny Wayne Shepherd**. Here, the riff takes more of a back seat, as it has been strongly established by now, and besides, by this point you'll have drawn a crowd anyway...

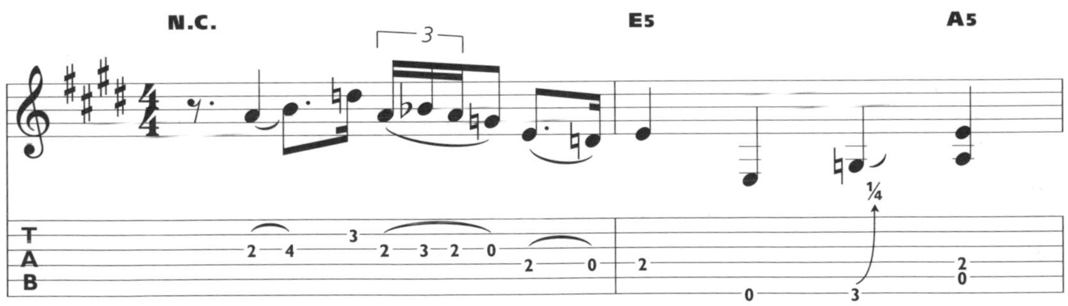

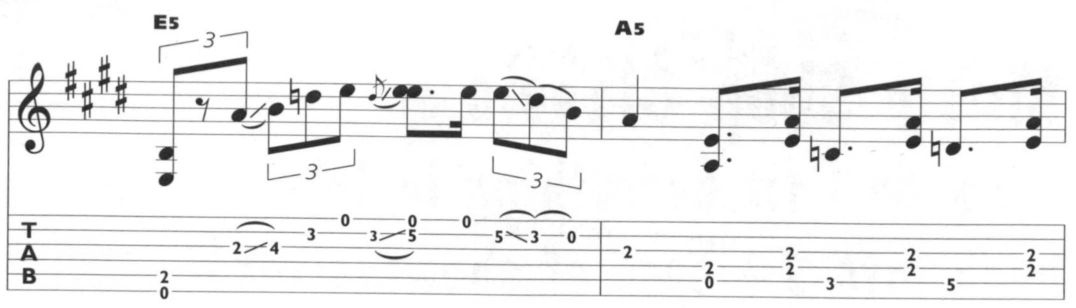
E5
A5

Em
A5
¼
¼

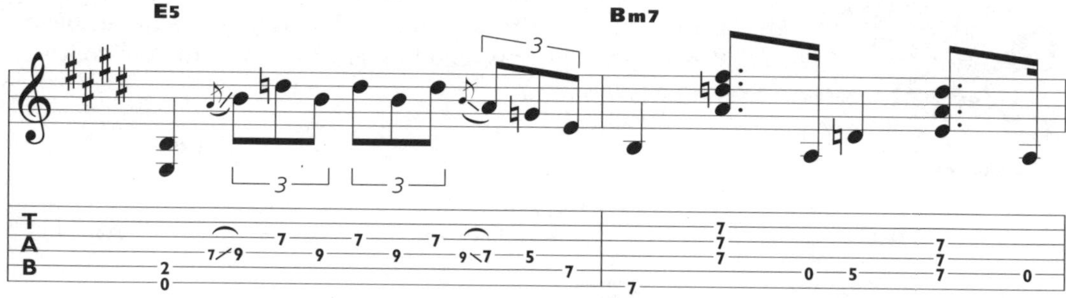
E5
Bm7

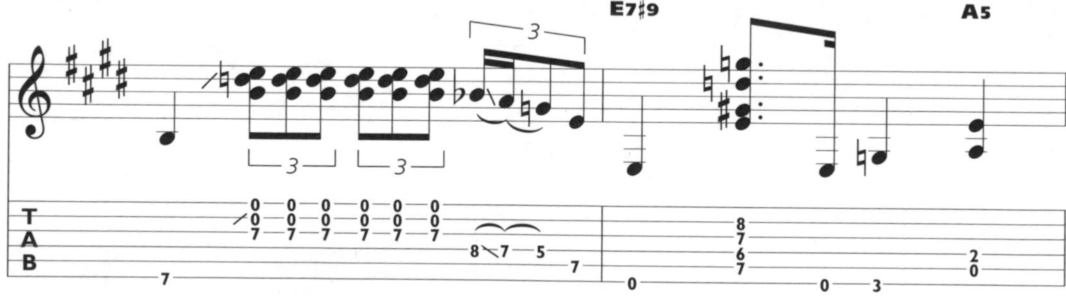
E7♯9
A5

E5
B
A5
Full
¼

E5
A5
E5
A5
8va
B
Full
¼
E5
A5
E5
Bm7
E5
A5
E5
Full
T
A
B

Blues Gear or "It's 106 miles to Chicago, we've got a full tank of gas, half a pack of cigarettes, it's dark and we're wearing sunglasses."

'The Blues Brothers' motion picture

If you're going to be a convincing blues player, you've got to have the right gear, which means thinking about everything from string gauge to guitar style to the type of hat you wear.

Iconography plays a big part in this - it's perfectly OK, for example, to say you bought a Gibson semi-solid because Freddie King plays one (even if you really got it because you like Oasis!).

In this section you'll find a list of all the gear you ought to buy, plus some tips on how to set up your equipment to recreate typical blues tones. Naturally, not everyone can afford a roomful of vintage amps, so there are also some tips on how to program a humble home multi-fx unit with a variety of blues guitar sounds.

If you do own a rack full of flashing lights and electronic sound-sculpturing equipment, stick the whole thing in an orange box or beer crate. If your amp is emblazoned with the words 'Authentic Tube Sound Blues King Valve Tone Classic', then it was almost certainly made by androids in a Korean micro-chip factory sometime last year, so you'll need to disguise it a little (take off the logo, wrap the whole thing in canvas, leave it out in the rain for a year or so etc).

Style Tip

As with most blues bluffing, how it all sounds is unimportant. Make sure that you and your gear look good on stage, and the audience will convince themselves that they've just seen a master at work.

Jake and **Elwood Blues** - the only gear they needed was a Cadillac, two pairs of sunglasses and a Mission from God.

What to Wear

HAT Any sort of headwear is instant cool in blues-land - this classic hat-trick has been used by John Lee, Jimi and Stevie Ray, among many others.

SHADES (black) Opinion is divided as to whether a blues dude should wear shades. They look cool, sure, but can put your bluffing at a disadvantage - the audience won't be able to see you wince convincingly when you're 'playing with feel'.

GUITAR Safe bets are the Gibson 335 (if you're black) or Fender Strat (if you're white). No-one's quite sure where this racial segregation began, but only a very small number of players have opposed it; Robert Cray and Jimi Hendrix (black guys with Strats), and occasionally Clapton (began with a Gibson 335, but even he gave in to tradition and went back to Strats in the 1970s).

JACKET Most classic blues players are pretty well-dressed - from Blind Lemon right through to Clapton, well-tailored jackets have always been the order of the day. Get one that's a couple of sizes too big - you'll look like you haven't eaten in a week.

TROUSERS Cotton suit trousers only. Denim takes you more in an R&B direction... anything leather, and you're an instant rock poseur.

SHOES Keep them clean. If you're feeling confident, you can make up a story about your days as a Chicago shoeshine boy in the 1950s (not recommended for young bluffers unless your audience has a serious problem with maths).

Guitars and Amps or Trainspotter's corner

With the current level of technology available to the guitarist, you could argue that it's possible to make any guitar produce just about any sound desired.

However, if this view were widely held by most players, the guitar manufacturing industry (not to mention the blues bluffing industry) would collapse. Endless hours of fun can be had debating whether the type of dot-marker on the neck of an **ES-335** improves its tone, or whether a '54 Strat would really beat a '57 in a straight fight. However, if you're going to prove your blues pedigree, a working knowledge of the guitars themselves is a must. There are three major contenders for the 'blues axe' crown – the **Gibson ES-335**, the **Fender Stratocaster**, and the **Gibson Les Paul**.

Eyes shut and frown!

Background information on each has been provided, including famous users, instant opinion, and a knowledgeable fact which you can use as evidence of your blues guitar aptitude. **All usage of jargon has, of course, been maximised for your convenience.**

Gibson ES-335

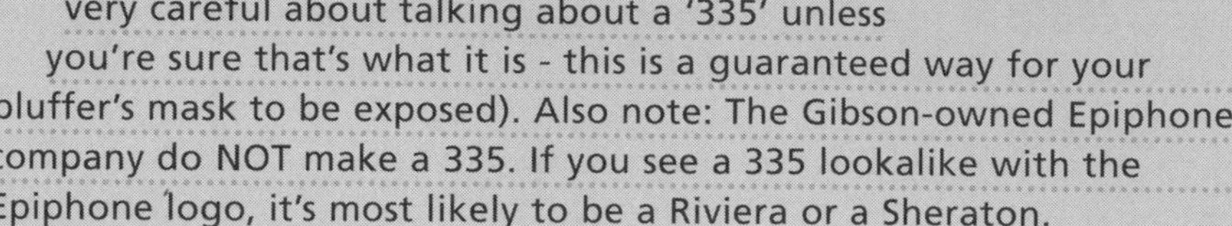

ANORAK DATA:
First introduced in 1958 as the ES-335T. Spawned the rest of the (similar) '300' series - the ES-355, 345 and 325 (so be very careful about talking about a '335' unless you're sure that's what it is - this is a guaranteed way for your bluffer's mask to be exposed). Also note: The Gibson-owned Epiphone company do NOT make a 335. If you see a 335 lookalike with the Epiphone logo, it's most likely to be a Riviera or a Sheraton.

FAMOUS NAMES:
BB King, Freddie King, Eric Clapton (with Cream), John Lee Hooker (with a bottle of beer), Alvin Lee.

DESIGN:
Solid centre block. Two humbucking pickups with three-way selector switch. Two volume plus two tone controls.

SOUND:
Despite the semi-solid construction, fundamentally a 335 sounds and feels like an electric guitar. Adjectives to use include 'warm', 'mellow' etc, plus more esoteric words like 'soulful', 'emotional', 'mild'. Or you can use the catch-all term 'evocative' - no-one will dare challenge its use in fear that they won't know exactly what a 335 evokes (in a crisis, this word can be used to refer to any guitar).

KNOWLEDGEABLE FACT:
Often called a 'semi-acoustic' but this is sometimes confused with 'electro-acoustic'. The correct definition is 'semi-solid', due to the solid centre block which runs along the length of the guitar to reduce feedback.

INSTANT OPINION:
"The trapeze tailpiece model definitely has more sustain." (untrue, but impossible to prove without an oscilloscope).

ACCEPTABLE CRITICISM:
A brand new ES335TD is phenomenally expensive (around £1600 in the UK or $3,300 in the USA).

Opinion is divided over whether those dot-shaped neck markers affect the tone...

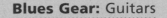

Gibson Les Paul

ANORAK DATA:
First introduced in 1952 ('Gold Top' model).
Designed by the eponymous guitarist.
Humbuckers replaced single-coil pickups in 1957.
Various off-shoots (Les Paul Junior, Les Paul Special, Les Paul Deluxe etc) but the two best-known are the Standard and Custom.

FAMOUS NAMES:
Eric Clapton (Bluesbreakers), Gary Moore, Jimmy Page, Paul Kossoff.

DESIGN:
Solid body (originally mahogany) with arched top, two humbucking pickups with three-way selector switch. Two volume, two tone controls.

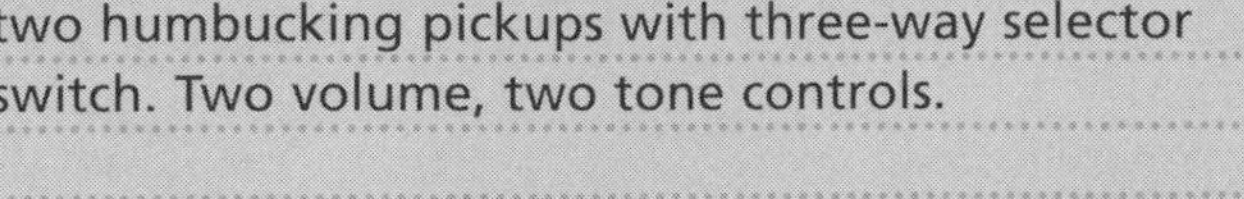

SOUND:
Les Paul wanted the guitar to have a 20-second sustain (hence the mahogany), and this is the instrument's most famous characteristic. Combination of solid construction and high-output pickups makes it suitable for high-gain, long distorted sounds (hence the rock-blues leanings of the above-named players). Typical adjectives include 'singing', 'ringing', 'stinging', 'swinging' (jazzers only), 'gunslinging' (guitar heroes only).

KNOWLEDGEABLE FACT:
Some 'Les Pauls' have double cutaways and a flat top - these are referred to as 'SG-style'. Generally, though, the name Les Paul is used by players to describe the arch-top, single cutaway guitar shown in the photo.

INSTANT OPINION:
Just say any old rubbish involving sustain, e.g. "the sustain on my old LP, it's incredible, but that's 'cos I got mine from a bloke who knew the milkman who used to deliver to Clapton's house back in '64."

ACCEPTABLE CRITICISM:
Try wearing a solid mahogany guitar on a shoulder strap throughout a 2-hour gig, then come up with your own...

The Les Paul Gold Top - ringing, singing, and gunslinging.

Fender Stratocaster

ANORAK DATA:
First introduced in 1954. Design has hardly changed in 45 years. Some models manufactured in Japan from early 1980s, under the Squier brand name. Strats are now made in the following countries (listed in order of price and quality): USA, Japan, Korea, Mexico, and China.

FAMOUS NAMES:
Jeff Beck, Eric Clapton (solo albums), Ry Cooder, Robert Cray, Rory Gallagher, Peter Green, Jimi Hendrix, Kenny-Wayne Shepherd, Stevie Ray Vaughan.

DESIGN:
3 single-coil pickups, double-cutaway, solid body. Floating bridge vibrato unit (though this is not used by many blues players).

SOUND:
Generally brighter than other blues guitars, due to its single-coil pickups. Adjectives to use include 'sparkling', 'glassy', 'sharp', 'honking', 'bell-like', 'squealing', 'crisp'...

KNOWLEDGEABLE FACT:
Single-ply scratchplates were replaced by three-play white/black/white versions in 1959. Impress other Strat users by noting that their single-ply scratchplate (very common on copies) is "based on the classic '57 design".

INSTANT OPINION:
"Early '80s Japanese Squiers were actually better made than the American Strats at the time." (true in some cases, and vague enough to convince everyone with your confident use of such a sweeping statement).

ACCEPTABLE CRITICISM:
They don't always stay in tune if you get carried away with the whammy bar.

This is a 1956 'Sunburst', but then you knew that by looking at the scratchplate, didn't you?

Backup Bluffs

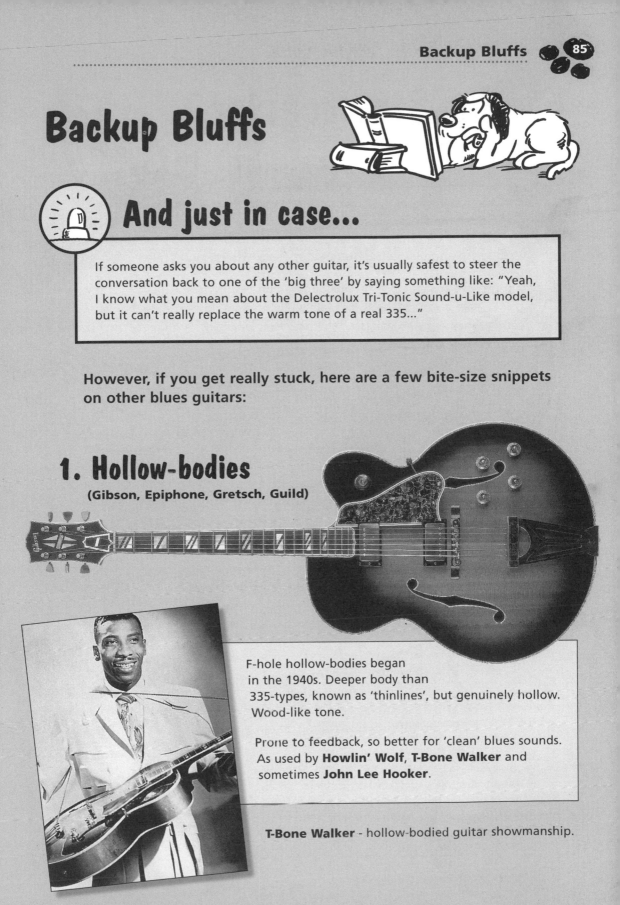

And just in case...

If someone asks you about any other guitar, it's usually safest to steer the conversation back to one of the 'big three' by saying something like: "Yeah, I know what you mean about the Delectrolux Tri-Tonic Sound-u-Like model, but it can't really replace the warm tone of a real 335..."

However, if you get really stuck, here are a few bite-size snippets on other blues guitars:

1. Hollow-bodies

(Gibson, Epiphone, Gretsch, Guild)

F-hole hollow-bodies began in the 1940s. Deeper body than 335-types, known as 'thinlines', but genuinely hollow. Wood-like tone.

Prone to feedback, so better for 'clean' blues sounds. As used by **Howlin' Wolf**, **T-Bone Walker** and sometimes **John Lee Hooker**.

T-Bone Walker - hollow-bodied guitar showmanship.

2. Gibson Flying V

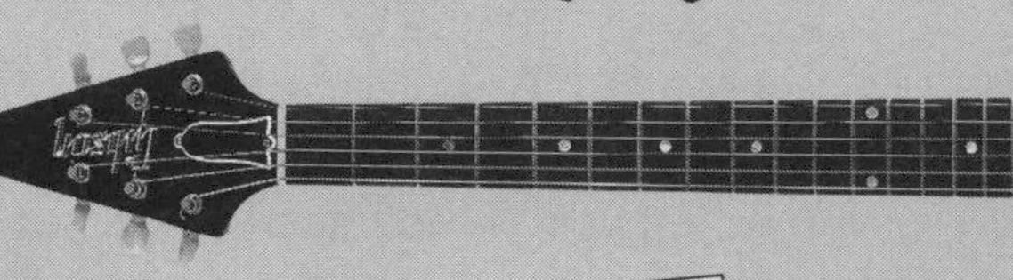

Solid-body, launched in 1958.
Not generally thought of as a blues guitar, but included here because it was played by left-handed bluesman **Albert King**.

Pickups and bridge identical to a Les Paul, but with V-shaped body.

The legendary **Albert King** - the most famous blues player ever to sport a **Flying V**.

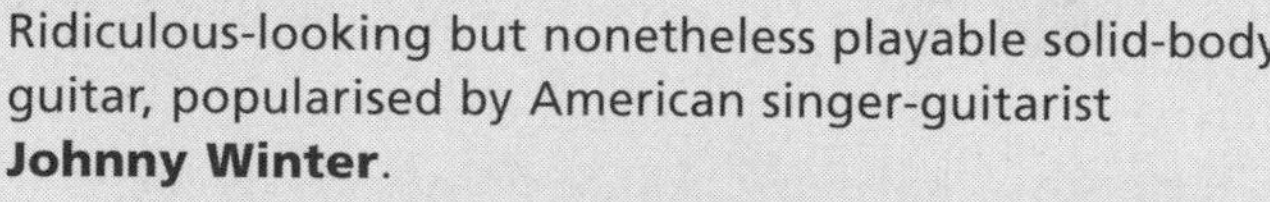

3. Gibson Firebird

Ridiculous-looking but nonetheless playable solid-body guitar, popularised by American singer-guitarist **Johnny Winter**.

Vintage models sometimes feature bridge vibratos. Available in 'standard' and 'reverse' models (presumably the original shape was so awful that someone suggested swapping it round. It didn't improve things.)

Ridiculous-looking but well-loved
(that's the **Gibson Firebird**, not **Johnny Winter**).

Multi-FX settings

Shown here are suggested settings for a multi-FX unit. As all of these products have different specifications and names for settings, each parameter setting is shown as a percentage which should be translated into numbers according to whatever scale your multi-FX unit uses.

The only effects shown are distortion/overdrive, EQ and reverb. Don't use any others - remember, you're using all of this technology to create the sound of an amp in a room! Although we've suggested a guitar type, don't worry if the one you own is different - just follow the pickup settings shown anyway.

Guitar	distortion type	drive (%)	level (%)	low (%)	mid (%)	high (%)	rev type	rev length	rev level	sound
Semi-solid (e.g. 335) any pickup	overdrive	40	50	40	50	65	Hall	1.8s	20%	**BB King** smooth lead
Semi-solid (e.g. 335) neck pickup	overdrive	10	60	50	50	40	Room	1.0s	10%	**John Lee Hooker** Rhythm
Strat neck pickup	overdrive	30	70	40	70	60	Hall	2.0s	40%	**Peter Green** slow blues
Strat neck pickup	overdrive	10	80	50	40	60	Room	1.2s	15%	**Robert Cray** '80s
Strat neck pickup	overdrive/ sustain/lead	65	50	40	70	35	Hall	1.8s	30%	**Clapton** '70s
Strat mid pickup	blues or overdrive	50	50	60	60	40	Room	1.0s	20%	**SRV** lead sound
Les Paul bridge pickup	overdrive	60	40	50	60	50	Hall	1.5s	20%	**Clapton** '60s 335 distortion
Les Paul neck pickup	overdrive/ sustain/lead	80	50	60	60	50	Hall	1.5s	30%	**Gary Moore** '80s

Blues Lyrics or 'My baby's still with me, I got a house and a car, and the sun's shining - guess I better join a pop band'

Most guitarists have a problem with lyrics, mainly because the words have a habit of filling that 24-bar section between the end of the intro and the start of the solo, taking up space which could easily feature more guitar parts.

However, it's a rare blues artist that makes his or her name purely from instrumentals, and sooner or later you're going to have to sing - or worse still, write - blues lyrics of your own.

Handy Hint

The first thing to remember is that (unlike any other type of songwriting) you don't have to avoid clichés. The classic blues idea of 'my baby left me' has been used by pretty much every guitarist mentioned in this book. Similarly, no rhyme is too obvious. **Stevie Ray** told his woman **"You can't change it, can't re-arrange it"**. **Peter Green** needed **"someone's hands to lead me through the night"** and **"someone's arms to hold me tight"**. **John Lee Hooker** even got away with rhyming the words **'Boom Boom'** with the words **'Boom Boom'**.

Repetition is actually desirable most of the time. Repetition is actually desirable most of the time. Not only can you almost always repeat verse 1 at the end of any blues to save you from writing another verse, you can actually repeat lines within the verse itself. The classic three-line blues is actually a two-line blues - the first two lines are the same.

Lyrical genius...

Check out **Blind Lemon Jefferson's** 'Matchbox Blues';
**"I'm sittin' here wonderin', matchbox hole in my coat,
I'm sittin' here wonderin', matchbox hole in my coat,
I ain't got no matches but I sure got a long way to go"**

Not exactly Shakespeare, and whoever said that 'coat' rhymes with 'go' anyway? However, one listen to Lemon's original (or even **Ringo Starr**'s painful version of **Carl Perkins**' version) and you'll be convinced that this man really *feels* that he, er, hasn't got any matches.

Contrary to popular belief, you can't just think about something that's upset you and assume it's good material for blues. Some subjects will lead you more towards Rock 'n' Roll (e.g. you can't have a blues lyric about automobiles, sex, high school etc). Others have already been snapped up by Country players (so avoid writing about orphans, dogs, disability, or deaf and blind dogs with no parents etc).

Sometimes even the way you describe the subject affects the style of music. 'Drink a wee glass of malt?' Scottish folk song. 'Take another cup of moonshine?' Country song. 'Need a shot of booze?' Heavy metal. And, of course, if you hadn't guessed already, the blues version should be 'got a bottle of bourbon'.

Generally, if you want to write blues lyrics, remember three things. Choose a subject that's a bit of a downer, but not life-threatening (say, running out of matches). Talk about it as if you were born in America, not Milton Keynes (don't 'pop to the supermarket'; instead, you should 'hang out in the local store'). And most importantly, sing it like you mean it. The more sincerity in your voice, the less anyone will pay attention to what you're actually singing.

It's Easy To Bluff
Rock Guitar

Chuck Berry: the Godfather of rock

Introduction

Whatever reasons a guitarist has for picking up an electric guitar, you can bet a truckload of leather jackets that rock was involved in some way or another. It's all very well to learn beautiful classical solo pieces to perform in front of your grandparents, or acoustic folk numbers to play at the local barn dance, but deep down, most players have a burning desire to get up on stage and yell at the audience "are you ready to rawwwwk?!".

Unfortunately, a great deal of rock guitar playing takes years - sometimes decades - of practice. To become truly proficient, you may have to learn (ugh!) scales and (yuck!) arpeggios and possibly even (aaaaargh!) to read music. Luckily, help is at hand. *It's Easy To Bluff Rock Guitar* explains how, with the right information, equipment, clothes, name-dropping skills and attitude, you can become an expert in all the local customs of 'planet rock'. Learn what to say and when to say it. Find out which players you can mention at a gig without ridicule. And play the riffs and licks that will have other musicians worshipping at your feet.

For example

Guitarists naturally have a tendency to judge each other by technical skill. The rock bluffer need show no fear, even when confronted with the most well-practised virtuoso. Any rival who can play stunning sweep-picking arpeggios at 10 notes per second can be dismissed as 'passé', 'retro', or 'a heavy metal dinosaur'. Players who achieve super-accurate scalic runs should be accused of 'having no feel' or 'missing the point'.

Of course, if you get stuck in a situation when your playing really is on the line, we've helpfully supplied just a smattering of impressive musical examples which you can throw into solos whenever you think the audience need reminding of your complete mastery of the instrument.

It's Easy To Bluff Rock Guitar **gives you an unfair advantage over other guitarists. It's an immoral, cheating, deceitful, unethical and deceptive way of improving your guitar playing. So now all you need to do is go out and buy up all the other copies so that no-one else gets their hands on them...**

The History of Rock or 'Who to name-drop, and when'

A true rock god will, when interviewed, make frequent reference to early blues. You know the kind of thing; "sure, we're into thrash-industrial-speed-punk-techno-metal these days, but sooner or later we're gonna go back to our roots and do an album of Robert Johnson covers". This is a perfectly valid bluffer's tactic, but doesn't really represent the truth in musical terms.

Origins

Rock music as we now know it is largely derived from R&B, so when you're name-checking influences the best era to start looking is the 1950s. Without a doubt the most influential guitar player from this era was **Chuck Berry**. Every rock player of the last four decades owes something to him, and many of the techniques we take for granted first appeared on his recordings.

Bluffer's rule #1: Whatever style you play, **Chuck Berry** is your biggest influence.

Aerosmith wouldn't be using palm-muted downstrokes were it not for Chuck. **The Sex Pistols** wouldn't have played their driving, 8-to-the-bar chord parts without the influence of the great man. And The Rolling Stones' **Keith Richards** alleges he would never have picked up the guitar in the first place if he hadn't heard those early Berry singles on Chess records.

Mostly, you'll bluff your way through any 'rock roots' conversation just by demonstrating your detailed knowledge about Chuck (see page 14), but it's also useful to have a sentence or two about some of his contemporaries, even though they will generally win you less cool points.

Eddie Cochran (perhaps the first rock guitar hero) and **Duane Eddy** (first rock guitar instrumentalist) are both worth a mention. Even **Hank Marvin** (not a name you'd normally bring up in a roomful of hairy rockers) was an innovator - he was the first Strat player in the UK, and also pioneered whammy-bar string bends.

Despite the fact that many classic rock acts started in the early '60s (**The Stones**, **The Kinks** and **The Who** to name but three), most of the choice name-drops occur in the later part of the decade. If you know your **Hendrix**, early **Pink Floyd**, **Jefferson Airplane** and **Cream**, you'll find that nine times out of ten you won't even have to go any further back than this.

The 1970s

This is by far the easiest decade to discuss for the would-be rock guru, because it's very difficult to put a foot wrong. No-one will argue against your assertions of the influence of Jimmy Page on your playing. Early Thin Lizzy and Van Halen recordings still command maximum cred amongst rock veterans.

Bluffer's rule # 2:
If you *have* to name-drop a 1970s HM act...

Even artists which were considered the height of naffness just a few years ago (**Slade**, **Marc Bolan**, **Kiss**, **Sweet**) can, if you bluff confidently enough, be used to demonstrate your unsurpassed appreciation of kitsch and irony in a rock context (hint: this is fairly advanced bluffing, and should only be attempted after you've spent some time on some entry-level concoctions).

Of course, it's not possible to ignore the fact that around this time, heavy metal was starting to claw its Satanic way into the album charts. It can be difficult to divorce the players from the paraphernalia (skulls, crucifixes, Viking helmets, rune-clad mystic symbols etc) so if you *have* to name-drop a 1970s HM act, at least try to choose one whose clothes you'd be happy to be seen in yourself.

... at least try to choose one whose clothes you'd be happy to be seen in yourself.

The 1980s

During this period, guitar sounds, stadium crowds, and hairstyles all got bigger at the same rate. Many bands who first recorded in the 1970s had continued success (Queen, AC/DC, Dire Straits, ZZ Top). However, the development of the synthesiser eventually led to the birth of rock music's all-too-legitimate offspring - the Adult Oriented Rock band.

Bluffer's rule #3: Don't admit to owning any albums by **REO Speedwagon**.

Whatever your personal view of AOR acts like **REO Speedwagon**, **Journey** and **Foreigner**, it is bluffing suicide to even mention one of their songs, let alone be caught in possession of an album. The other phenomenon that appeared during this decade was the fretboard tapping virtuoso, now universally referred to as 'widdlers'. Just a few years after **Van Halen**'s first album, the likes of **Vinnie Moore**, **Joe Satriani**, **Jennifer Batten**, **Steve Vai** and **Paul Gilbert** were wowing the guitar-playing community with their instrumental technique.

Warning: it's extremely difficult to navigate your way through a conversation about these players with your status intact. Some are safe to mention and will guarantee admiring glances etc, others will earn you promises that you'll never work again in this town... that's if you don't have your fingers broken for alluding to them in the first place.

To give an example, **Yngwie Malmsteen** and **Steve Vai** are both very fine players (even having played in the same band at different times), yet Vai's name is positively celestial to guitarists, whereas citing Malmsteen as an influence will (at best) result in you being firmly directed to the nearest exit. There's no real rule of thumb to help you here - you'll just need to learn which players are 'safe ground'.

Bluffer's rule #4: Learn your widdlers.

The 1990s

In recent years, advanced guitar techniques have, to some extent, taken a back seat. This is great news for a rock charlatan like oneself, because it's now possible to look cool with considerably less time spent in the practice-room.

Bluffer's rule #5: You don't have to practise too hard...

Kurt Cobain and **Noel Gallagher**, for example, are guitar heroes to millions, and yet neither of them are particularly adept players. Concentrating too much on the subject of technique can actually damage your reputation in some circles; the worst criticism you can make of another player is to say "he's good, but *so* 'eighties'." Admittedly, there are still some advanced players on the current scene - **Kim Thayill** of Soundgarden, The Chilis' **Dave Navarro**, Ex-Living Colour guitarist **Vernon Reid** etc, but in the main the big rock guitar heroes (**Eric Clapton**, **Jimi Hendrix**, **Mark Knopfler**) have hardly changed in the last 20 years.

Bluff your way through the 21st century

So the rock bluffers of the 21st century need to be good players - but not too good. If you're technique's already pretty hot, try toning down the quality of your playing by adding so much distortion that no-one can hear it properly.

If you're not an advanced player, you'll still need a few flash licks now and again so you can demonstrate to the audience that your incessant strumming of one chord is actually down to a sense of musical restraint rather than a lack of ideas. Eventually, of course, the pendulum will swing back and technique will reign supreme again. But by that time you'll have had more time to practise, won't you?

Bluffer's rule #6: ... but if you get *really* good, make sure no-one can decipher what you're playing.

Jeff Beck: a true rock pioneer and still one of the most innovative players around

The Players

Bite-size biogs

Rock purists will consider it blasphemy to have a player's entire life summarised in two pages, but in reality, you can bluff your way through with a surprisingly small amount of knowledge. In this chapter you'll find an instant guide to five top rock guitarists.

Remember that these aren't necessarily the most important or famous players - we haven't included **Ritchie Blackmore** or **Mark Knopfler**, for example - but they are the names which crop up most frequently in rock gig-speak.

For each artist, I've included some basic **biographical information**, notes on **playing style**, plus (most importantly) which **techniques** you should steal in order to facilitate your bluffing career. Of course, you have to know the **gear** they used - equipment trainspotters are everywhere and could pounce at any time.

To save you from having to wade through a truckload of albums, I've also picked out one **essential album** for you to mention (not necessarily the best-known - it can sometimes pay dividends to bluff your way by showing you listen to the obscure stuff). If you're actually asked to prove that you've heard the artist, you'd be stuck without the quick and easy **'finest moment'** reference.

Finally, it's always useful to have a few oven-ready opinions up your sleeve. For each player, I've included an 'instant opinion' (usually ambiguous enough to cover all situations) and an 'acceptable criticism'. If you're cool enough to intelligently criticise one of the greats, your status as a blackbelt bluffer is assured.

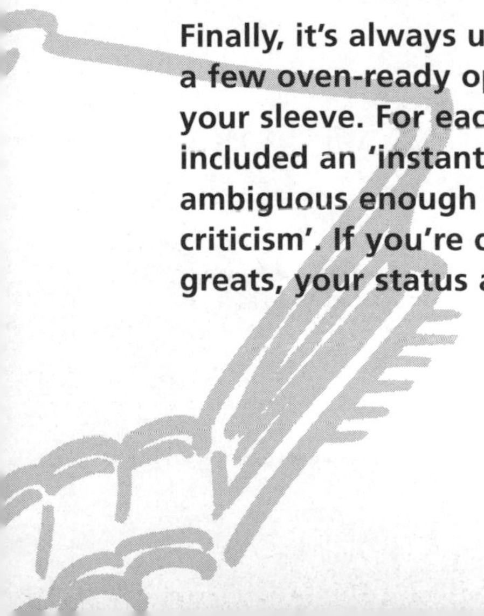

Chuck Berry

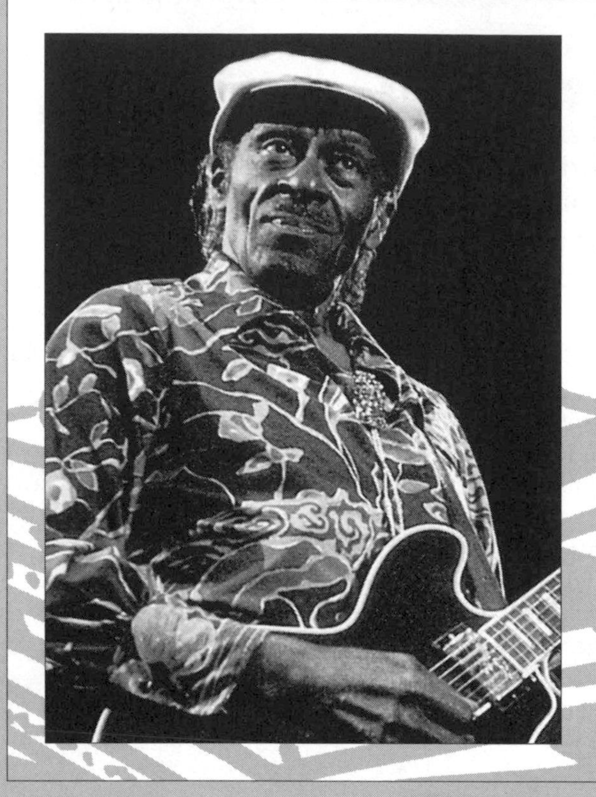

HISTORY AND BACKGROUND:

Born 18th October 1931 *or* 15th January 1926. Like many aspects of Chuck's shady past, his birthdate is still the subject of controversy (he's had various brushes with the law, including armed robbery and 'transporting a minor across a state line for immoral purposes'). 1955 single 'Maybelline' was an instant R&B hit - perhaps the first ever rock recording. Early recordings ('Around And Around', 'Come On', 'Rock And Roll Music', 'Roll Over Beethoven') were heavily covered by British acts - **Rolling Stones, Beatles, Animals, Yardbirds**. Famously eccentric live performer. As well as his trademark 'duckwalk', (see page 92) Chuck is known for always insisting on being paid cash for every performance. He doesn't travel with a band, preferring to hire and fire players local to the venue, and expecting them to learn his entire repertoire before the gig.

PLAYING STYLE:

Plectrum downstrokes, 8-to-the-bar. Double-stops (two strings played together) using first finger flattened over the first two strings, or over the second and third. Occasional lead lines harmonised in thirds. Semi-distorted tone. Almost always plays solos in minor pentatonic box shape.

TECHNIQUES TO STEAL:

Double-stops are great for making solos sound energetic and exciting, and best of all they're even easier to play than single-note lines. The duckwalk should be mastered by every guitar player because it's such an essential bit of showmanship - simply put all your weight on one leg and bend it, then kick the other heel into the floor as you hop along (whilst playing 8-to-the-bar downstrokes). Not as difficult it sounds.

GEAR:

Gibson semi-solids, mainly cherry red ES-335. Often uses Fender combos, but doesn't set much store by amp types 'so long as it works'.

BLUFFER'S ALBUM:

Any compilation 1955-95, but you should also buy a few vinyl singles, regardless of whether you have the equipment to play them. Chess label recordings are still available in second-hand record shops, and if you can get an ex-jukebox one with the centre removed, so much the better.

FINEST MOMENT:

The intro from his classic 'Johnny B Goode' (which is almost identical to many others, including 'Roll Over Beethoven' and 'Bye Bye Johnny') or possibly the main riff from later hit 'No Particular Place To Go' (which is the same song, basically, as another hit 'School Days').

INSTANT OPINION:

"The Godfather of Rock 'n' Roll - he's my biggest influence."

ACCEPTABLE CRITICISM:

Didn't break any new ground after about 1960.

Jeff Beck

HISTORY AND BACKGROUND:

Born 24th June 1944. First big break came when he replaced **Clapton** in the Yardbirds (1965). Formed his own self-titled group the following year. First (pop) hit 'Hi Ho Silver Lining' was his biggest single, and inspired some players to experiment with twin lead lines (so he is partly to blame for the existence of **Iron Maiden**).

Never worked consistently with a vocalist, despite sessions or albums with **Donovan**, **Rod Stewart**, **Tina Turner**, **Kate Bush**, **Brian May**, **Jon Bon Jovi** and **Robert Plant**. Two jazz-rock albums mid '70s - *Blow By Blow* and *Wired*. Current output is roughly one or two albums per decade. Very rarely gives interviews, and spends much of his time restoring classic American cars.

PLAYING STYLE:

In a word - stunning. One of the true masters of the electric guitar. Unreal string bends, whammy-bar harmonics, trills, tapping, country-picking. Usually plays with fingers. Despite the flash stuff, though, he's always willing to play more laid-back lead if the song demands it.

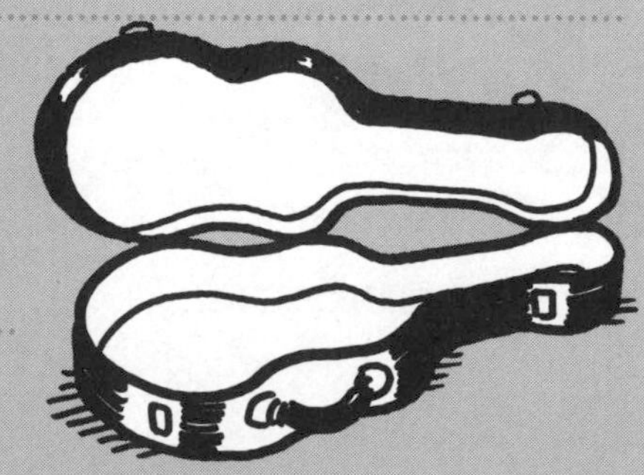

TECHNIQUES TO STEAL:

The most interesting is probably whammy-bar harmonics. Hit an open harmonic (say, 5th or 7th fret) and practice bending that one note around using the bar to create melody. It's difficult but the effect is worth it in audience-wowing terms.

GEAR:

Started on Teles, Strats and Les Pauls, but now synonymous with the Strat. Marshall amps.

BLUFFER'S ALBUM:

Jeff Beck's Guitar Shop (1989) is one of his most accessible, while still showing off that technique. But for true cred points you should own the largely dance-inspired *Who Else* (1999).

FINEST MOMENT:

'Where Were You' from *Jeff Beck's Guitar Shop* features a typical Beck-ism; although it uses lots of repetition, he never plays the same phrase twice with the same tone, using the pickup selector or his picking technique to modify the sound.

INSTANT OPINION:

"Check out the new stuff - he's still one of the most innovative players around."

ACCEPTABLE CRITICISM:

Doesn't release enough material to keep the fans happy.

Brian May

HISTORY AND BACKGROUND: Born 19th July 1947. Worked in a college band called Smile with drummer **Roger Taylor**, before forming Queen in 1971 with singer **Freddie Mercury** and bassist **John Deacon**. His early influences as a player were originally the **Everly Brothers** and the **Shadows**, but like many rock guitarists he soon learned to bluff his way through by namechecking **Chuck Berry** and **Bo Diddley**.

Queen's 25-year career needs little documentation (at the time of writing there are rumours of a reunion with the three remaining members). But Brian's also been an active solo performer both during and after Queen - his 1984 *Starfleet Project* was recorded with **Eddie Van Halen**; he's also done various guest spots and sessions, plus two solo albums.

PLAYING STYLE: Famous for multi-layered harmony guitar parts. These are more intricate than many players first think; often several harmonised lines work against each other. Uses very light strings and picks delicately. Adds whammy bar vibrato to chords.

TECHNIQUES TO STEAL: The harmony thing is pretty tough to copy - even Brian had to use a long delay to duplicate the sound when playing live. Many multi-FX units have harmonisers on-board, but don't attempt to use one of these unless you really know what you're doing with music theory. The results can be truly painful. Try using the whammy bar as a subtle addition to your vibrato, rather than always using it for mad dive-bombing antics.

GEAR: Any rock bluffer should know how to identify The Three Eras Of Brian from pictures and album covers. If he's shown with long curly hair, playing a red home-made guitar through a Vox AC30, it dates from the mid-1970s; long curly hair, red home-made guitar and Vox AC30, and it's from the 1980s. If you see him these days, though, it'll be with long curly hair, a red home-made guitar and a Vox AC30.

BLUFFER'S ALBUM: Queen's *A Night At The Opera* is standard issue for any rock music fan, though there's enough water under the bridge now for you to get away with owning the outrageously overblown but guitaristically impressive 1974 album *Queen II*.

FINEST MOMENT: The 'chiming' layered solo from 'Killer Queen' (from the album *Sheer Heart Attack*) is one of Brian's faves, and most fans agree. However, it's impossible for one player to duplicate on their own, so if you're looking for ideas to steal, try the long delay-based 'Brighton Rock' from the same album.

INSTANT OPINION: "Don't buy that Brian May signature guitar - the sound isn't just about his gear, you know - it's in the way he plays."

ACCEPTABLE CRITICISM: Solo material has tended towards the bland compared to more adventurous guitar work with Queen.

Edward Van Halen

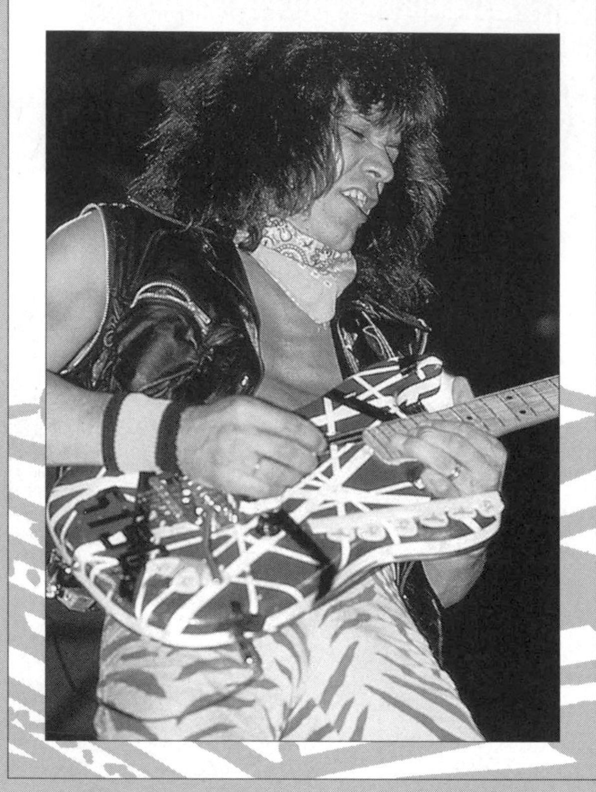

HISTORY AND BACKGROUND:
Born 26th January 1957. Dutch in origin. Learned drums originally (brother Alex played guitar) but swapped instruments with him before forming Van Halen in 1974. First album *Van Halen* in 1978 was (perhaps!) the first to feature picking-hand fretboard tapping, although this is one of the great bluffers' debates of rock guitar. It appeared briefly on Queen's *It's Late* a year previously, and was allegedly used by **ZZ Top** even earlier (although no-one seems to be able to identify on which track).
Whether or not he was technically the first to tap, EVH still deserves his status as one of the most influential electric guitarists of all time. Has confessed that he doesn't listen to music much these days, as shown by the fact that his material has hardly developed in the last decade or so. Members of the band have publicly apologised for the poor quality of the 1998 album *Van Halen III*.
Note: the initiated now refer to him as 'Edward', rather than 'Eddie' Van Halen. Like Dave 'David' Gilmour, he's gone back to the full version of his name for what we can only assume are reasons of musical maturity.

PLAYING STYLE:
Tapping, harmonics and combinations of same, using distorted and delayed sound, plus flangers, phasers etc as appropriate. Solos are not always just speed-based - he plays some fine melodic material too, especially on the early albums.

TECHNIQUES TO STEAL:

Try to avoid basing your whole style on tapping, but as with all of the show-off techniques, it is worth learning a few basic examples to throw into solos now and again. The Van Halen guitar sound (bridge humbucker through distortion pedal and valve amp with medium-length delay added) was a blueprint used by rock players for years afterwards.

GEAR:

Originally, he used a single-pickup hybrid guitar made from spare parts with an old-style Fender floating bridge, into a Marshall stack. More recently, Ernie Ball and Peavey have made signature models for him. He now uses his own signature Peavey 5150 amp.

BLUFFER'S ALBUM:

Without question, the band's debut is the one to own, but you might also want to be seen with some of their other material from the same era with **Dave Lee Roth** on vocals. The mid-80s Sammy Hagar stuff is derided by many for its US-rock production sheen.

FINEST MOMENT:

The instrumental 'Eruption' from *Van Halen* is responsible for some of the greatest aural pain ever to be visited upon the ears of guitar shop assistants, but when you listen to the man himself play it, you can see what all the fuss was about.

INSTANT OPINION:

"Combining melodic playing with tapping - he was the first and still the best."

ACCEPTABLE CRITICISM:

Should get out more and listen to some new music.

Steve Vai

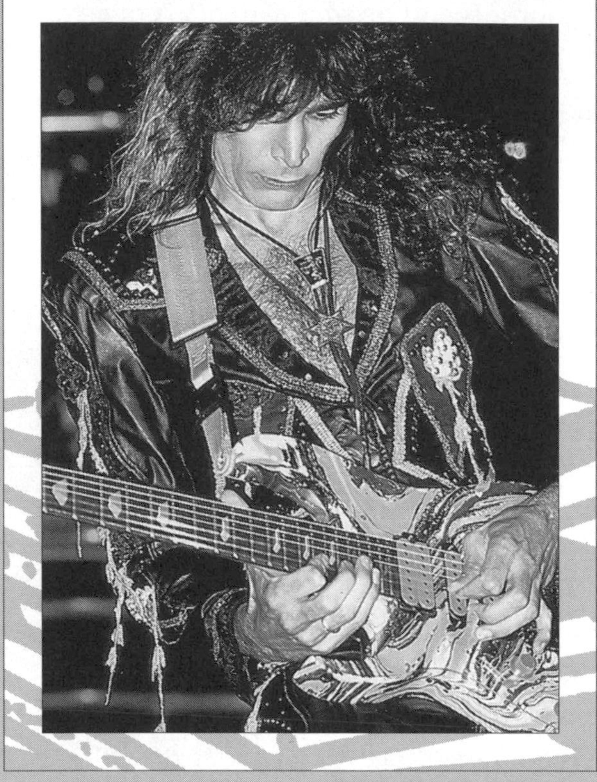

HISTORY AND BACKGROUND:

Born 6th June 1960.
First big break came when he worked as a transcriber and then guitar player for the infamously-meticulous **Frank Zappa**. During the 1980s he went on to replace **Yngwie Malmsteen** in flash-metal band **Alcatrazz**, then worked with **Dave Lee Roth** (who had recently quit **Van Halen**).

Solo album *Flex-able* was followed by a stint with **Whitesnake**, with various solo recordings since, all exploring the arty side of virtuoso rock. The man's studio and practice techniques are unconventional, to say the least. He's into meditation, fasting, and using recordings of animals on backing tracks.

PLAYING STYLE:

Whether or not you're into squealy widdle-metal, you have to admit that Steve is possibly the world's most technically accomplished rock guitarist. He uses all the techniques popularised by **Van Halen** (whammy bar dives, tapping, pinched/ natural/artificial harmonics) and many others besides (multi-layered harmonics in harmony, bar-flicking or 'gargling', weird tunings on six- and seven-string guitars).

TECHNIQUES TO STEAL:

Start with gaining as much pitch control over harmonics as you can, then work on your whammy technique, then be prepared to give up your job and go and live in a rehearsal room for 10 years or so - that's the only way you're going to steal from Steve...

GEAR:

Ibanez Jem and 7-string Universe guitars, designed by Steve (see page 93). Amps mainly Marshall and Soldanos, though he's currently endorsing Carvins.

BLUFFER'S ALBUM:

If you can stand the sexist lyrics, massive 80s-rock production and sparkly keyboard sounds, the guitar playing on Whitesnake's 'Slip Of The Tongue' is wonderful. However, if you do buy this album, keep it in a brown paper bag under the bed in case anyone finds out. Vai recordings suitable for the CD rack include *Passion and Warfare* and *Flex-able*, plus any early 1980s Zappa albums.

FINEST MOMENT:

For pure showmanship, watch the movie 'Crossroads' - Steve plays a 'gunslinger' guitar-player character who takes part in a musical duel at the end of the film. For bluffing purposes, though, you're better off extolling the virtues of one of the solo album tracks - For The Love Of God (from *Passion and Warfare*) is a good starting point.

INSTANT OPINION:

"Sure, technically he's pretty good, but he can't play with the feel of Kurt Cobain" (almost certainly untrue, but like all good bluffs, it makes you look knowledgeable, starts an argument, and can't be settled one way or the other).

ACCEPTABLE CRITICISM:

Fashion only, I'm afraid, but there's a wealth of scope there - blue hair (including back-combing), distressed jeans, spandex pants, lace cardigans...

Emergency backup bluffs

Here are some bluffing basics on a further six players, just in case you need additional reference to prove your depth of knowledge.

1. Scotty Moore

The most famous of **Elvis Presley**'s guitarists. Was working as a session player at Sun Studios in the early 1950s, before teaming up with **The King** in 1954. Used Gibson archtops (including L-5s and Super 400). He's responsible for many of the rockabilly double-stopped licks that we know and love today. If anyone plays a rock 'n' roll lick that doesn't sound like **Chuck Berry**, simply describe it as "very Scotty Moore" for instant respect from those in the know.

2. Jimmy Page

Like, you need any information about the man who played 'Stairway to Heaven', right? Well, we should thank our Jim for a lot more than merely adding to the guitar shop repertoire. Check out Led Zep's work and you'll hear open acoustic tunings, time signature tricks, and modal improvisations, plus a range of influences from English folk to Indian classical music.

Most famously played sunburst Gibson Les Pauls, but also had several Telecasters and of course the 6/12-string double-necked ES1275 (pictured). Generally he plays electric through a Marshall stack. What else?!

3. Joe Satriani

Probably the biggest guitar hero of the late 1980s. His popularity's taken a bit of a dip lately, partly due to a less-than-great album in 1996, partly due to a lack of commercial interest in instrumental rock generally.

He knows the instrument inside out, though, and his tracks, despite featuring more than a dash of flash, actually have *good melodies*. Ibanez player, mainly through Marshalls. The 'Satch' sound is a very warm, thick, midrange-heavy tone, with compression and delay. Also notable for teaching **Steve Vai** and Metallica's **Kirk Hammett**.

4. Kurt Cobain

When you consider that your average street-corner session player or pub rock musician is likely to be a technically better guitarist than Kurt, it might seem unfair that he's featured on the same page as, er, **Page**, but there's a good reason for it. His aggressive guitar style and Nirvana's sparse sound were defining factors in the development of rock music in the 1990s. Plus, of course, with his self-imposed martyrdom back in 1994, he's become one of the most bluffed-about guitar players of the decade.

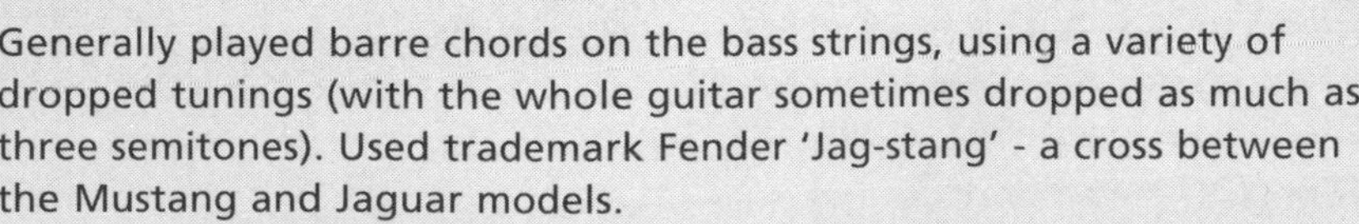

Generally played barre chords on the bass strings, using a variety of dropped tunings (with the whole guitar sometimes dropped as much as three semitones). Used trademark Fender 'Jag-stang' - a cross between the Mustang and Jaguar models.

5. John Squire

Contemporary Indie-rock icon. First came to our attention in 1989 on the **Stone Roses'** debut album. Impersonated **Jimmy Page** outrageously on their next recording, 'Second Coming'. Technically, he's not an especially interesting player (usual pentatonics and barre chords) but much-discussed due to the way he uses the guitar as part of the mix, often layering several different guitars, amps, tones, and tunings to create the overall effect.

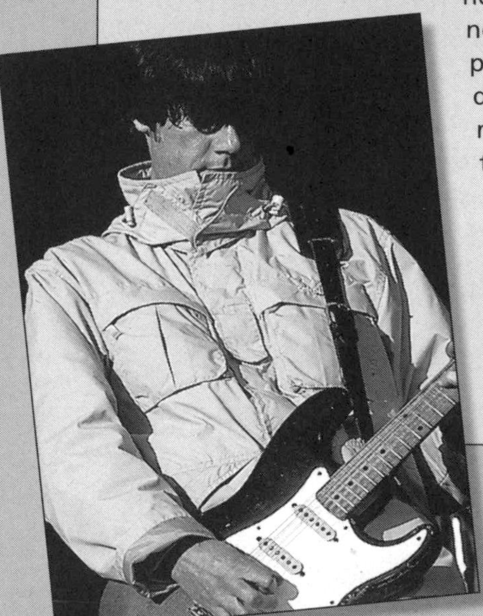

Played a Gretsch Country Gent and Fender Jaguar with **the Roses** - currently favours Les Pauls. Bizarrely, you'll find it difficult to criticise his technique in a bluffing environment - everything he does seems to be sacred, despite the fact that he's only done three albums in 13 years.

6. Noel Gallagher

Controversial Britrock player, and possibly the most successful rock bluffer of all time. Has continued to play the same six or seven chords and the same two pentatonic scale shapes throughout his recording career, and consistently has chart success, despite refusal to attempt anything new on the guitar. Depending on whether or not you like Oasis, you can choose to bluff either side of the technique debate - if you're a fan, then anyone who criticises Noel's playing 'just doesn't get it'; if you're not, simply learn three or four Oasis solos note-for-note, and point out to your opponent how similar they are.

Noel plays a 1970 Epiphone Casino almost exclusively, although there's a current signature model you can buy. He's loved and hated by the guitar world - on the one hand, he's responsible for tens of thousands of young people getting into the guitar; on the other, he made them think it sounds OK to thrash away at an open C chord through a wall of distortion.

Spinal Tap

"How much more clichéd can this be..."

In 1980 film director Marti Di Bergi made this classic documentary, or if you will, rockumentary, about an English rock band on their comeback tour of the US. It's become the most quoted movie of all time among rock musicians, and as such the bluffer should know every word of the script by heart.

However, if you've never seen it, here are the most common 'Tap' references you'll hear at gigs, together with the required response.

Situation	Tap reference	Your response
Guitarist has very loud amp - refers to the band's modified Marshalls whose controls go up to 11	**"It goes up to eleven"**	**"That's, like, one louder"**
Drummer is late for the gig - refers to Tap drummers who commonly die under mysterious circumstances	**"He's probably dead"**	**"..in a bizarre gardening accident..."**
The band hasn't rehearsed, or a key member hasn't turned up - refers to Tap gig shortly after Nigel's resignation	**"There's nothing for it"**	**"we'll have to play Jazz Odyssey"**
Somebody comments on your guitar - refers to interview between Marty and Nigel	**"I'll just take a look..."**	**"Don't even look at it. Don't even point"**
Band, stage set, album, guitar or amp is coloured black - refers to all-black cover for Tap's 'Smell The Glove' album	**"How much more black can this be?"**	**"None. None... more black"**

Jimmy Page: stairway to technical mastery

Rhythm Patterns or 'He doesn't want to make it cry or sing'

If you have to bluff your way through a whole rock gig, you'll need to convince everyone in the band that you know your 'rock chops', so it's vital that you can play some basic accompaniment styles.

In this section you'll find six rhythm and picking patterns, in progressive order of difficulty, that rock guitarists use when playing in a band context under a singer or lead player.

Rhythm Tips

- Almost every rock player uses a pick rather than fingers for rhythm work. And If you're playing in 4/4 time, you should generally favour downstrokes rather than upstrokes.
- **Rest the picking-hand palm gently on the strings near the bridge to create palm-mutes, then use 8-to-the-bar downstrokes with the plectrum. This is essential for heavier rock styles.**
- Generally, avoid open major chords like G, C, D etc - they don't sound anything like as good as 'power chords' (see page 144).
- **There's a common misconception that the more distortion you use, the heavier it will sound. This is rarely true, because if you bury the whole mix in distortion, the attack of the chord is lost, so the whole mix doesn't 'rock'.**
- Don't strum all 6 strings, all the time. Most rock rhythm parts only use the bass strings.
- **Experiment with tunings for a heavier sound. Try dropping the bass string down to D, or tuning the whole guitar a semitone lower.**
- Don't use lots of reverb on rhythm parts - it turns the whole sound into a mushy mess.
- **There is no such thing as a tuning that's 'close enough for rock and roll'. If your guitar's out of tune, your rhythm playing will *always* sound wrong. Get an electronic tuner and use it!**
- Use accents. Why should every chord in your rhythm pattern be played at the same volume?
- **Be disciplined. Don't let your concentration wander even if what you're playing is really simple - a good rhythm part often features very little variation.**

'No Latin Quarter'

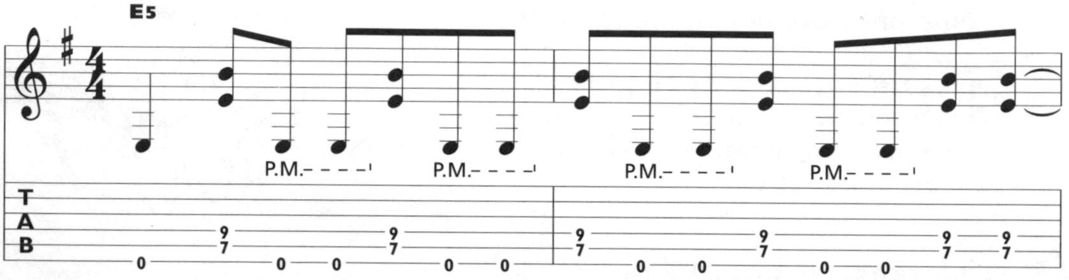

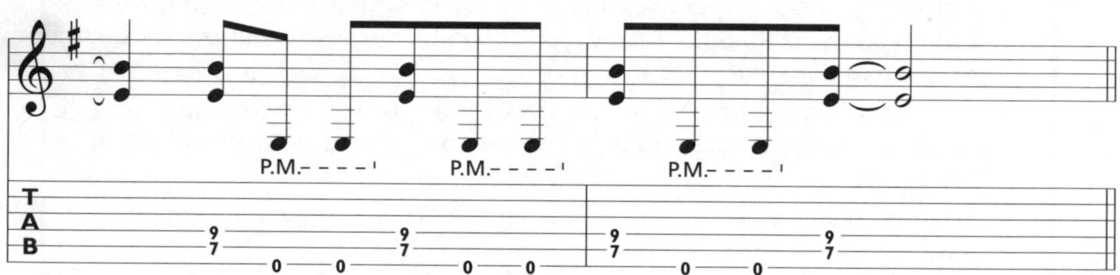

Highlighting the contrast between muted/ringing notes by playing them in different octaves, this example would be right at home driving along an early 80s style Heavy Rock/Metal track.

Ironically, the rhythm has an almost Latin American quality. However, with the correct (i.e. extreme) volume, distortion and posturing, you can be sure *nobody* will be wuss enough to attempt the cha-cha...

'Skipping Scallies'

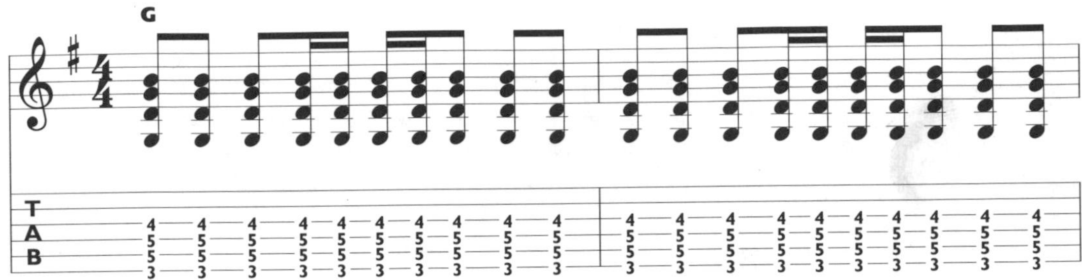

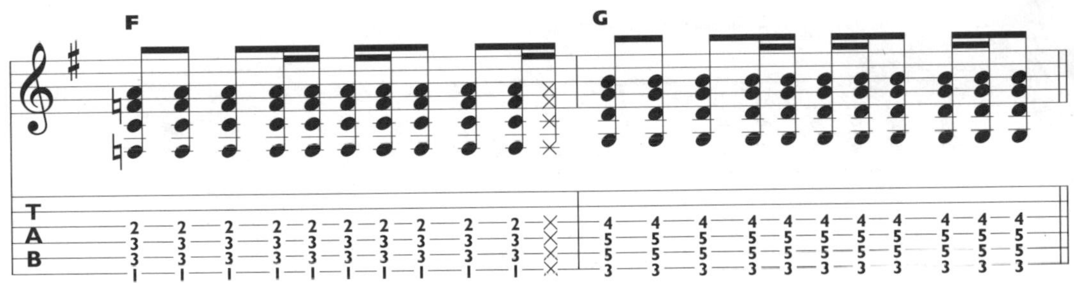

This rhythm features a more contemporary 'skipping' beat feel, in the style of **Oasis** et al - use up and down strums throughout.

There is no need to stick religiously to the same pattern for more than a bar at a time, though it could be argued that you are trying to produce a repetitive 'hypnotic' feel, if inspiration deserts you in the heat of the moment!

'Highwayman On The Gallows'

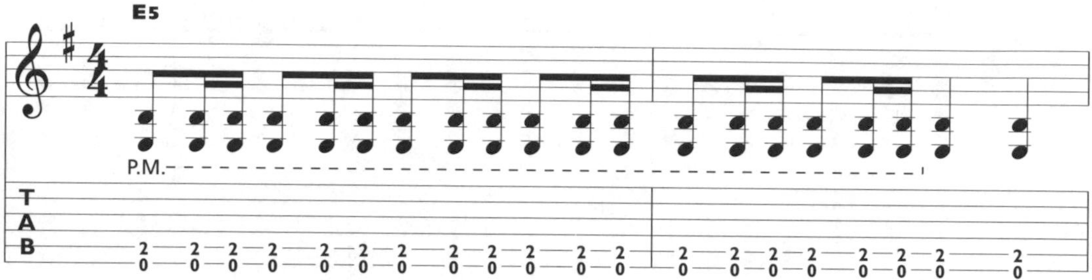

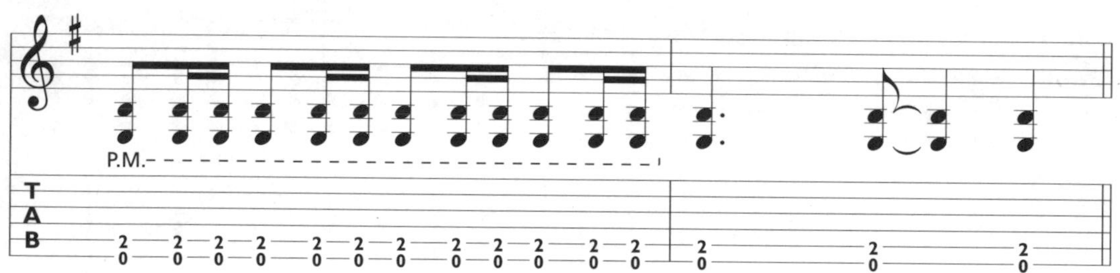

This 'galloping' rhythm has been used on many **Iron Maiden** songs, giving a driving feel, like you're really 'leaning on the beat'.

Maximum Impact!

For maximum impact, punctuate the fast bits with ringing chord accents, as featured in bars 2 and 4. How fast you play it depends on the limitations of your stamina... and your drummer's.

'Smells Like Kurt'

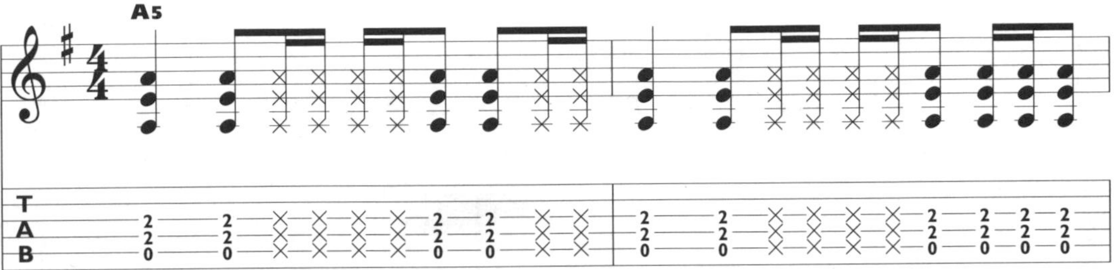

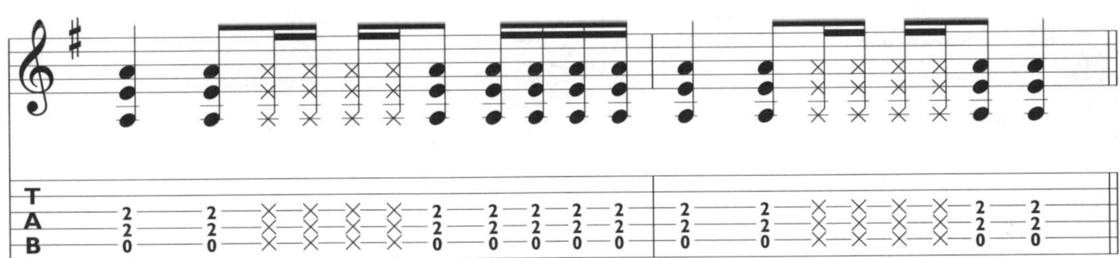

Based round a loose '**Nirvana**' style rhythm feel, this example features a large amount of percussive muted strumming. This keeps the rhythm moving nicely as well as giving you extra time to make your 'seamless' chord changes.

As a general rule, keep these strums from ringing or you will lose the feeling of contrast.

'Cult Following'

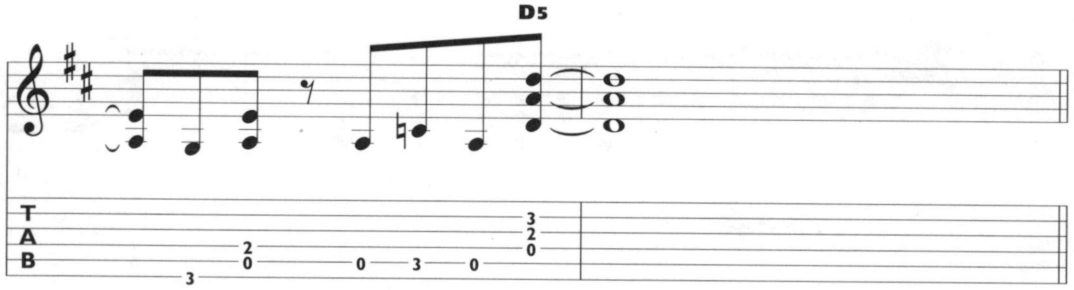

This staccato style calls to mind **Billy Duffy** from The Cult, making as much use of space as it does punchy power chords.

Remember

Without bursts of silence, there is no reference point to demonstrate how staggeringly loud and raunchy your rhythm tone really is!

'Since You Lost Your Eyesight'

Take a big pot of **Rainbow**'s 'Since You've Been Gone' and sprinkle in a little of **Queen**'s 'One Vision', and you'll instantly get a taste for this riff. (Obviously, if you're dealing with a more modern metal situation, quote the names **Pantera**, **Metallica**, **Korn** etc, who do exactly the same thing but with the gain turned up higher!).

For maximum effect, try to make sure the silence between chord stabs is unbroken by string noise or feedback. Onlookers' gasps of awe, however, are perfectly acceptable.

Keith 'The Human Riff' Richards - most Rolling Stones tracks would be unlistenable without his guitar part.

Rock Riffs or 'Play it over and over until it sounds good'

Rock wouldn't have got anywhere without the guitar riff. Try to imagine 'Smells Like Teen Spirit' without those 'dum-dum, k'chung chung...' chords at the beginning, or 'A Design For Life' without the picky bits before the vocal comes in. And the strange thing about most riffs is - they're so simple, you can't believe you didn't write them yourself.

What's a riff?

A riff is a short guitar phrase, almost always one, two or four bars in length, which repeats at various points throughout the track. It can be transposed (moving into different fingerboard positions when the chords change) or it may be slightly modified to take account of the changes.

In this section, we've also included rock 'licks'. A lick is a lead guitar part that you learn beforehand, and then include as part of a so-called 'improvised' solo. It follows that licks are, of course, vital to a bluffer's defensive equipment, because they can be inserted in a lead part without anyone knowing that you prepared them before the gig.

The difference between a riff and a lick is basically that you may only use a lick once (pretending it's a great phrase you just thought up) but you can use a riff over and over (demonstrating how you can make one simple idea into a whole musical experience).

In this section you'll find riffs and licks of varying levels of difficulty, together with tips and suggestions about when - and when not - to use them. If you're a complete beginner on guitar, don't be afraid to concentrate purely on the easy examples - some of them sound more difficult than they actually are.

'Chuck Van Gallagher'

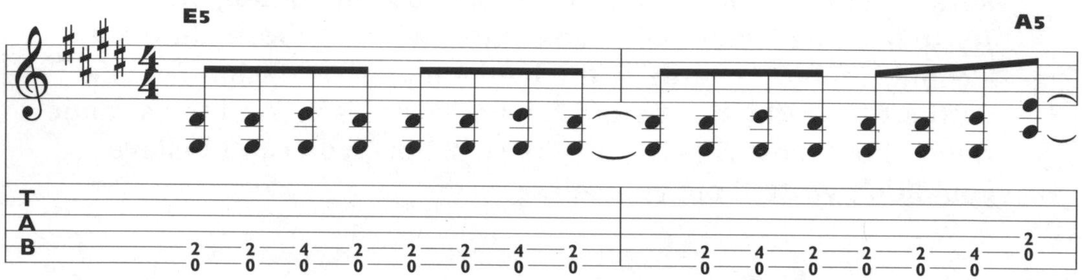

From **Chuck Berry** to **Van Halen** to **Oasis**, this riff has a long history. It's suitable for a wide range of dynamic purposes, so try it ringing wide open or palm muted with accents. This approach will also work in the keys of A and D, without any fingering alterations.

'Arriving Early'

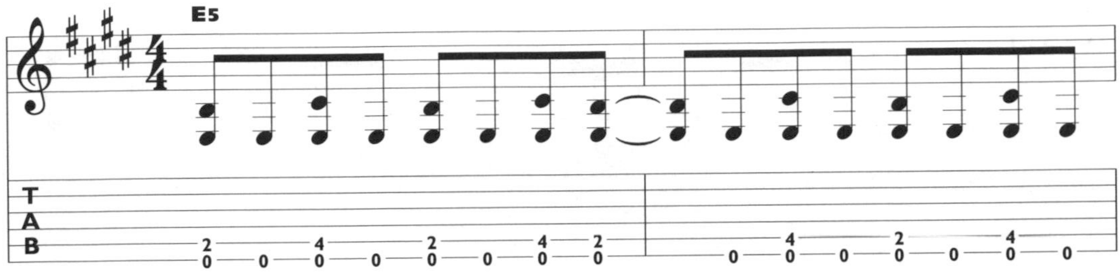

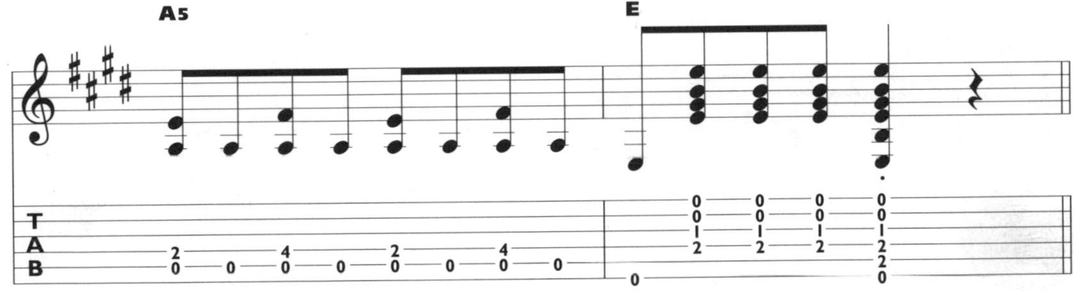

Here's a similar idea, using a more varied picking hand approach.

Check out the anticipations of the following beat before the barline - this gives a little more rhythmic movement and stop the backing becoming too 'straight'. Including the occasional full E chord adds another dimension and gives a further range of dynamics to choose from.

'Who Said Rock Was Difficult?'

This is an easy riff, but play it with your back to a wall of Marshalls and rock deity status is yours for the taking. Using the open position E minor pentatonic scale (see page 71), this riff passes through the chords of E5, A5 and B5, changing the content and style slightly for each.

Play the same riff in a fretting position (without the open strings) and use the opportunity to add shedloads of taste-free vibrato!

'Mauve Haze'

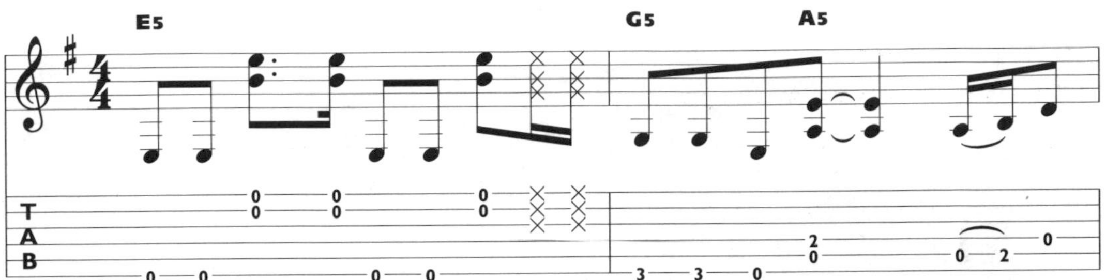

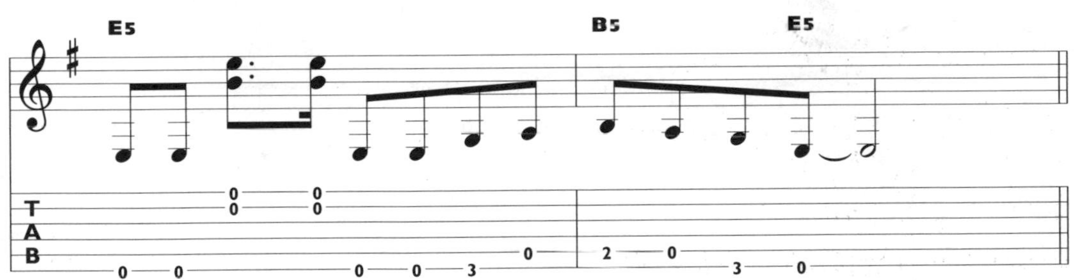

Taken from the **Hendrix**/late 60s school of rock rhythm playing, this kind of riff, though never out of style, is currently enjoying a resurgence of mainstream popularity.

To avoid unwanted notes sounding from the open E chord, try lightly holding down an E major shape, preventing the fifth, fourth and third strings from sounding. A semicircular side-to-side movement of the head is optional, but recommended.

'Machine Gun Metal'

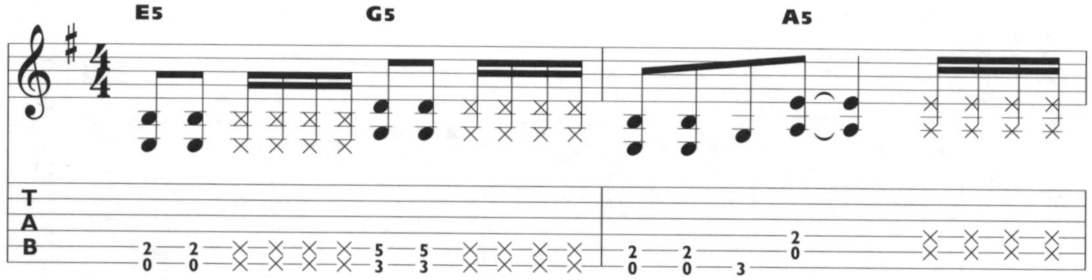

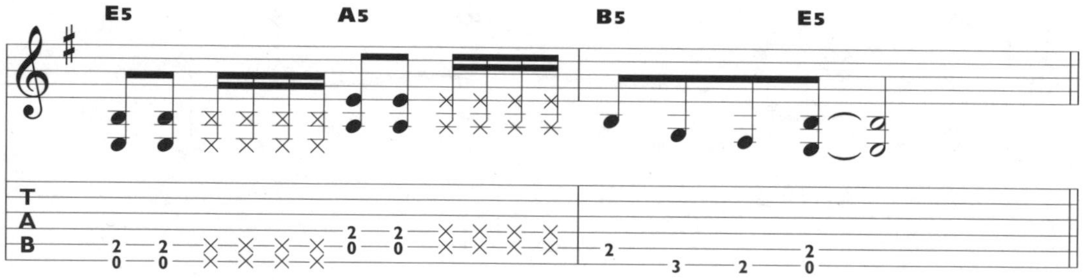

Dial in a really dirty distorted sound and tell the crowd to stand well back before you lurch into this riff.

The string noise is every bit as important as the chord accents, so don't let your muting hand relax until exactly the right moment. Because the left hand part is fairly easy, you should be able to get this up to a high enough speed to convince other players that you are not to be messed with.

'Leading Astray'

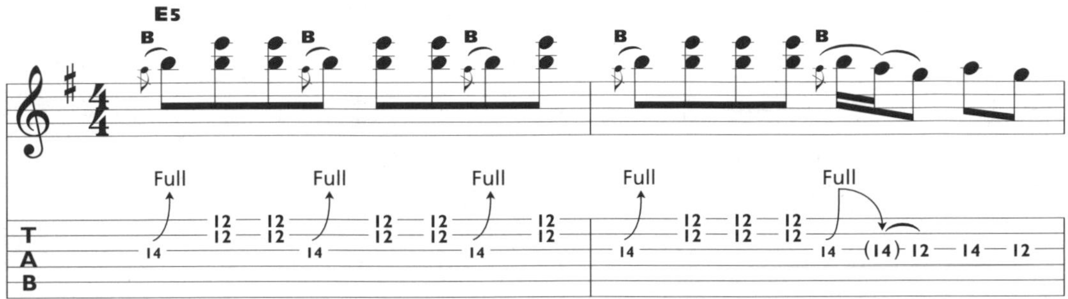

Moving into outright 'lead' territory, this authoritative, attention-grabbing phrase will have everyone hanging on your every note throughout your solo!

The 'double-stop' approach is also very useful if you have a lot of musical space to fill e.g. with a 'power trio' (just bass and drums backing you up). Don't forget to name-check **Chuck Berry** if anyone asks...

'Lizzie's In The Pink'

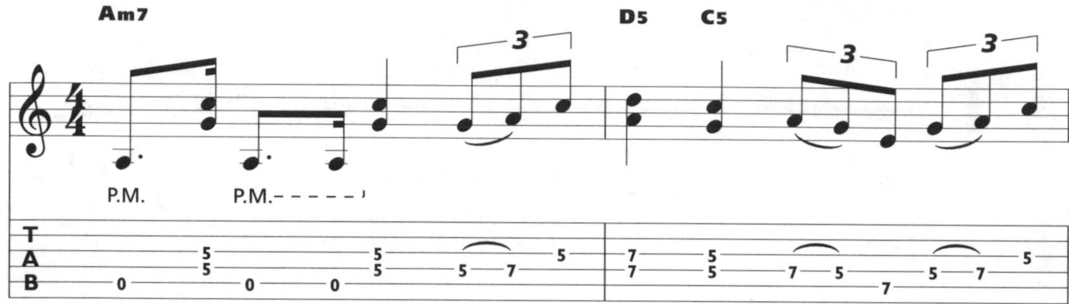

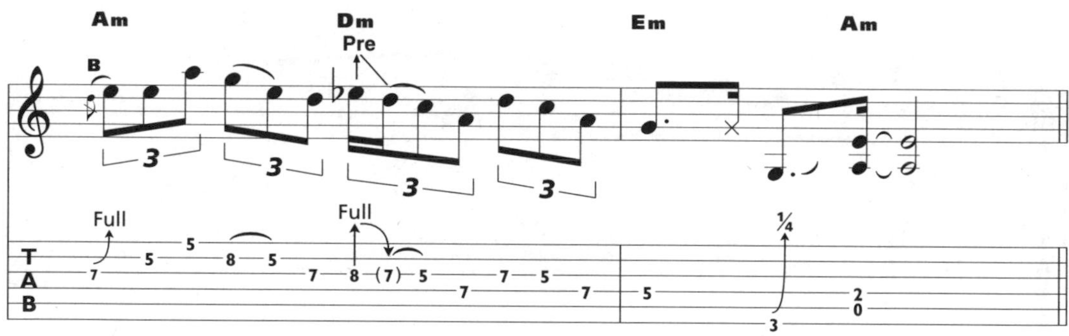

This riff crosses over between lead and rhythm techniques, beginning with a **Thin Lizzy**-style groove which segues into a descending pentatonic phrase.

Remember

This is pure **David Gilmour** - remember, when you're backed into a corner by a faster player, assume a dignified stance and think of the majesty of the 'Comfortably Numb' solo!

A tricky-sounding bluesy rock pentatonic lick - think of **Aerosmith**'s 'Walk This Way' on steroids! Don't rush this one or the intricacy will be lost on the listener. Rehearse slowly in private, then dash it off carelessly in public.

Try playing this one up at the 12th fret and then using the notes to make up a classy-sounding solo.

'Emergency Speed Lick in G'

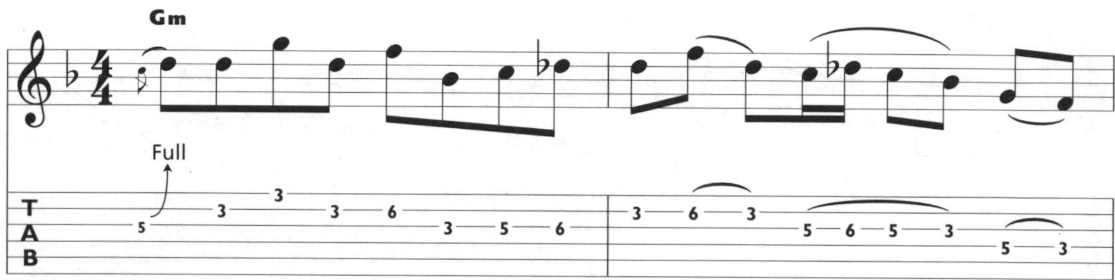

Every now and then, we all run out of ideas during a solo. Keep this one on hand if you ever get stuck when you're jamming in G.

Played at a high enough speed, it should dispel any doubts about your natural soloing ability. Even at a steadier pace, the hammer-ons and pull-offs in bar 2 give a degree of fluency that is hard to beat, especially when you nail the pull-off at the end of bar 3.

Use your little finger for this, just before jumping over with the first finger for the concluding hammer-on.

'Superhuman Picking'

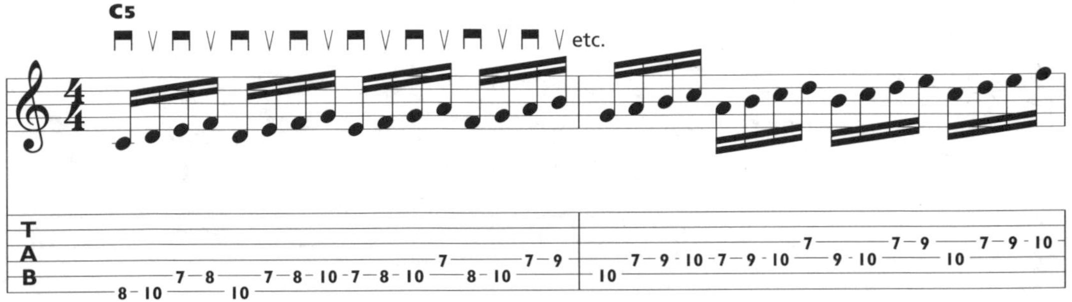

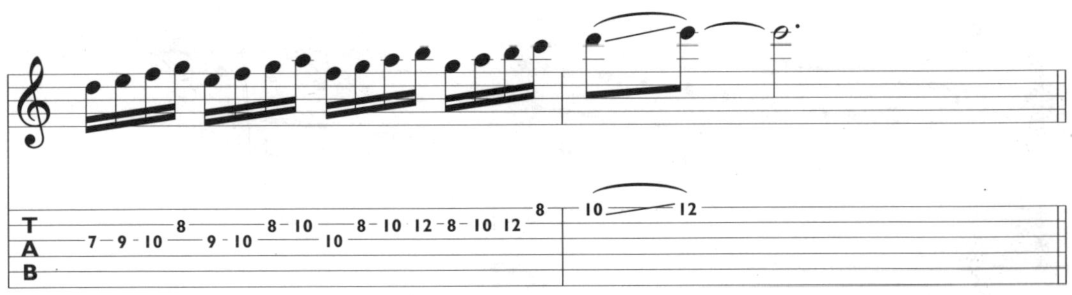

When you need one of those impressive, long alternate picked runs that seems to go on forever, this is just the sort of thing to play.

As with most fast playing, a large proportion of its content is repetition, so it's not nearly as tough as it first appears. Work slowly through the phrase, choosing a comfortable and logical fingering, building up the speed gradually. **Then, rip it up!**

'Sounds Good - Looks Better!'

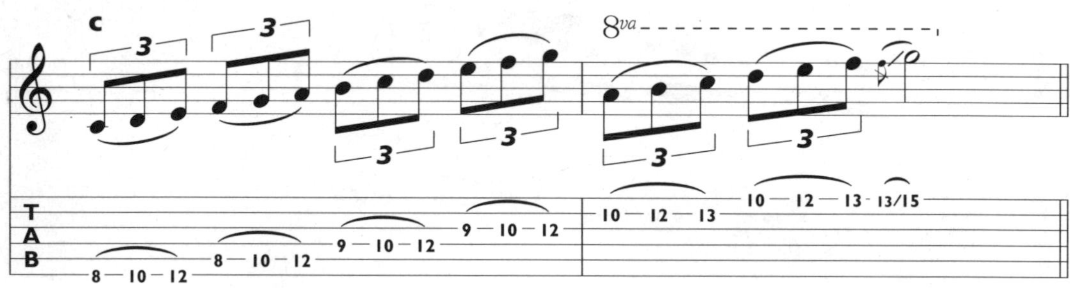

Using three-note-per-string hammer-ons is a great way of adding 'flash' to your solos.

This example also incorporates some position shifts: I've never understood why, but audiences always seem to think you're a better player if they see your hand move along the neck a bit. Once your fingers have learned the shapes, playing this at speed is relatively easy.

Just remember to be ready with a blistering pentatonic phrase to follow it up!

Led Zeppelin were responsible for some of the greatest rock riffs of all time.

'Tapping Without Taste - lick 1'

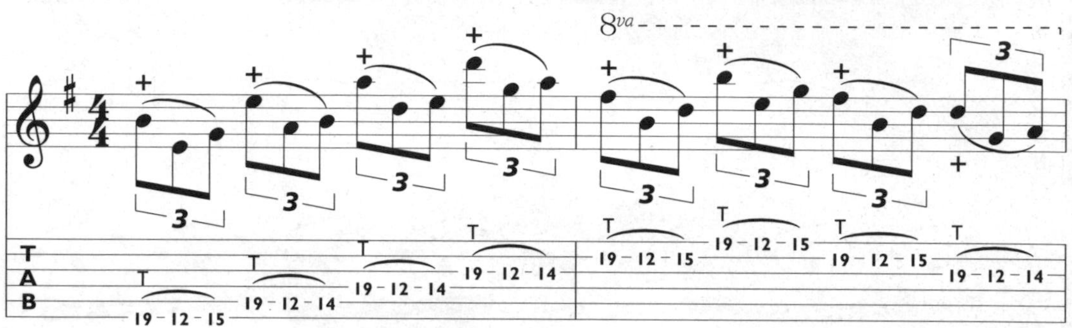

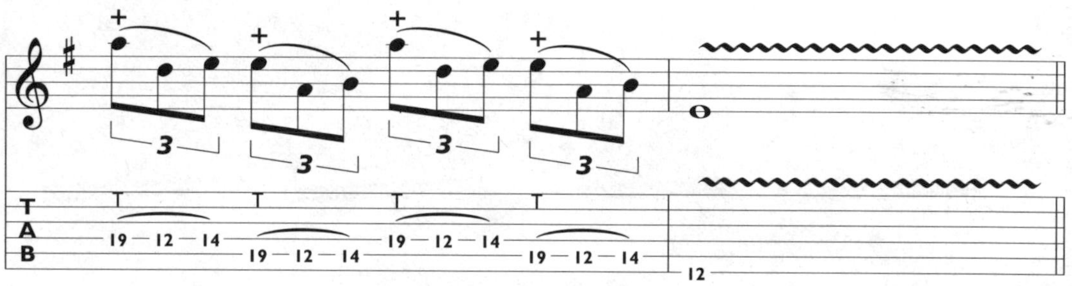

A cascade of arpeggiated patterns will emerge from your guitar when you run through this deceptively simple tapping sequence.

Looking closely, you will see that the fretting hand part is none other than the simple E minor pentatonic scale. The tapping hand part is even easier, staying at the 19th fret throughout. **Trust me - it's hard to get a bad sound from this lick.**

'Tapping Without Taste - lick 2'

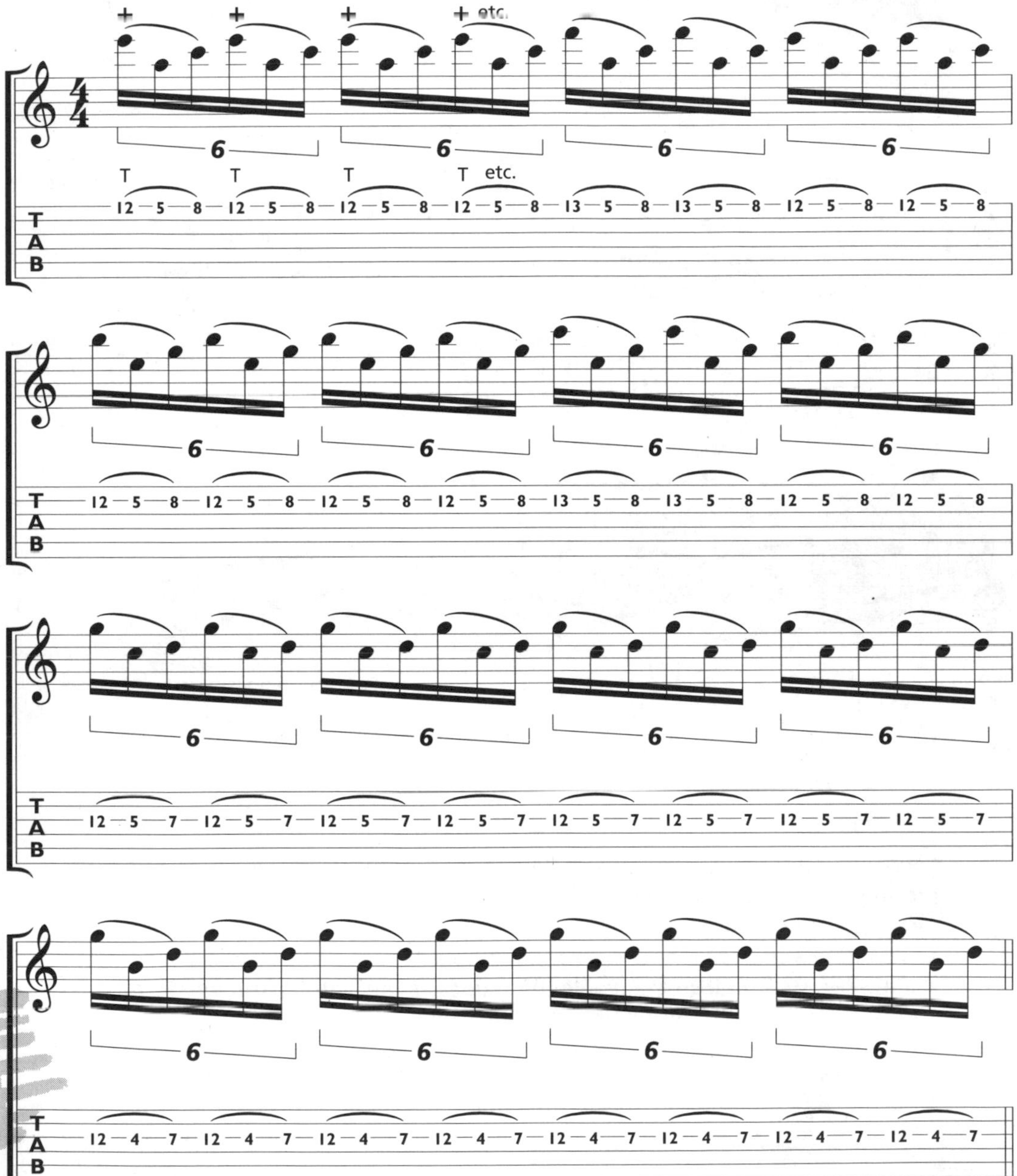

```
+   +   +   + etc.
6   6   6   6
T   T   T   T etc.
12–5–8–12–5–8–12–5–8–12–5–8–13–5–8–13–5–8–12–5–8–12–5–8
T
A
B

6   6   6   6
12–5–8–12–5–8–12–5–8–12–5–8–13–5–8–13–5–8–12–5–8–12–5–8
T
A
B

6   6   6   6
12–5–7–12–5–7–12–5–7–12–5–7–12–5–7–12–5–7–12–5–7–12–5–7
T
A
B

6   6   6   6
12–4–7–12–4–7–12–4–7–12–4–7–12–4–7–12–4–7–12–4–7–12–4–7
T
A
B
```

Tapping frenzy ahoy! This classical-sounding pattern is reminiscent of **Eddie Van Halen** and **Randy Rhoads**. In this case, the tapping finger is moved to provide a shifting melody at the top line, which changes slightly as the line moves across the strings. **Steve Vai** and **Joe Satriani** have taken this technique to even further extremes, based on the same blueprint.

'Sweep Picking Made Easy(ish)'

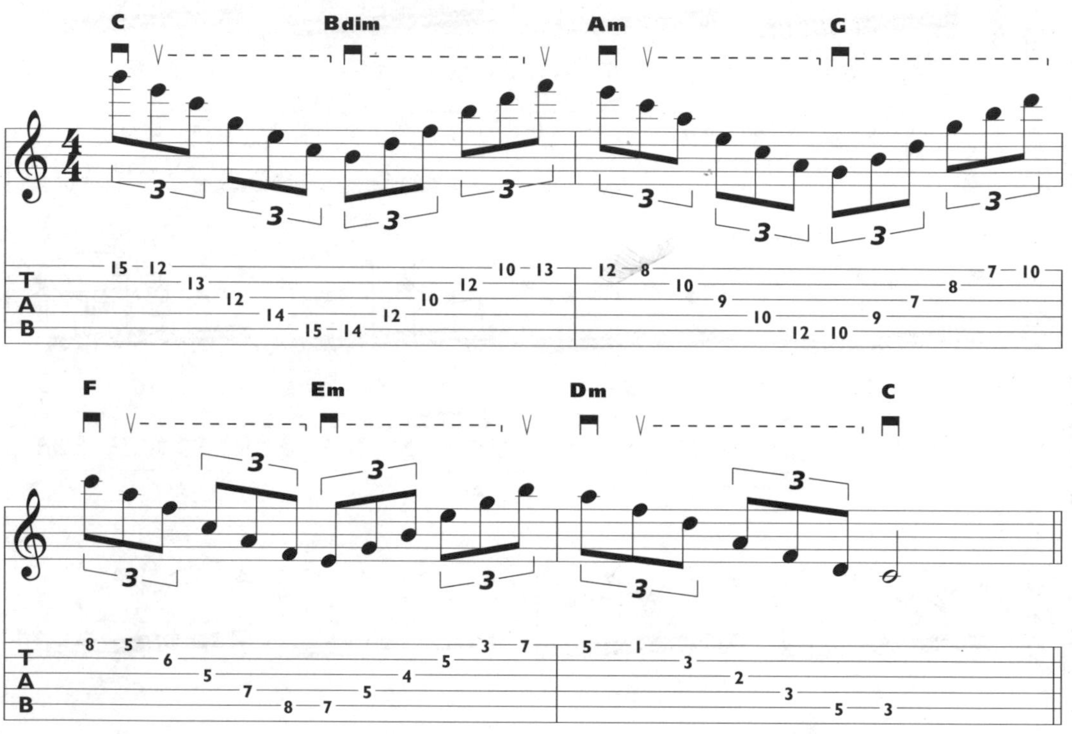

Sooner or later any conversation between rock guitarists comes round to sweep picking, so it's worth knowing at least a couple of shapes. Here's how you do it: pick one note, then pick across the strings *all in the same direction*, fretting each note as you go. As soon as a note has sounded (and as you pick the next one), slightly release pressure on it so the whole thing doesn't blur into a strummed chord.

It takes a few months to get the effect, but the obscene sounds you can get from the guitar with it are well worth the effort.
Note the picking direction -

 means up, and  means down.

'Abuse At The Bar'

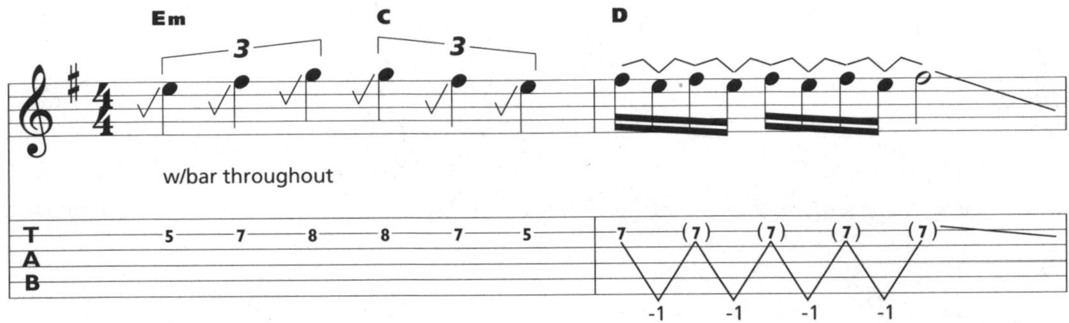

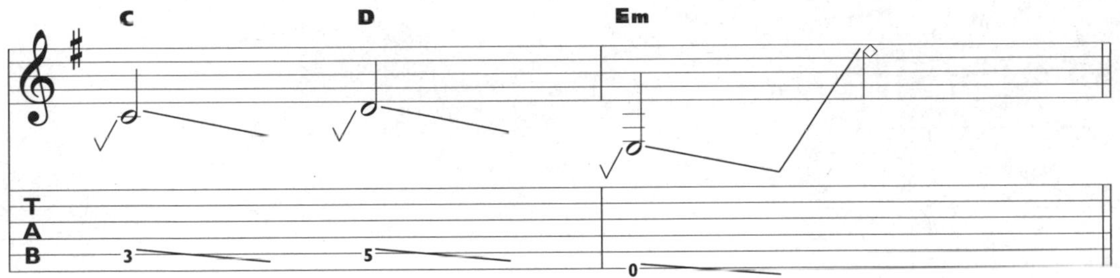

An essential part of the rock guitarist's equipment during the mid/late '80s was a locking tremolo, engineered to take all manner of abuse without going out of tune.

It's all extremely addictive once you start, so here is one example featuring a few tricks. In the last bar, touch a fifth fret harmonic on the sixth string, while it is slack, then let it raise back up to pitch.

Many players learn **Satriani** licks by heart and pass them off as their own. Hey, it works!

'Outrageous!'

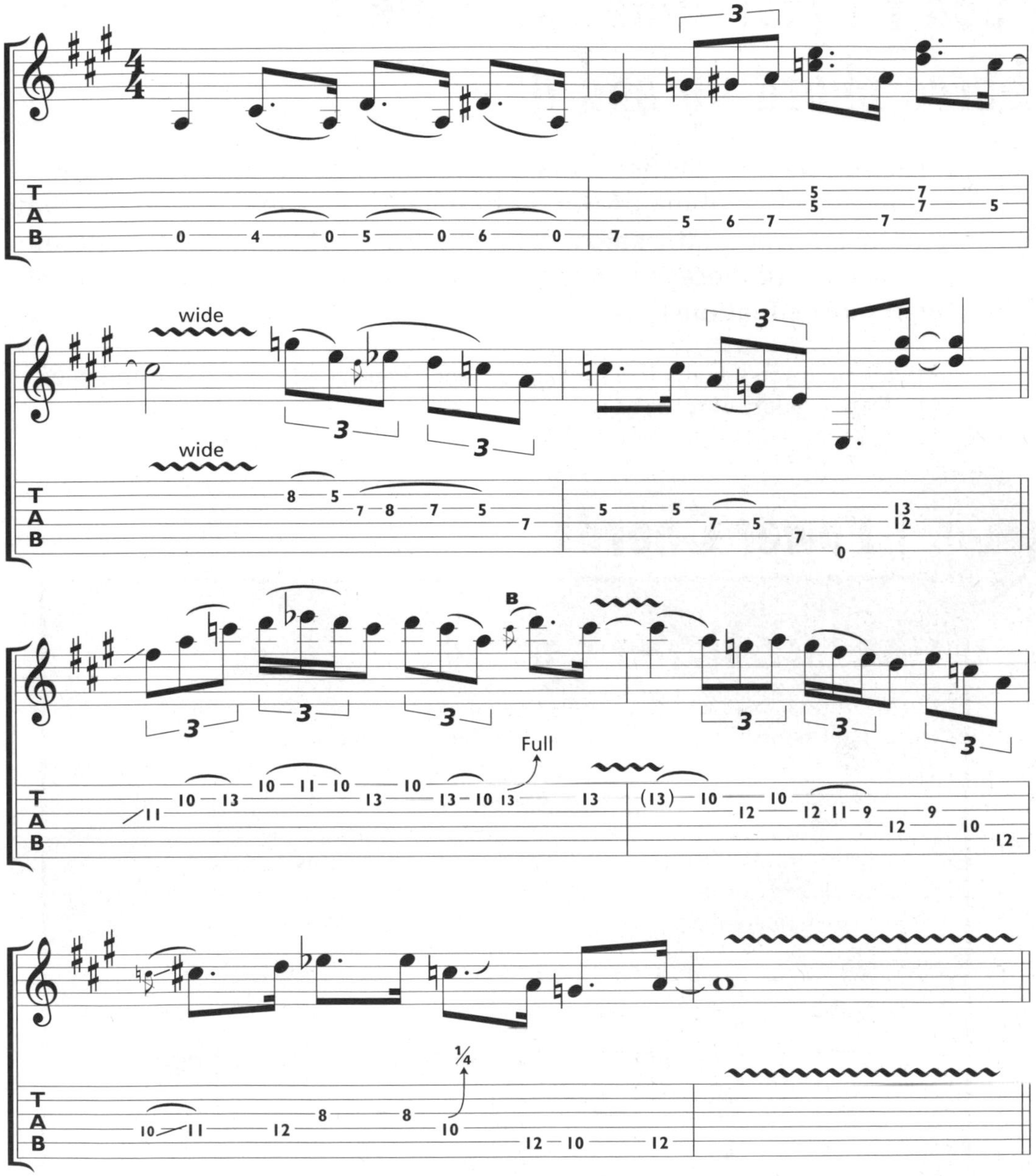

And to finish this section, here is a longer difficult phrase, giving a little more room to demonstrate some of the tricks/phrases in context. Make sure you choose the most convenient and comfortable fingering pattern for each of the phrases - start on the premise of 'a finger per fret' and modify it to suit from there. Perhaps the overall feel can be compared to **Ritchie Blackmore** circa 1970, or **Joe Satriani**'s 'Satch Boogie'.

Chord Sequences or 'Can't I just slide the same barre chord up and down?'

Rock players are notoriously lazy when it comes to learning chord sequences - they think of the rhythm backing as the 'boring bit' that gets in the way of the solos. Also, many only learn one barre shape for each chord (because, in true bluffing style, this will help you get by in most situations!).

In this section you'll find a few simple two- and three-chord sequences which you can use in a variety of rock styles.

Power Chords

The rock bluffer's friend

Power chords, or '5 chords' as they're sometimes known, are the most essential rhythm weapon in the rocking rhythmist's arsenal. They contain only two notes per octave, leaving out the major or minor third (so if a chord of C major, or C, contains notes of C, E and G, a chord of C5 will contain only C and G). They have two great advantages – one, they sound better (i.e. more powerful!) through distortion or overdrive; and two, they're usually easier to play. Shown in the fretboxes are four examples of common power chord shapes – these are in the key of A but can be moved to any fret. Learn 'em!

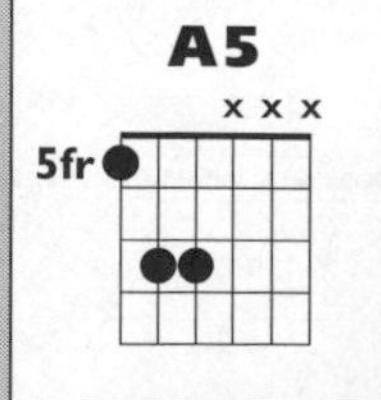

BASIC A5
Kurt Cobain
Metallica
Sex Pistols

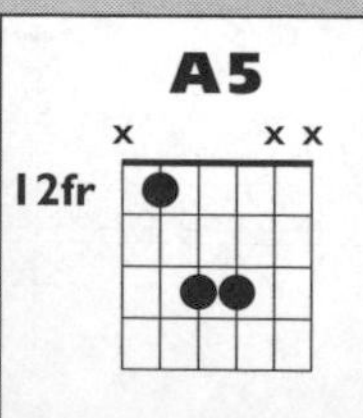

CLASSIC HIGH A5
Black Sabbath
Stereophonics
Queen

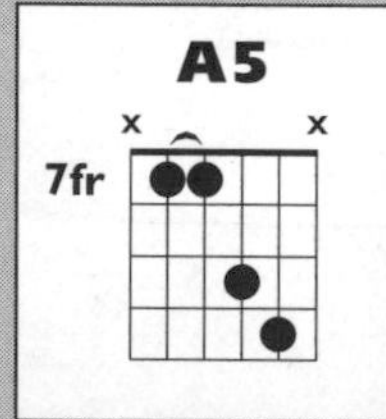

MIDDLE A5
Deep Purple
Led Zeppelin

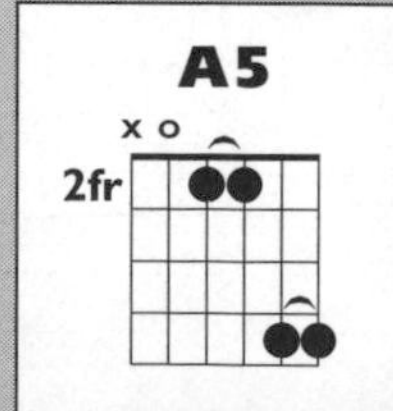

PINKY SHAPE A5
Free
U2

'Room To Flaunt It'

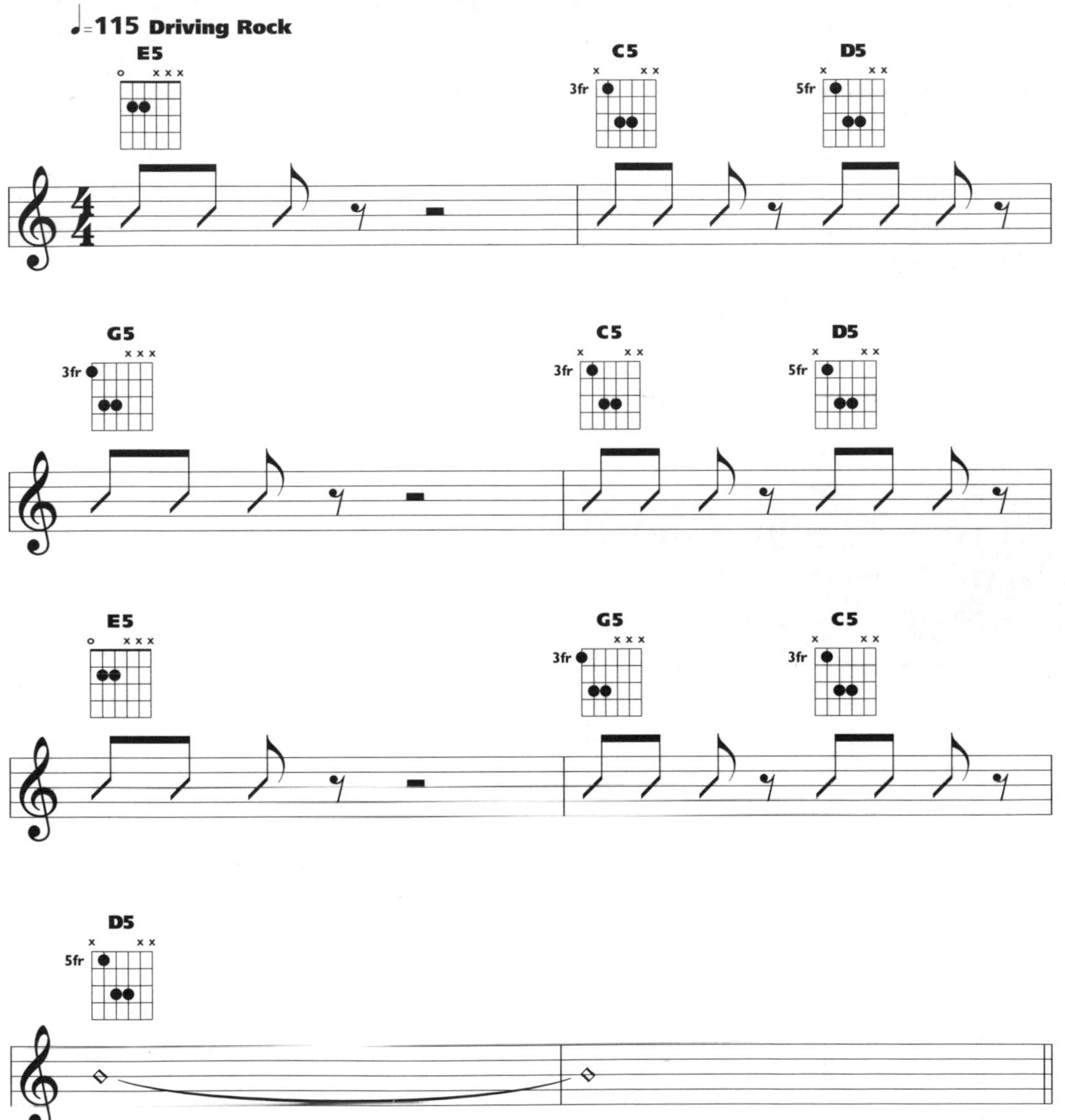

A typical driving rock sequence, with characteristic gaps punctuating bars 1, 3 and 5. Any ideas based around the E minor Pentatonic, blues scale, or minor scale will fit with no problems. Try to persuade your bass player and drummer to keep quiet during the gaps, so your hard-learned lead licks are certain to be heard without anything clouding the picture.

'Maximum Potential'

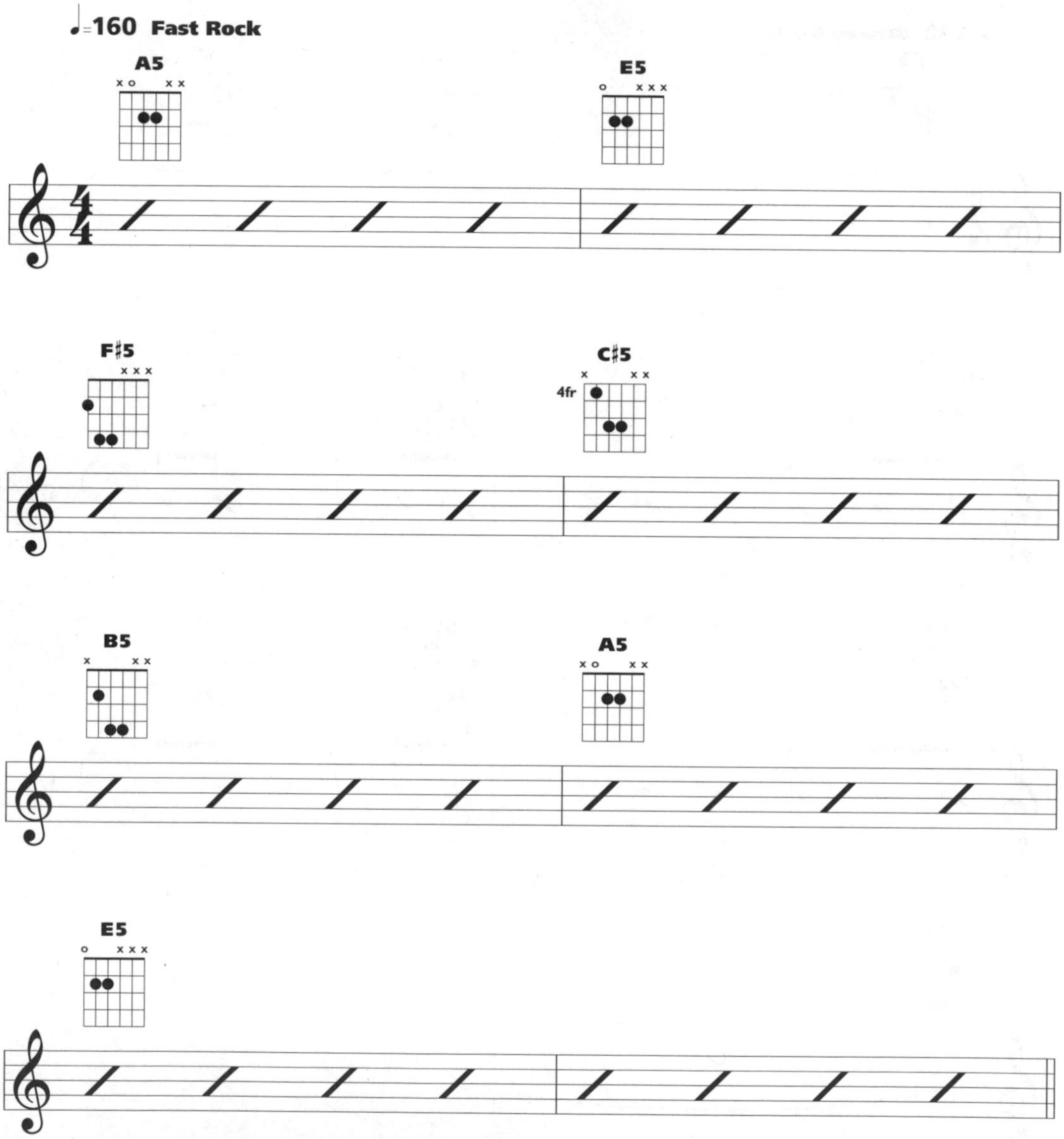

♩=160 **Fast Rock**

A5 | E5

F♯5 | C♯5 (4fr)

B5 | A5

E5 |

This is notated as a straight four to the bar, but should be played using a few of the rhythm patterns you've already tried. For soloing, the F♯m pentatonic or blues scale will fit anywhere, with all the usual bends available. The reason for choosing this key is that it allows maximum choice of cool rock licks at all times.

'Classical Era'

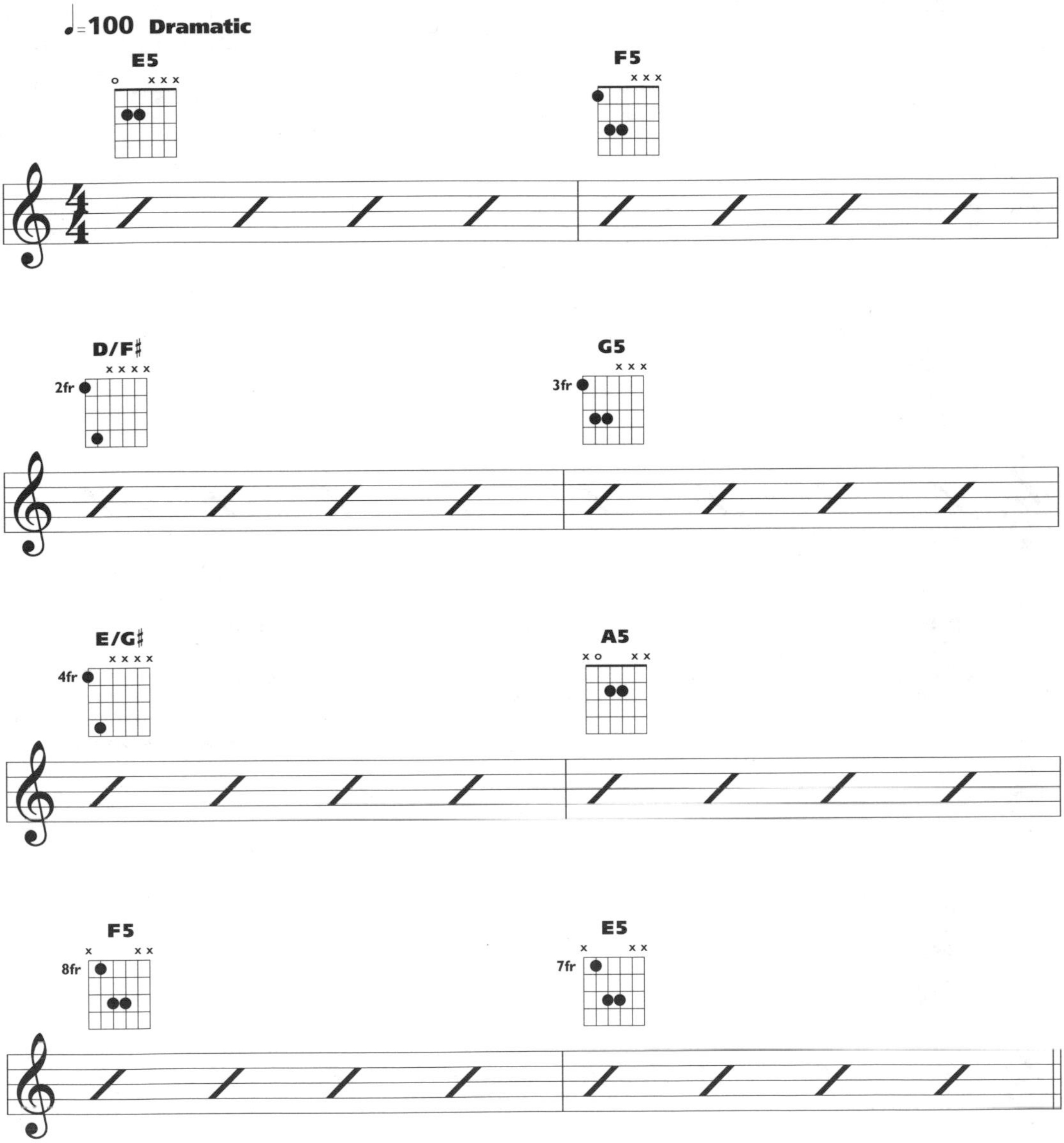

♩=100 **Dramatic**

E5 | **F5**

D/F♯ | **G5**

E/G♯ | **A5**

F5 | **E5**

Ascending in a dramatic and menacing manner, it's time to rise to the challenge with a couple of neo-classical flourishes. Tapping is always good in a situation like this, but another option could be the 'eastern' sounding harmonic minor scale. In this case it would work best over the suspended, or 'slash' chords - you can, of course, mix it up with the ever-present A blues scale!

'Hearing Voices'

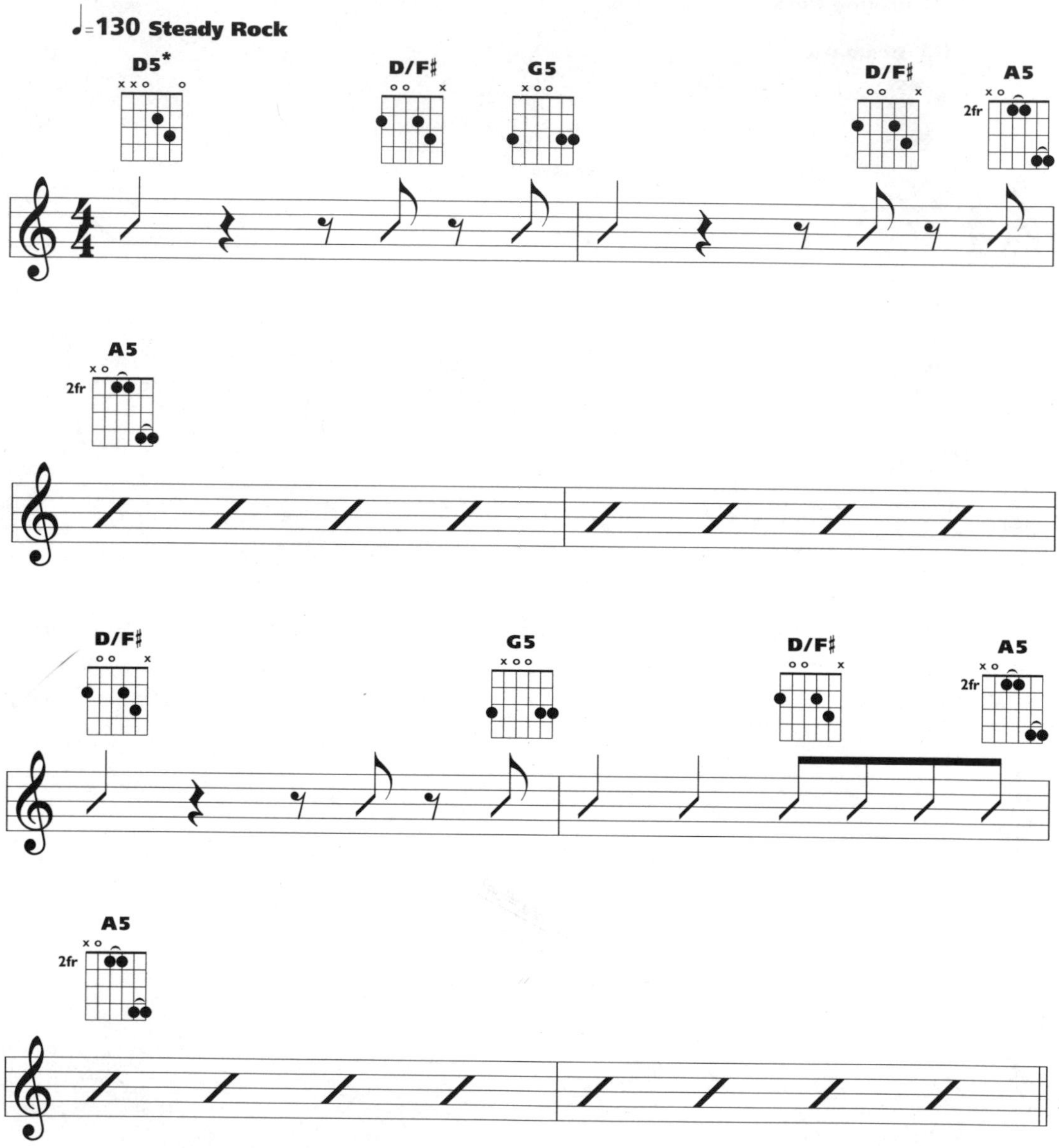

♩=130 **Steady Rock**

D5* D/F♯ G5 D/F♯ A5

A5

D/F♯ G5 D/F♯ A5

A5

This one's straight out of **AC/DC**'s 'Very Small Book Of Rhythm Patterns'. Sometimes the 'voicing' of a chord - as these alternative versions show - can make them really stand out as something very different from the standard versions. If you're soloing, try the B blues or pentatonic scale, along with the A Mixolydian mode.

'Jackson Five'

♩=140 **Driving Rock**

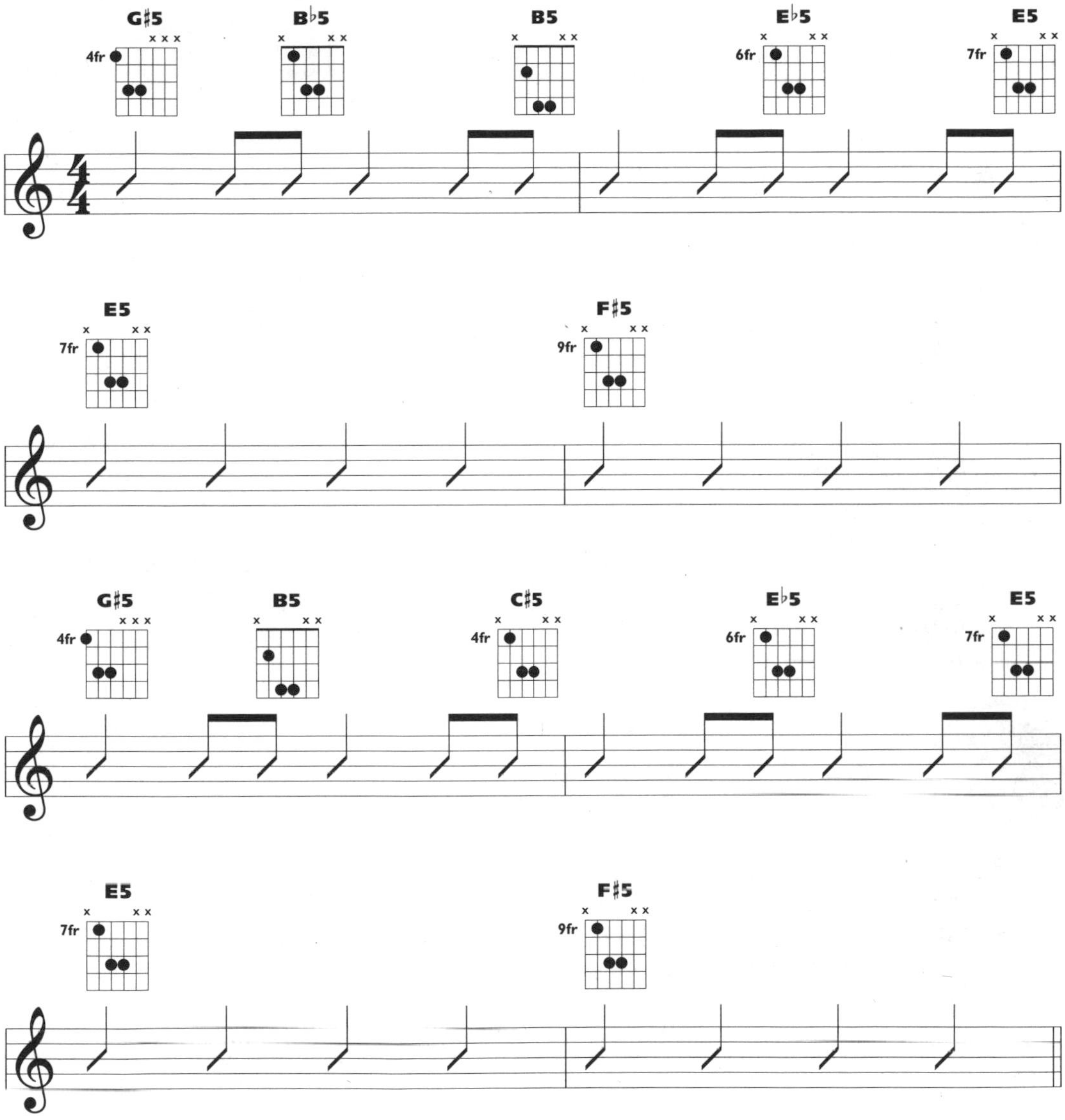

G♯5 B♭5 B5 E♭5 E5

E5 F♯5

G♯5 B5 C♯5 E♭5 E5

E5 F♯5

Most rock music features '5' chords - also known as '**power chords**'. These consist of root and fifth only, meaning they're neither major nor minor. This, of course, makes them indispensable to the rock bluffer, because you can get away with a whole bunch of scale choices without the audience hearing any wrong notes. This example, in the key of G♯, would work best with G♯m pentatonic, G♯ Dorian mode, or G♯ blues scale.

Scales or 'It may not sound too good - but look how fast I can play it...'

A great deal of nonsense is talked about scales by guitarists, so it's usually possible to fool the assembled company with very little knowledge. Ask any reasonably experienced player to perform the major scale, or any of the modes, and nine times out of ten they'll zip up and down the fingerboard at high speed. Ask the same player to take a solo, and they'll go back to the same simple blues licks they've been playing for years.

So it's a dead cert that you'll produce gasps of awe just for creating a solo out of these scales. The ones featured here are the most foolproof - it's difficult to put a foot wrong with some of them - and will be more than enough to take you through 95% of the soloing situations that the average rock track puts you in.

Scales Tip

You'll also have the added advantage of being able to devise nonchalant phrases such as "I just take a simple natural minor pattern and modalise it via the Dorian and Mixolydian with a couple of basic position shifts. Kids' stuff, really, but I guess it works." And if you get a smack in the face, they're just jealous...

All scale fretboxes are shown upright, with the headstock at the top, and the strings ascending in pitch from left to right: i.e. **the lowest E string is on the left.**

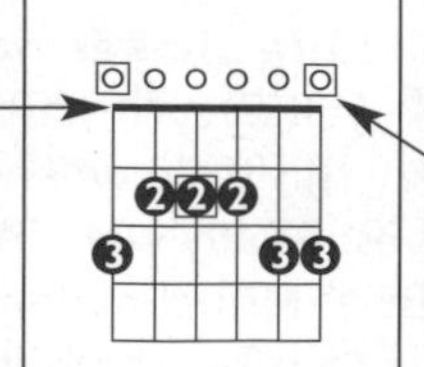

A box around a note or open string simply means that note is a 'root' note. I.e. **in A major any boxed out notes will be A.**

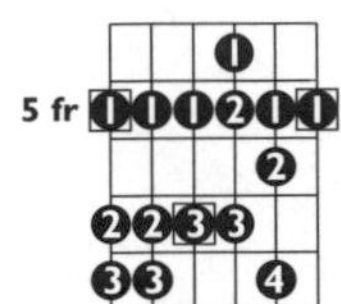

A natural minor - spoilt for choice

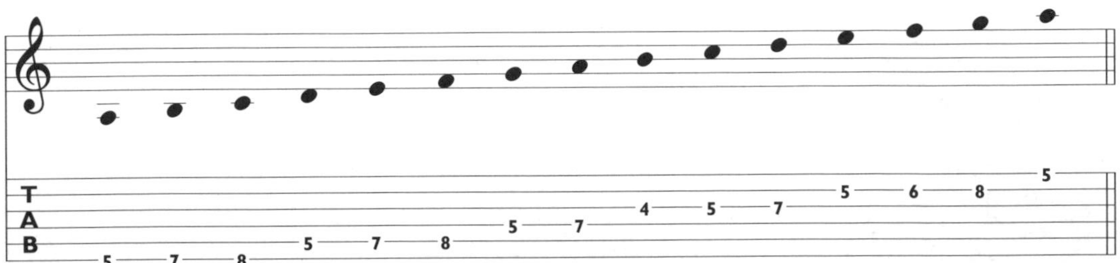

Keyboard players don't understand this one, because they don't do it in their grade 1 exam! However, next to the minor pentatonic and blues scales, it's one of the most useful for 'sensitive' rock solos. If the backing chords are basically minor, this scale works a treat for those 'big ballad' moments of the set.

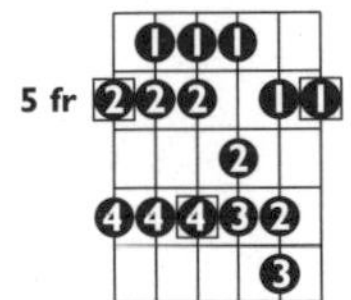

A Mixolydian mode - wizardry and wands

Some say **Jimmy Page** and **Kula Shaker** wouldn't have had a career without this scale, and it does work well over 'mystic' drone notes, but it's actually much more versatile than that. Try this scale whenever the main backing chord is a 7th (in this case, A7) - it works especially well on R&B, rock 'n' roll, and some jazz/rock tracks. Theoretically, it's just a normal major scale with the 7th note flattened, but you should always refer to it by its modal name to command maximum appreciation of your 'years' of rock study.

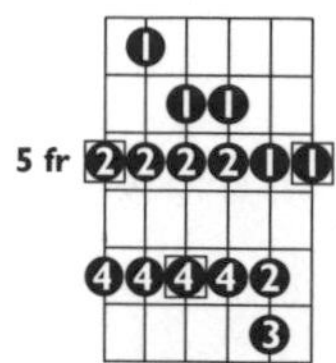

A Dorian mode - spinning in space

Due to the fact that modal theory is often taught fairly badly, many guitarists think of this exclusively as a 'D minor' mode, but like any scale, it can be played in every key. Think of it as a natural minor scale, but with the sixth note raised by one fret. Dorian phrases can work well to add interest to a straightforward minor pentatonic solo. Its 'spacious' sound can be heard in tracks by **The Eagles**, **Pink Floyd**, **Satriani** and **Santana**.

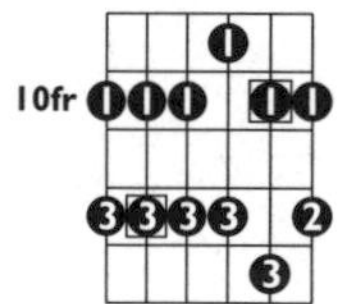

A Minor Pentatonic - position shift

This alternative position of A minor pentatonic starts at the tenth fret of the sixth string. This pattern offers a slightly different take on the same licks you've tried with the 'basic' shape. As the notes fall on different strings, there are a few surprises as to what will and will not work using hammer-ons and string bends. This is a very easy shape to use, but you'll be amazed how many guitar players never bother to learn it.

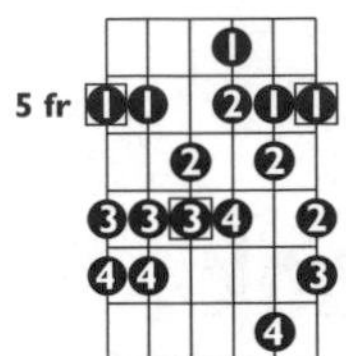

A Harmonic Minor - Full of Eastern Promise

Using this scale instantly gives the impression that you are classically trained. If you play it throughout a solo, it starts sounding a bit 'Eastern', so if that's not the effect you want, then just use it over the fifth chord (i.e. if you're in A minor, play A harmonic minor when there's an E or E7 in the backing).

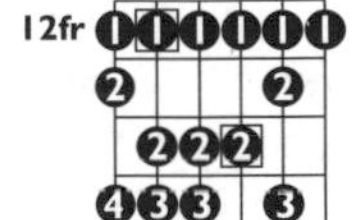

A Minor Pentatonic - position shift 2

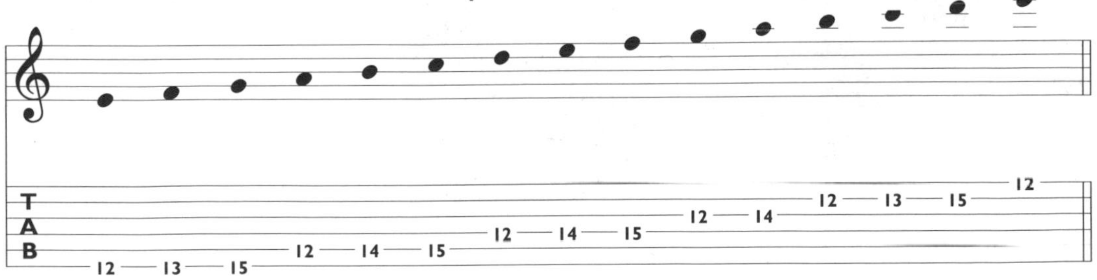

The rock player can never learn too many minor pentatonic shapes, and this one is great for single-note melodies with plenty of bent notes. Because the first finger is always anchored at the 12th fret, there are some awesome hammer-ons and pull-offs available with very little effort.

Music Shop Classic or 'How do I fit everything in this book into 24 bars of showing off?'

This custom-designed showpiece should amaze any onlookers and cynical staff at your local guitar shop. It's been specially devised to be utterly without the shackles of musical subtlety, emotional validity or artistic good taste.

First of all, be sure to play it at a tempo which enables you to make all the position shifts evenly - it's far better to nail a lick perfectly at a slower tempo than make a mess of it at high speed (unless you're playing *very* fast, that is, in which case any old rubbish will do). There are a few tricks in here to help you out, too. It uses lots of open bass notes to aid fast position shifts.

The **Led Zep**-meets **Aerosmith** riff section should wake up the staff and draw a crowd (which usually takes 11-12 bars or so), then when everyone's watching, the flashy single-note solo licks can become more frequent.

Warning

At no point should you show undue strain, so make sure you're so well-practised that you can play it without breaking into a sweat. That way, everyone in the shop will be secretly imagining what you could do if you were *really* trying.

E5
A5 G5 E5
T
A
B

G5 A5 E5
B
B
6
6
Full
Full
T
A
B

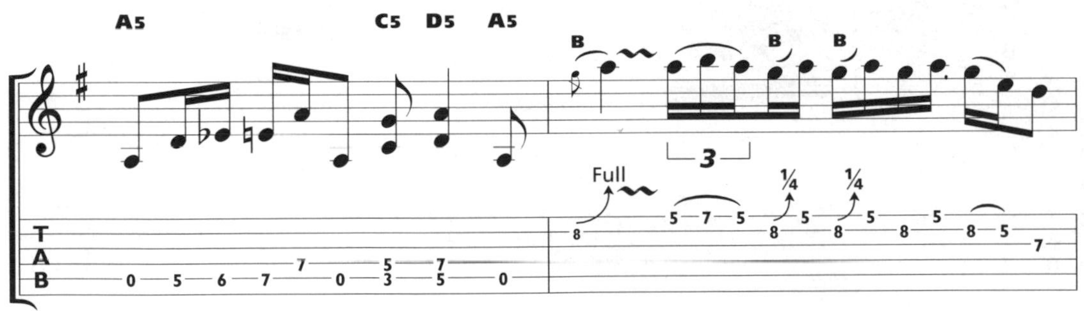
A5
C5 D5 A5
B
B
B
3
Full
¼
¼
T
A
B

E5
A5 G5 E5
3
B
B
Full
Full
T
A
B

B5
A5
T
A
B

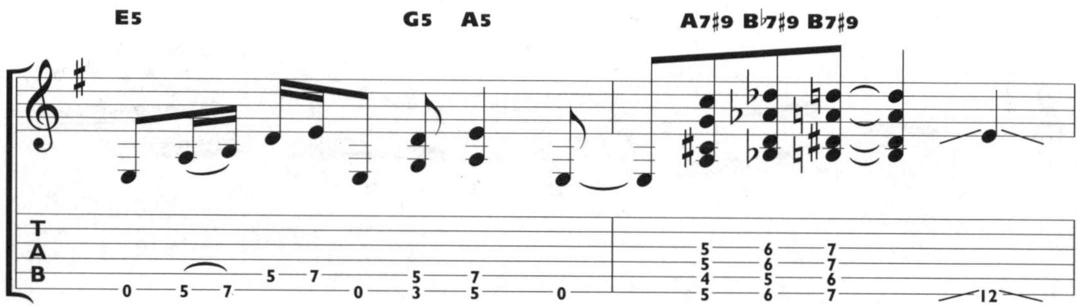
E5
G5
A5
A7♯9
B♭7♯9
B7♯9
T
A
B

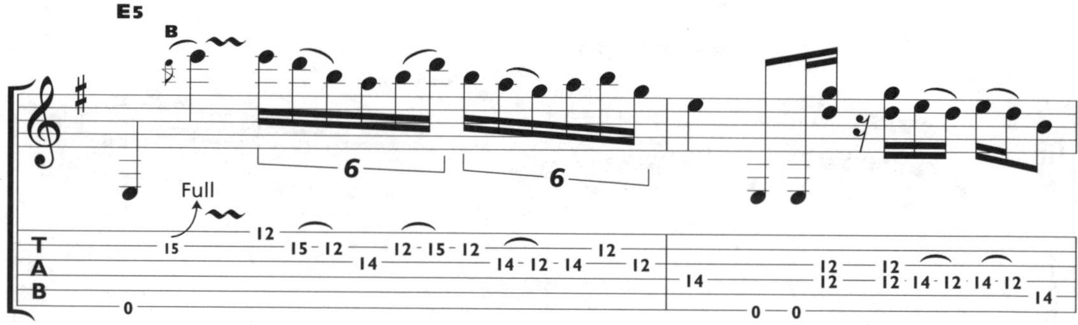
E5
B
6
6
Full
T
A
B

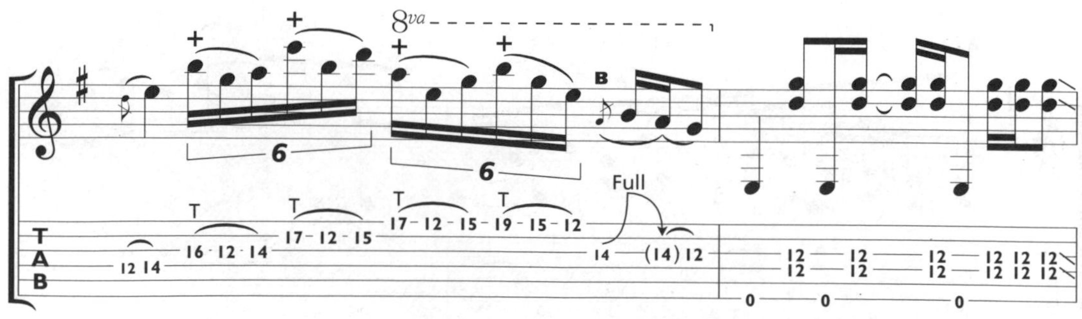
8va
6
6
B
Full
T
A
B

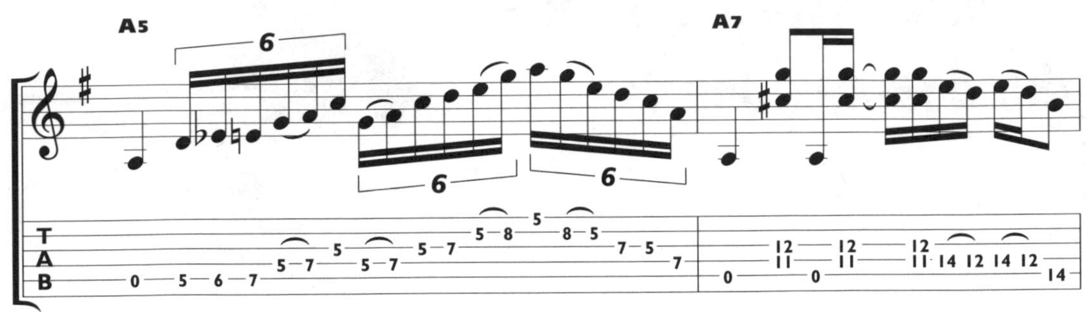
A5
6
6
6
A7
T
A
B

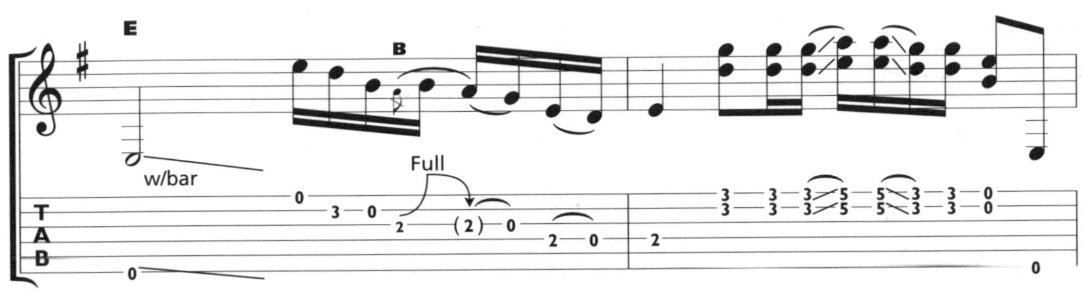
E
B
w/bar
Full
T
A
B

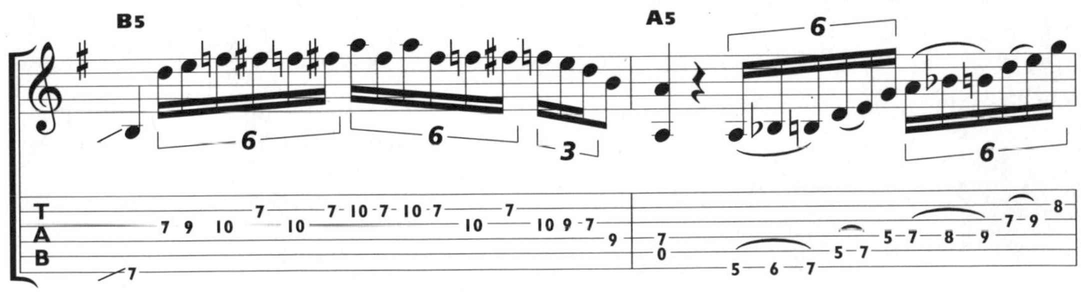
B5
6
6
3
A5
6
6
T
A
B

E5
3
T
A
B

Music Shop Riffs - the dos and don'ts

If you *have* to play well-known riffs in a music shop, you might as well choose one of the best. On these pages, I've listed the top 20 rock riffs currently being played in UK music shops.

You can get away with some of them yourself - indeed, several are expected of you - but others will result in banishment to cliché hell. Next to each riff is listed an advisability rating (10 means it's essential repertoire, 1 means you'll be lucky to leave the shop with your nose still attached to your face) and tips on which bit to play.

Title	Artist	Advisability rating	Tips
Stairway To Heaven	Led Zeppelin	**0**	One of only two intros to be banned absolutely by international treaty. Never, EVER play this song.
Smoke on the Water	Deep Purple	**1**	And this is the other one. Tip - most people start it on two open strings - it's actually a double-stop at the 5th fret. Point this out to others, but DO NOT play it yourself.
Smells Like Teen Spirit	Nirvana	**4**	Intro chord riff. Quite useful for the basic player who wants to sound authentic, but should only be played a maximum of twice through.
Enter Sandman	Metallica	**7**	Intro picking. Over 10 years old and still going strong.
Every Breath You Take	The Police	**5**	A bit worn, this one. Message in a Bottle is more difficult but worth the effort.
Design For Life	Manic Street Preachers	**7**	Recorded in 1996, and still very popular. C major 7, 3rd fret. Dead easy. Make sure you stop before the difficult E♭ bit.
All Right Now	Free	**1/8**	Intro - if you can play it *exactly* like the original, then go for it, otherwise steer well clear.

Title	Artist	Advisability rating	Tips
Layla	Eric Clapton	**2**	Without a big backing, this one always sounds weedy played solo. Avoid.
Eruption	Van Halen	**6**	A bit passé now, but still bloody impressive if you put in the work to learn it all the way through.
Ain't Talkin' Bout Love	Van Halen	**8**	Rejuvenated by Apollo 440's sampled version, this one wins extra points.
Purple Haze	Jimi Hendrix	**3**	Main riff. You might get away with it if you've got just the right fuzz sound.
Sultans of Swing	Dire Straits	**2**	Intro chord/lead part. OK for clean sounds, but difficult if you're a plectrum player. Insist on a compressor pedal.
Wonderwall	Oasis	**1**	Between 1995 and 1998, this evil beast stalked the music shop community like an... awful chord riff. The only consolation is that it's played on acoustic.
Back In Black	AC/DC	**4**	Main chord/lead riff. AC/DC will always be in these charts, but *please* make sure the guitar's in tune before you start.
Paranoid	Black Sabbath	**3**	1-bar intro. And don't play any more than that.
Sweet Home Alabama	Lynyrd Skynyrd	**6**	Chord intro. Everybody knows it, but no-one can quite remember what it is. Easy to play if you know D, C and G.
Whole Lotta Love	Led Zeppelin	**9**	Main riff. Possibly rock's most famous guitar line, known equally for the original as for its status as the Top Of The Pops theme.
Parisienne Walkways	Gary Moore	**6**	Main melody. Lots of people play this, but few play it well. Only to be attempted if your string bends are accurate.
Hotel California	The Eagles	**5**	Well-known, but not as clichéd as 'Stairway...'. Acoustic players should go for the fingerstyle intro. Electric players try the pull-off arpeggios at the end.
Blackbird	The Beatles	**6**	Whole song. A good one if you're new to fingerstyle, but only to be attempted if you can play it all the way through. Yes, even the middle bit!

Amps or 'The foolproof guide to guitar tone'

Hopefully by now you should know that the most important things in rock music are visual. Having a guitar with a Fender logo is, in the eyes of players, better than one with a Squier logo. When Oasis released their first album, many people thought that they sounded like the Beatles - primarily because Noel was seen in a John Lennon-style hat. And, of course, two Marshall stacks look twice as good as one.

However, some will try to convince you that the most important thing about a guitar is its tone. And to know about tone, you need to know about amps. In days gone by, an amp was designed to reproduce the guitar sound as cleanly as possible. Not any more. These days having the right amp is as important as... well, having the right colour plectrum.

Opening a valve

You'll be told throughout that valve or 'tube' amps are preferable to transistor or 'solid-state' models, and even though many people who say this wouldn't have a clue in a blindfold test, you can't call yourself a rock guitar player unless you take a stance on the issue of valves.

Generally, it's safer to take the tube option - firstly, most of the pro players do choose valve amps, so you're in safe company, and secondly, it's easier to defend old technology by describing it as 'classic' and 'legendary' than to attempt to praise current items because they're 'small' or 'reliable'. Think of your amp as a car - would you rather be seen in a 1960s Aston Martin or a brand new Nissan Micra?

The mighty Marshall stack. Sounds great, but you wouldn't want to take it on the bus.

Tone Tips

10 tips for the ultimate Rock guitar tone

1. Use the right guitar! Les Paul-type or other humbucking pickup for fat, thick rock tones, Strat-type for bluesy biting sounds. You won't get satisfying rock sounds out of a Strat. Unless you're **Jimi Hendrix**. Or **Carlos Santana**. Or **The Edge**. But apart from those guys, it's impossible to get a decent rock tone out of a Strat. Oh, yeah, and there's **Ritchie Blackmore** too.

2. **Use the right pickup! Neck pickup is great for warm, middly leads, but the rest of the time, if you really want pounding rhythm parts and squealing lead, the bridge pickup is the one to choose. Tone control all the way up, please!**

3. Remember, the more distortion you use, the more difficult it is to hear what's going on. This can totally destroy a rhythm guitar part...

4. **...however, if you're playing single-note lead, a really high gain setting can improve sustain, create fantastic harmonics, and make your guitar sound more expensive than it really is.**

5. If you use a compressor, put it *before* the distortion in the effects chain to avoid microphonic feedback. If you value your eardrums, that is.

6. **To smooth out your lead sound, add a delay of about 200-400ms to the distorted tone, and mix it between 20% and 50% of the main signal. This turns any solo from a sputtering moped in a pothole to a Ferrari being driven on a frozen lake. By Sean Connery.**

7. Rock lead parts can sometimes be improved by boosting the midrange a tad...

8. **...and rhythm parts by cutting some mid from the sound.**

9. You can get away with a dreadful guitar tone if your vibrato's good...

10. **...and vice versa.**

Guitars! or 'Surely it's more important to be a good player?'

More important than your technique, amp tone, even hairstyle, is the type of guitar you're seen with. A player can get away with horrendous musicianship if they own an instrument to die for. The reasoning goes something like this; if you see someone with a guitar which cost more than your house, you get to thinking that they wouldn't have spent all that money unless they could really get the best out of it.

All too often, of course, it just means that they've got more cash than you. But admit it, for a second, when you saw that guitar in its case, you thought the owner was a better player than you, didn't you?

Mouth open and RAWWK!

Here, then, is a selection of the guitars to own if you want to command maximum respect amongst the rock community. All usage of jargon has, of course, been maximised for your convenience.

Gibson Les Paul

ANORAK DATA:
First introduced in 1952 ('Gold Top' model). Designed by the eponymous guitarist. Humbuckers replaced single-coil pickups in 1957. Various off-shoots (Les Paul Junior, Les Paul Special, Les Paul Deluxe etc) but the two best-known are the Standard and Custom.

FAMOUS NAMES:
Gary Moore, Jimmy Page, Paul Kossoff, Joe Perry, Slash, James Dean Bradfield.

DESIGN:
Solid body (originally mahogany) with arched top, two humbucking pickups with three-way selector switch. Two volume, two tone controls.

SOUND:
Les Paul wanted the guitar to have a 20-second sustain (hence the mahogany), and this is the instrument's most famous characteristic. Combination of solid construction and high-output pickups makes it suitable for high-gain, long distorted sounds (hence the rock-blues leanings of the above-named players). Typical adjectives include 'singing', 'ringing', 'stinging', 'swinging' (jazzers only), 'gunslinging' (guitar heroes only).

KNOWLEDGEABLE FACT:
Some 'Les Pauls' have double cutaways and a flat top - these are referred to as 'SG-style'. Generally, though, the name Les Paul is used by players to describe the arch-top, single-cutaway guitar shown in the photo.

INSTANT OPINION:
Just say any old rubbish involving sustain, e.g. **"the sustain on my old LP, it's incredible, but that's 'cos I got mine from a bloke who knew the milkman who used to deliver to Clapton's house back in '64."**

ACCEPTABLE CRITICISM:
Try wearing a solid mahogany guitar on a shoulder strap throughout a 2-hour gig, then come up with your own...

The 1952 Les Paul Gold Top - ringing, singing, and gunslinging.

Fender Stratocaster

ANORAK DATA:

First introduced in 1954. Design has hardly changed since. Some models manufactured in Japan from early 1980s, under the Squier brand name. Strats are now made in the following countries (listed in descending order of price and quality): USA, Japan, Korea, Mexico, and China. Technically, its low-output pickups and high frets shouldn't make it a rock machine, but plenty of players have put in the effort and got results.

FAMOUS NAMES:

Jimi Hendrix, Ritchie Blackmore, The Edge, Jeff Beck, Crispian Mills, Eric Clapton, George Harrison, David Gilmour.

DESIGN:

3 single-coil pickups, double-cutaway, solid body. Floating bridge vibrato unit (though for serious whammy-bar madness you'll need a locking unit).

SOUND:

Generally brighter than other rock guitars, due to its single-coil pickups. Adjectives to use include 'sparkling', 'glassy', 'sharp', 'honking', 'bell-like', 'squealing', 'crisp'...

KNOWLEDGEABLE FACT:

Single-ply scratchplates were replaced by three-ply white/black/white versions in 1959. Impress other Strat users by noting that their single-ply scratchplate (very common on copies) is "based on the classic '57 design".

INSTANT OPINION:

"Early '80s Japanese Squiers were actually better made than the American Strats at the time." (true in some cases, and vague enough to convince everyone with your confident use of such a sweeping statement).

ACCEPTABLE CRITICISM:

Cheaper copies are often prone to microphonic feedback, and most Strats will give you mains hum unless you get replacement pickups.

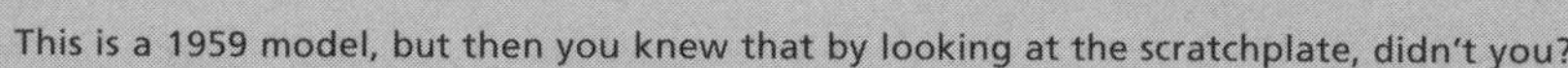
This is a 1959 model, but then you knew that by looking at the scratchplate, didn't you?

Fender Telecaster

ANORAK DATA:
First introduced in 1948 as the 'Broadcaster' but this was changed because the Gretsch company made a drumkit of the same name. Various options were available later, including humbucking pickups, semi-solid body and even a paisley finish, but the basic Tele we now know and love is almost exactly the same as it was 50 years ago.

FAMOUS NAMES:
Keith Richards, Bruce Springsteen, Chrissie Hynde, Graham Coxon.

DESIGN:
2 single-coil pickups, 3-way switch, one volume, one tone. No tremolo block. No complex switching options. No fancy contours. A Tele is basically a plank with strings on it.

SOUND:
A little fatter than a Strat, but not as rounded in tone as a Les Paul. Used through the right amp/pedal, the bridge pickup can create a rich 'growling' sound that no other guitar can imitate. Adjectives include 'cutting', 'gutsy' and 'biting'. You get the idea.

KNOWLEDGEABLE FACT:
There's a Fender guitar called an Esquire which is basically a Tele with bridge pickup only (it's cheaper, and most rock players rarely use the neck pickup anyway). But for some reason, people still prefer the Tele...

INSTANT OPINION:
"It's a solid, functional piece of equipment, like a Sten gun..." (Keith Richards).

ACCEPTABLE CRITICISM:
Only 21 frets, but if you want to play widdly metal nonsense at the top of the neck, you're looking at the wrong guitar...

The Fender Telecaster - a solid, functional... plank with strings.

And just in case...

If someone asks you about any other guitar, it's usually safest to steer the conversation back to one of the 'big three' by saying something like: "Yeah, I know what you mean about the Delectrolux Tri-Tonic Sound-u-Like model, but it can't really replace the warm tone of a real Les Paul..." However, if you get really stuck, here are a few bite-size snippets on other rock guitars:

1. Gibson SG

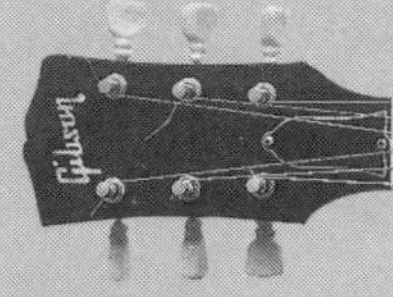

Double-cutaway, twin-humbucking flat top solid-body. As played by **Frank Zappa**, Black Sabbath's **Tony Iommi** and AC/DC's **Angus Young**.

Tiny neck width has been known to annoy big-fingered rock players.

2. Gibson Flying V

Possibly the first deliberately-designed 'rock' guitar, even though it was introduced long before heavy metal was anything more than a buzzword for nuclear physicists. Fixed bridge, solid body, twin humbuckers.

Hendrix owned one, but it's also been played by many a metaller, including **Michael Schenker** and **J. Geils**.

3. 'Superstrats'

During the 1980s, the US company Jackson had the bright idea of taking the world's most popular guitar and giving it a turbo-charge. So they whacked a high-output humbucking pickup in the bridge and put a 'locking' tremolo unit in, allowing all sorts of whammy-bar shenanigans at high volume without feedback, mains hum or tuning problems.

You don't see them so much nowadays, but the Superstrat is still one of the most versatile guitars around.

4. DIY guitars

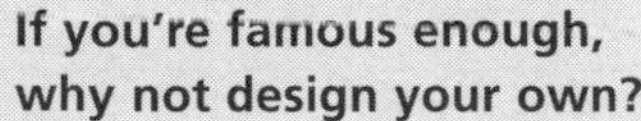

If you're famous enough, why not design your own?
Mind you, if you're that well-known, you've bluffed your way to the top already, so you won't be needing this book...

Although some players play 'signature' versions of classic designs, others actually have their own models. **Bo Diddley**, **Joe Satriani**, **Steve Vai**, **Randy Rhoads**, **Eddie Van Halen** and **Nuno Bettencourt** all have had guitars made for them by the manufacturers, like this 7-string Ibanez Universe á la Steve Vai.

Guitar Sounds or 'Who Cares How It Sounds When It's This Loud?'

Players often convince themselves that they need the exact same gear as their heroes before they can create convincing sounds. In fact, with a guitar that plays in tune, a reliable amp, and a selection of effects, you can get a useable version of every guitar tone you ever wanted.

On these pages, we've shown diagrams of a typical pedals setup for three basic sounds. (Note - multi-FX owners should assume that all values are out of 10, except for delay times - our delay pedal shown has a maximum time setting of 1000ms, so if the dial's at 12 o'clock, that means a 500ms, or half-second delay).

Blues-Rock Setup

Use middle pickup

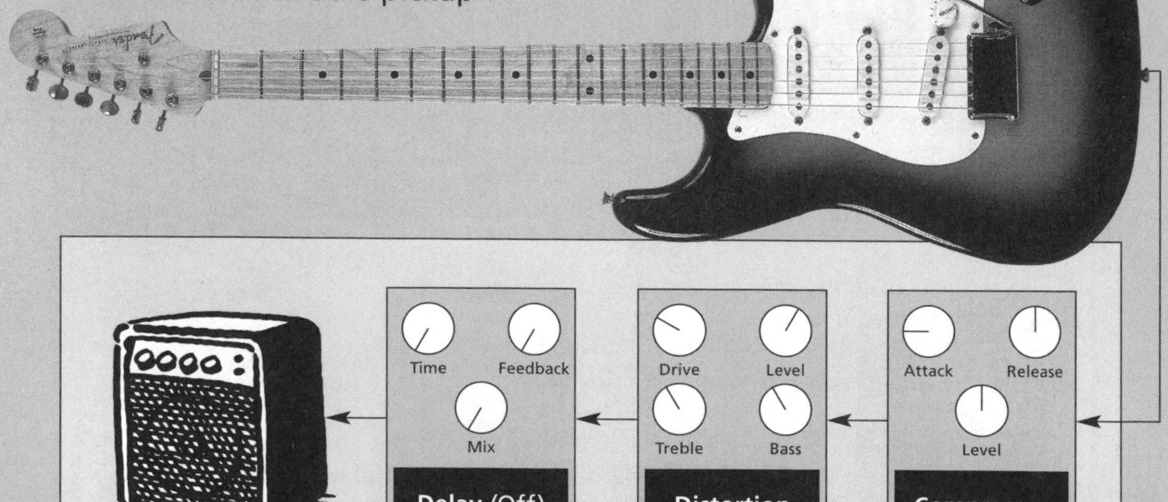

Thrash Setup

Use bridge pickup

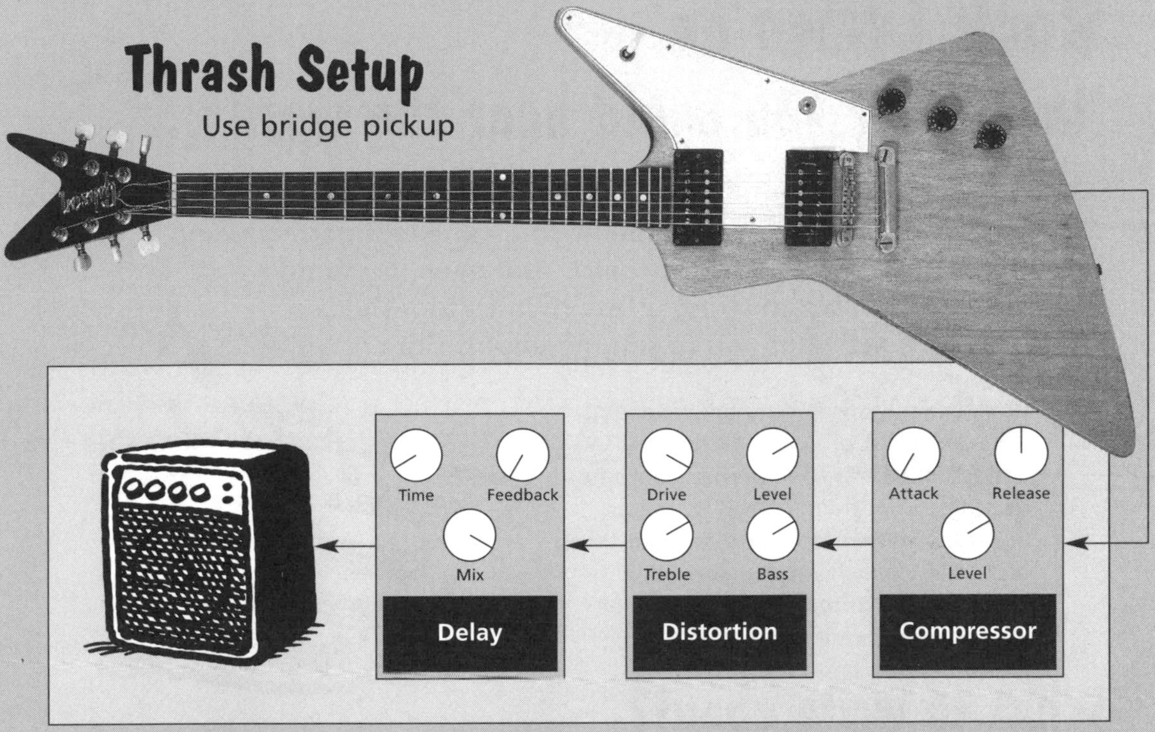

Time
Feedback
Mix
Delay
Drive
Level
Treble
Bass
Distortion
Attack
Release
Level
Compressor

Funk Metal Setup

Use both pickups

Time
Feedback
Mix
Delay (Off)
Drive
Level
Treble
Bass
Distortion
Attack
Release
Level
Compressor

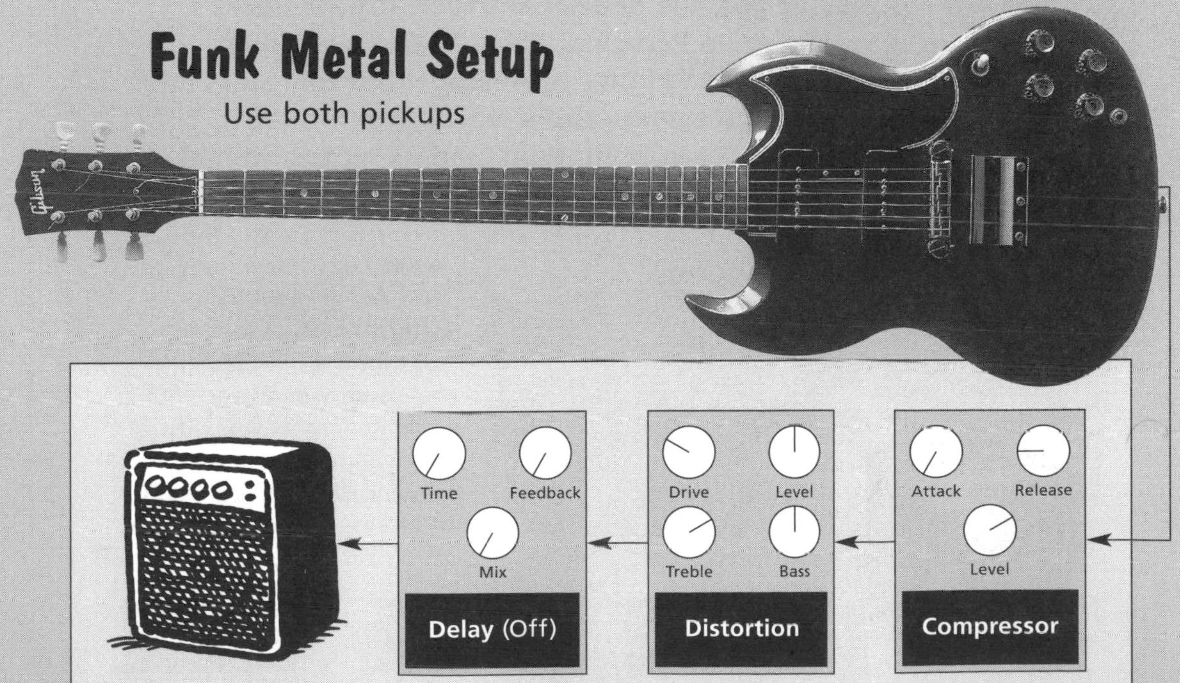

Rock Lyrics or 'In my day you could hear the words...'

No-one likes writing lyrics. Hey, you didn't get into rock to be a poet - if you had, you'd spend your time wandering round fields of daffodils in a frilly shirt. And even if you do take the trouble to string a few rhymes together, no-one cares what you're singing about, right?

Well, broadly-speaking that's true, and in recent (post-grunge) years, many bands' rock lyrics have perhaps become even less important. However, there are some subjects that you need to cover, and others which you must avoid, if you're going to convince anyone that you're a 'proper' rock songwriter.

What to write about?

Anything which mentions motor vehicles is instant cool. And the less wheels they've got, the heavier the rock. Chuck Berry's 'No Particular Place To Go' was drivin' along in its automobile, but ten years later Steppenwolf's motorcycle anthem 'Born To Be Wild' had its motor runnin' out on the highway.

Meat Loaf - two-wheeled rock

Steppenwolf - born wild

Meat Loaf's been defying the laws of gravity atop a Harley Davidson for years. But that doesn't mean it's cool to be seen in your gran's Robin Reliant – even with black windows, flames up the sides and **Metallica** blaring out of every window...

If you're going to write about historical subjects, it needs to be 500 years ago or more. Anything to do with mediaeval torture, thunder crashing over castle ramparts and maidens being saved from certain death is fine for some types of rock and metal. Just don't mention dragons or you'll be accused of being a **Genesis** fan.

Politics is OK, as long as you don't mind being branded 'alternative rock' (**Rage Against The Machine**, **Skunk Anansie** etc). Keep it contemporary, though. If you start writing about the hangman's noose or 18th century Luddism, that's fine, but keep in mind that these days there's not an awful lot of work for **Jethro Tull** tribute bands.

Rock lyricists have been writing about sex for years, and it's all been done, so don't bother to try and shock anyone. If **Whitesnake** can get away with songs like 'Slide It In' (subtle use of metaphor) and the **Stones** can do 'Brown Sugar' (sexism and racism all in the one track) there's not a lot of point in taking things any further.

Lyrical Genius

Generally, your love story should go - boy meets girl (**verse 1**), boy asks girl for a dance (**verse 2**), they 'rock' all night long (**chorus**), stopping only for a guitar **solo** before we're reminded how they met (**repeat verse 1**).

So our ultimate rock lyric needs to feature a rock dude on a motorbike - wait, let's be really heavy and make it a unicycle - in the year 1500. He's gotta save his girl from the clutches of the evil Zarg (random sci-fi is usually OK too) who lives in a castle in the ancient land of Gandalf (or pick any other word from The Hobbit).

She's exploited by the despotic power of MTV, which is oppressively sapping her sense of political self-determination (might be tricky to make that bit scan), but by the end of the middle eight she meets up with our unicycling hero and they rock the night away. Classic!

It's Easy To Bluff...

Acoustic Guitar

Bob Dylan's songs are still as good as they ever were.
Unfortunately, so is his guitar playing.

Introduction

Electric guitar players have it too easy, don't they? They just plug in, turn everything up to '11', then stomp on the latest Japanese talent-booster effects pedal. Hey presto - instant Pink Floyd. That's all very well, but what do guitarists do when they're sat under the stars with nothing but a bottle of beer and a Martin D-28?

The whole problem with acoustic guitar is that everyone can hear it. Hit a wrong note on your electric and you can bend it up until it sounds OK, or hit the whammy bar to turn a musical mistake into a Jimi Hendrix reference. On acoustic the note stays where it is, for all to enjoy. This makes it one of the most difficult instruments to bluff with. However, help is at hand.

It's Easy To Bluff... Acoustic Guitar shows you how you can bluff your way through the cruellest campfire sessions and the fiercest folk clubs with a little knowledge and a few simple tricks. As long as you name-drop the right albums, talk about the right players and know which songs you should be playing, your status as an aficionado of all things acoustic is assured. Keep this book with you at all times, but don't let other people see it - you wouldn't want anyone to find out that you're just bluffing...

"What, No Classical?"

You may be surprised to see a distinct lack of references to the classical guitar and its players in this book. That's because, in terms of construction and musical style, it's a totally different instrument from the 'acoustic' steel-strung. The main differences are:

- **The classical guitar uses nylon strings (even the 'metal' ones are in fact nylon with a metal winding round the outside).**
- The steel (or steel/bronze wound) acoustic guitar strings produce more tension, so the acoustic guitar needs a 'truss rod' - a metal bar going up the inside of the neck to prevent it from bending or breaking.
- **The steel strung guitar is usually louder and has more sustain, due to the increased tension, truss rod and metal strings.**
- Classical guitars are generally easier to play due to the lower string tension.
- **Classical guitars are almost never played using a plectrum.**
- Vibrato and strumming techniques are different due to string materials.
- **Classical players very rarely use alternate tunings apart from dropped D.**
- The acoustic steel-strung has a rounded 'radius' to its fingerboard (the classical guitar has a flat fingerboard), which is one of the reasons why you've never heard bottleneck classical guitar!

The Story of the Acoustic Guitar
or 'Who to name-drop, and when'

Although classical guitars have been around for centuries, the steel-strung acoustic has only been with us for 150 years or so. To all intents and purposes, the instrument started with the American Martin company in the 1850s.

You will hear true acoustic trainspotters mention **Lyon** and **Healy** (responsible for the Washburn brand), and of course **Gibson** (who made some of the earliest f-hole acoustics) but basically, if you want to name drop guitar-makers, **C F Martin**'s the man. The company is still making guitars today, and its reputation hasn't dwindled - you'll still see these instruments in the hands of top folk, rock and country players the world over.

However, if you do get accidentally stranded between two acoustic wild bores in their native habitat, you might wish to aid your escape by also mentioning **Gretsch** (early 12-string maker) and perhaps **National/Dobro** (whose guitars featured a metal dish in the centre to amplify the sound). And by the time you've brought up the subject of 1930s **Maccaferri** jazz guitars, you'll probably have made it as far as the door anyway.

The Players

Bluffer's rule #1: You play acoustic, your dream guitar is a Martin.

Of course, the only guitarists that any of us can say we've heard are from this century, because no-one was recording before then (you'd think some bright spark record producer would have seen the sense in getting some of those early players down on tape, but maybe CD manufacture was too expensive back in the 19th Century!).

With this in mind, your first points of reference have to be the early blues players. Many less experienced bluffers will try to name-check the legendary **Robert Johnson** as an early acoustic blues player, but remember that there was literally a generation of players before him. **Blind Blake**, **Charley Patton** and **Blind Lemon Jefferson**'s recordings all pre-dated Johnson, so mentioning their names in the right company guarantees an air of authority.

Above: c.1850 Martin 'Stauffer' with curly headstock and abalone inlay

Acoustic Jazz and the Teddy Bunn clause

Bluffer's rule #2: Use the **Teddy Bunn** clause when in difficulty - no-one will be able to challenge you.

As the 20s and 30s wore on, jazz guitar became increasingly popular, and like it or loathe it, you can't say you know your acoustic roots unless you're familiar with some of the early jazzers.

Many people know about **Django Reinhardt**, but how about **Lonnie Johnson** or **George Van Eps**? Don't worry yourself with details, though - you can get by with very little knowledge of these people.

Luckily for the acoustic bluffer, all of the early acoustic jazz players had a similar career - single-note acoustic soloing was combined with tasteful rhythm work, but recognition of their talent was limited by the fact that the instrument wasn't amplified. Even more conveniently, you'll find that very few guitarists actually own a recording by acoustic jazz pioneer **Teddy Bunn**.

Thus, you can achieve mastery of any conversation instantly by saying something like "well, you've got to give it to **Reinhardt**, but his tracks just didn't have the unique timing of those early **Teddy Bunn** recordings". Like all the best bluffs, it demonstrates your encyclopaedic knowledge while making you impossible to challenge.

First folk and classic country

The earliest country guitarist you need to know about is Maybelle Carter. In the 1930s she invented the technique called 'Carter picking' (so it was just as well she had the same surname...) which consists of picking the melody on the bass strings whilst strumming chord accompaniment in the gaps between notes.

The next most significant, in technique terms, is undoubtedly **Chet Atkins**. His thumb-and-three-fingers technique has since acted as a blueprint for thousands of acoustic fingerstyle players.

The earliest British folkie you'll hear mentioned is probably **Davey Graham**. As well as inventing the DADGAD acoustic tuning in the 1950s, he also penned the classic instrumental 'Angie', but more importantly laid the groundwork for the many players that followed - **John Renbourn**, **Gordon Giltrap**, **Leo Kottke** and **Bert Jansch** to name but four.

Lots of people who couldn't play guitar very well but got away with it because they had some good songs.

In the mid 1960s, a whole bunch of players arrived who did nothing but strum three chords. Whilst any guitarist would be hard-pushed to call these people an 'influence' on their technique, you'll find that theirs are among the songs you'll be asked to play most often.

So make sure you've got a smattering of **Bob Dylan**, **Neil Young**, **Joan Baez**, **Don McLean** and **Leonard Cohen**. Shouldn't take you too long to learn the material.

Bluffer's rule #3: If your songwriting's any good, no-one will notice how badly you play acoustic.

The Fingerpickers

The late 60s and early 70s were something of a heyday for the acoustic guitar. Songwriters like Paul Simon, Joni Mitchell, Donovan and even The Beatles were using an alternating thumb technique based loosely on Chet Atkins' style, and writing material using the guitar as the sole or primary accompaniment.

Bluffer's rule #4: It's OK to play acoustic even if you're really a rocker at heart...

Pretty much every acoustic guitarist has played their songs at one time or another, so if you haven't got a transcription of **Paul Simon**'s 'The Boxer' or **Joni Mitchell**'s 'The Circle Game', now would be a good time to put things right.

Conversely, things looked pretty bad for acoustic players in the 1980s. Synthesisers and electric guitars reigned supreme, and it seemed that people cared more about hairstyles than hammer-ons. It was left to a few brave souls to save the day, and they did, in a spectacular fashion.

A stream of virtuoso players appeared, including **Michael Hedges**, **Adrian Legg** and **Al Di Meola**. If you're brave you might want to check out their recordings, but if you want to learn their material, might I suggest a ten-year holiday and an island retreat?

The Unplugged Generation

These days, thanks partly to one MTV show, acoustic guitar is reigning supreme again. It seems any artist, however noisy their music, can gain instant cred by doing acoustic versions of their songs (although the acclaimed 'Nirvana Unplugged' session, bizarrely, featured an electric guitar through a fuzz pedal).

Bluffer's rule #5: ...and when you get old, you can always retire to MTV.

Even the angry young men of yesteryear have now settled down with pipe, slippers and acoustic flat-top; remember that **Paul Weller** was practically a punk in his Jam days, and **Eric Clapton** was in one of the 60s' loudest, heaviest rock bands.

Bluff your way

So there you have it - a potted history of the instrument.

If you remember half of what's written here, it's probably more bluffing material than you'll need to use in a lifetime. And remember, if another player name-drops someone who doesn't appear in this book, just ask them what they think of **Teddy Bunn**. Works every time.

Nirvana's MTV Unplugged set famously used a fuzz pedal. Doh!

The Players

Bite-size biogs

In this section you'll find an instant guide to six top acoustic guitarists. Remember that these aren't necessarily the most 'important' players, but they are the most 'significant' (i.e. these are the ones to mention if you want to impress people!).

For each artist, I've included some basic **biography** information, notes on **playing style**, plus, more importantly, which **techniques** you should steal in order to facilitate your acoustic career. Of course, you have to know the guitar they used - acoustic guitar trainspotters are everywhere and could pounce at any time.

To save you from having to wade through a truckload of CDs, I've also picked out one **essential album** for you to mention (not necessarily the best-known - it can sometimes pay dividends to bluff your way by showing you listen to the obscure stuff). If you're actually asked to prove that you've heard the artist, you'd be stuck without the quick and easy '**finest moment**' reference, and you'll find it helpful to casually mention your handy '**knowledgeable fact**'.

Finally, it's always useful to have a few oven-ready opinions up your sleeve. For each player, I've included an 'instant opinion' (usually ambiguous enough to cover all situations) and an 'acceptable criticism'. If you're cool enough to criticise one of the greats, you can consider your acoustic acumen to be truly foolproof.

Chet Atkins CGP

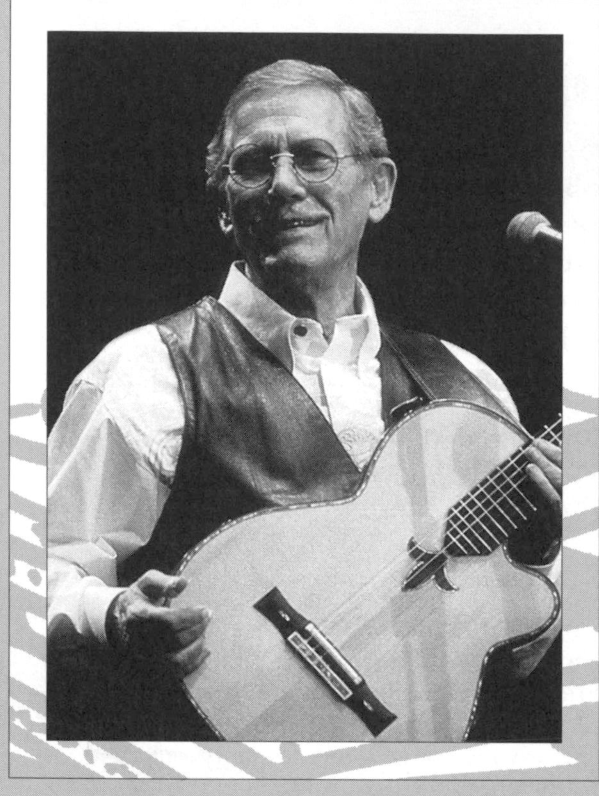

HISTORY AND BACKGROUND:

Born June 20th 1924, Tennessee, USA. Started playing fiddle in country bands while still at school, but soon moved to guitar. His advanced thumb-and-three-fingers technique meant that he could create whole arrangements with bassline, chords and melody on one instrument. After a string of successful albums he went into A&R for RCA records, so he was instrumental (ahem) in launching the careers of **Elvis Presley**, **The Everly Brothers** and **Jim Reeves**, among others. One of the few acoustic guitarists to have consistent top 40 success purely with instrumentals. Added the initials CGP ('Certified Guitar Player') to his name in 1983.

PLAYING STYLE:

Thumb (or thumbpick) covers the bass notes, playing two or four to the bar, while the fingers take the melody. Even if he uses a backing band, the basic idea is the same. Some hits feature the thumb straying onto the top strings occasionally.

TECHNIQUES TO STEAL:

If you play any fingerstyle at all, the odds are that you're indirectly influenced by this man. If you can get your hand round some basic alternating thumb techniques, you're doing pretty well, but listen out for some pyrotechnic stuff too. Our Chet uses banjo rolls (fast melodic runs created across several

strings by plucking with three fingers in a 'rolling' motion), harmonics, tremolando picking, and some seriously jazzy chords in his work.

GUITARS:
Although his technique suits acoustic so well, we've seen a variety of guitars in the Atkins armoury. For years he was a Gretsch semi-acoustic endorsee (he now says they "sounded like they were made out of orange boxes") but acoustic-wise he's always been a Gibson man, having recorded with a thin-bodied electro-classical and a Country & Western flat-top.

ESSENTIAL ALBUM:
1975's *Chester And Lester*, a duet with Les Paul, was a massive success, and does contain some great playing, but you'll give yourself several years of study if you just buy any compilation of his '50s and '60s RCA recordings.

FINEST MOMENT:
His famous arrangement of 'The Entertainer' is a great crowd-pleaser, as is his detuned version of 'Vincent', but you can't beat the simplicity of his own tune 'Maybelle' - normal tuning, open C and barre G7 chords, and a country melody to die for. And it was written about country picking pioneer **Maybelle Carter** (see page 9) so it's always a good one for showing off your knowledge of two players during the same conversation.

KNOWLEDGEABLE FACT:
His single 'Yakety Axe' was later used on British TV as the 'Benny Hill' theme.

INSTANT OPINION:
The most influential fingerstyle guitarist of all time.

ACCEPTABLE CRITICISM:
Adding CGP to your name is conceited, grandiose and pretentious.

Bob Dylan

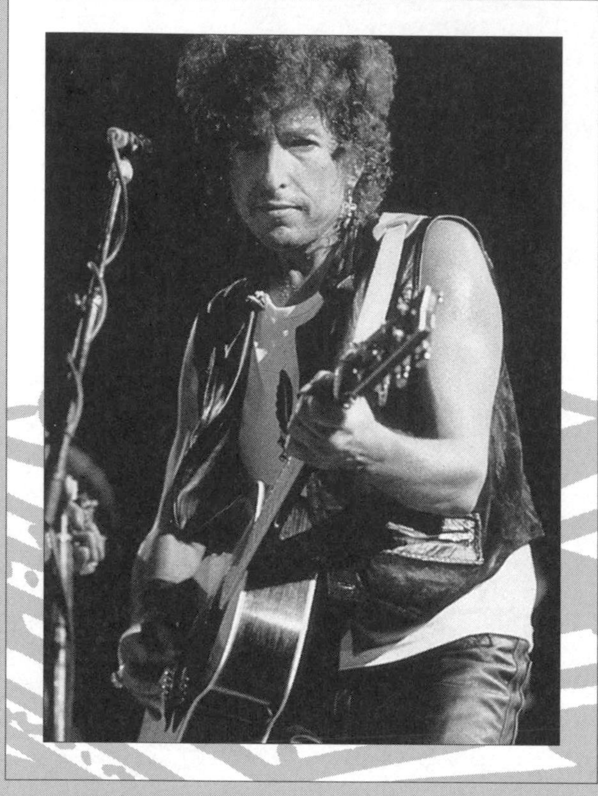

HISTORY AND BACKGROUND:

Born Robert Allen Zimmerman, Minnesota, USA, May 24th, 1941. Influenced by 1930s US folkie **Woody Guthrie**, and successfully revived the folk protest song in the mid-1960s. Remained a three-chord acoustic strummer until the mid-60s when he controversially appeared on stage with an electric guitar, prompting booing from assembled folk purists. His guitar playing (and singing) was always pretty ropey, and many other '60s artists had bigger hits with Dylan songs than the man himself, including **The Byrds** ('Mr Tambourine Man'), **Peter Paul and Mary** ('Blowin' In The Wind') and **Jimi Hendrix** ('All Along The Watchtower').

Bob's still recording and writing, having recently released a compilation of songs by country legend **Jimmie Rodgers**. His own songs are as good as they ever were. Unfortunately, so is his guitar playing.

PLAYING STYLE:

Lots of capo'd strumming, but he has had fingerstyle moments too ('Don't Think Twice'). Treats the guitar as vocal accompaniment, hence the basic level of technique. Timing is sometimes very loose, reminiscent of his folk, blues and country influences.

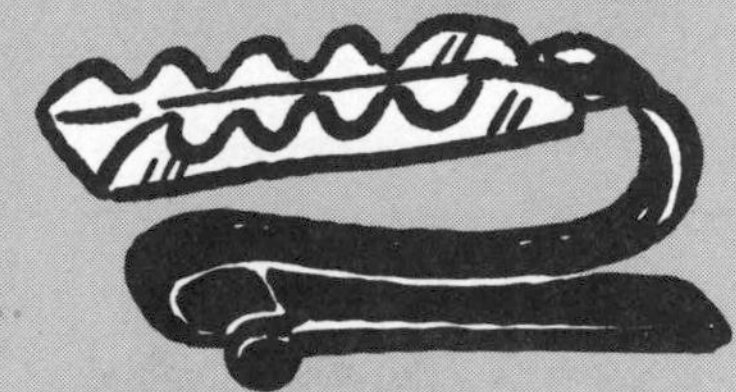

TECHNIQUES TO STEAL:

Fingerstyle, perhaps, but the most important technique we should all learn is to write such good lyrics that no-one notices the standard of our guitar playing.

GUITARS:

Over the years has been seen with Martins, Guilds and Gibsons, plus of course that controversial Fender Strat.

ESSENTIAL ALBUM:

For early acoustic hits, check out 1963's *The Freewheelin' Bob Dylan*, but the Dylan album that is standard issue amongst most musicians is 1975's million-selling *Blood On The Tracks*.

FINEST MOMENT:

Loads of 'em... apart from the obvious standards like 'Blowin' in the Wind' and 'The Times They Are a-Changin', 1969's 'Lay Lady Lay' is a four-chord acoustic anthem to make any songwriter weep, and 'Subterranean Homesick Blues' is great to play at your local jam session - if you can remember all the lyrics without cue cards.

KNOWLEDGEABLE FACT:

A bunch of 1970s terrorists named themselves 'The Weathermen' after Dylan's lyric "You don't need a weatherman to know which way the wind blows" from the song 'Subterranean Homesick Blues'.

INSTANT OPINION:

Other people play his songs better than he does.

ACCEPTABLE CRITICISM:

Sings like a vacuum cleaner.

Joni Mitchell

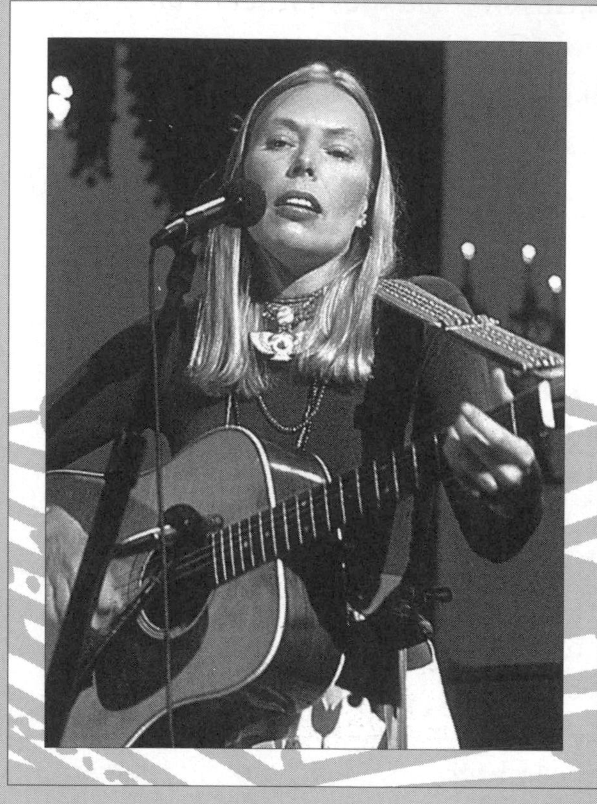

HISTORY AND BACKGROUND:

Born Roberta Joan Anderson in Canada on 7th November 1943. Joni, along with **Chet** and **Bob**, is one of very few acoustic guitarists famous enough to be referred to by first name only. Started playing and singing solo in local coffee bars in the mid-1960s. First album recorded 1967, and by 1969 she was a regular on the Californian hippy-drippy scene. Her song 'Woodstock' was **Crosby, Stills & Nash**'s first single. She's experimented with plenty of different styles over the years, including jazz, rock and choral music, but keeps coming back to her stock in trade - the open-tuned, fingerpicked solo guitar song.

PLAYING STYLE:

Early albums featured very precise, specific fingerstyle parts, which became more strummed and ambiguous on later albums. She has, to date, used 51 tunings, including old favourites like open G and double dropped D, but has also devised many of her own.

TECHNIQUES TO STEAL:

Try making up your own tuning, then making up your own chord shapes, and just see how it sounds. Many of Joni's greatest songs have been written this way. Her early stuff featured non-alternating thumb technique (i.e. you just keep striking the same bass note with the thumb whilst picking the treble strings).

GEAR:

Generally Martins, but she also owns a Klein custom acoustic, and has recently been using a Roland VG-8 synth guitar system.

ESSENTIAL ALBUM:

For the acoustic parts, go for 1970's *Ladies Of The Canyon*, but the follow-up *Blue* has been bedsit material for hippy student guitarists for over 30 years.

FINEST MOMENT:

'The Priest' from *Ladies Of The Canyon* has a masterful fingerpicked intro using DADGAE tuning, or possibly the intros from early open G songs 'Morning Morgantown' and 'The Circle Game'.

KNOWLEDGEABLE FACT:

Her tunings have been dropping over the years as her vocal range has changed - e.g. 'Big Yellow Taxi' was written in open E, but she now plays it in open C, tuned four semitones lower.

INSTANT OPINION:

She didn't recapture the great acoustic playing of the early material until *Turbulent Indigo* (1994).

ACCEPTABLE CRITICISM:

Some of her more left-field mid-1980s material is tough going for the traditional folkie.

Paul Simon

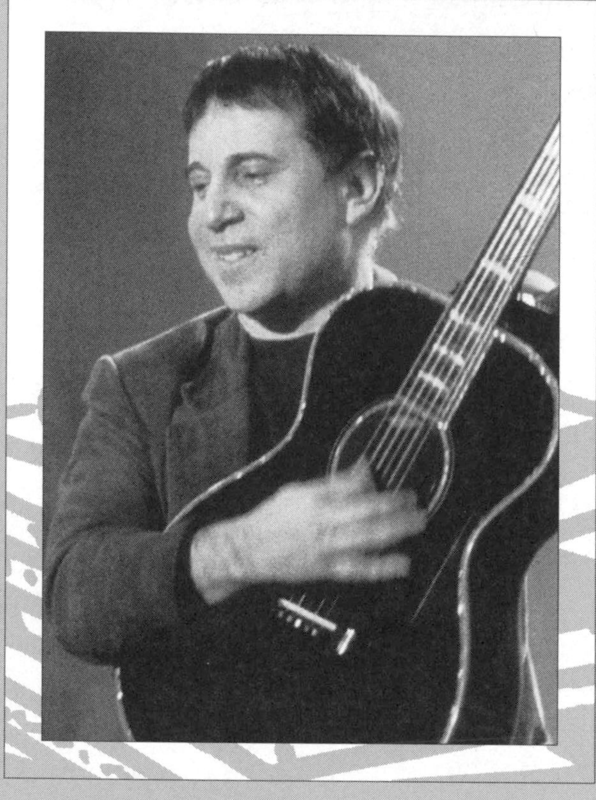

HISTORY AND BACKGROUND:

Born November 5th, 1941, New Jersey, USA. Got together with singer **Art Garfunkel** while still at school, and had a minor hit in 1957 as teen duo Tom and Jerry. First album *Wednesday Morning 3am* was not a big success, but subsequent 60s albums were huge, including *Sounds Of Silence*, *Bookends* and 1970's *Bridge Over Troubled Water*. After the duo split, solo material moved away from acoustic-based arrangements - in the 1970s and 80s, he plundered reggae ('Mother and Child Reunion'), gospel ('Loves Me Like a Rock'), and South African styles ('Graceland'). Even so, he could always cut it as a straight guitar-vocalist - the 1982 Simon & Garfunkel concert in Central Park contained some great acoustic picking. His songs are still campfire and folk club perennials, and the picking intro from 'The Boxer' still flummoxes the majority of players.

PLAYING STYLE:

Mainly straight fingerstyle in regular tuning ('Homeward Bound', 'Scarborough Fair'), frequently with capo, but he's also written some pretty nifty rhythm parts (the intro to 'Mrs Robinson' or the backing from 'Me And Julio Down By The Schoolyard').

TECHNIQUES TO STEAL:

Many fingerstyle players get by with only three or four right hand patterns, but Paul uses dozens. If you can train your fingers to play so many variations, people will actually start to think your fretted parts are more complex than they really are. Foolproof!

GEAR:

Yamaha custom, Ovation, Gurian, Guild and of course Martin.

ESSENTIAL ALBUM:

The one with the most prominent acoustic guitar playing is probably *Live Rhymin'* (1974) because it's got all the hits on it and Paul plays throughout. *Bookends* is also a great example of how his playing can take on folk, pop and jazz influences.

FINEST MOMENT:

Although the simple 3/4 picking from 'Scarborough Fair' is not difficult to play once you've mastered the thumb part, it's an amazing sound considering that he's just using regular tuning and a capo. Learn it - but don't let anyone see how easy the chord shapes are.

KNOWLEDGEABLE FACT:

Hundreds of artists have recorded his songs, including **Joan Baez**, **Shawn Colvin**, and **Davey Graham** (whose instrumental 'Anji' was recorded by Paul, and who himself later covered 'Bridge Over Troubled Water' and 'Homeward Bound').

INSTANT OPINION:

The best folk-rock songwriter of the 1960s.

ACCEPTABLE CRITICISM:

Plays his own recordings in the background when he holds parties at his house.

Jimmy Page

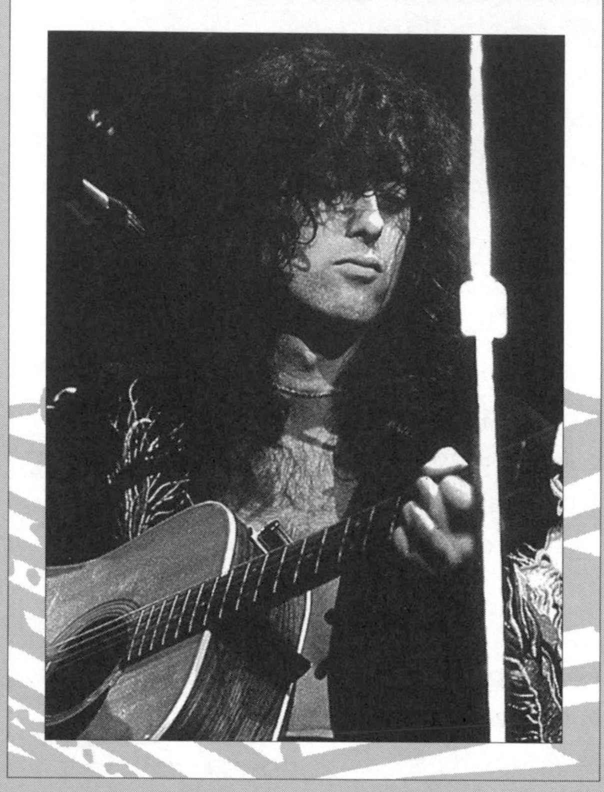

HISTORY AND BACKGROUND:
Born 9th January 1944, London. Started playing guitar aged 14. Worked as a session player in the 1960s before joining the **Yardbirds**, then formed **Led Zeppelin** in 1968. Despite the band's electric blues-rock hits, he also contributed some stunning acoustic playing, using many open tunings and a variety of picking styles. In post-Zep years, he's worked with Paul Rodgers of **Free** and **Whitesnake**'s David Coverdale, and is currently back with **Robert Plant**, a collaboration which began in true old-men-of-rock style at a 1994 MTV unplugged session.

PLAYING STYLE:
Lots of straight fingerstyle, but he is never afraid to go in the other direction and strum the life out of the instrument. Often takes a simple two or three note riff and plays it in different rhythmic ways to add interest. 80% of tunings include DADGAD, open G (DGDGBD) and open C6 (CACGCE). He's not a perfectionist, often leaving mistakes in on recordings - some of his time sig changes may or may not be intentional! Has been seen using thumbpick, pick and fingers, or just fingers.

TECHNIQUES TO STEAL:
Keep one open string ringing on while you slide an octave shape around the fingerboard, strumming all six strings and muting any that you're not using. This is the classic Page acoustic sound. He's referred to this as his 'CIA' connection - Celtic, Indian and Arabic.

GEAR:

Most of the early Zeppelin stuff was done on a Harmony acoustic, until he got a Martin D-28 in the early '70s, but he also uses (deep breath) a Yamaha acoustic; a 1920s Cromwell 'cello guitar; a Vega 5-string banjo; a Gibson A4 mandolin; a '60s 'Everly Brothers' black Gibson flat top given to him by **Ron Wood**; a Gibson '20s harp guitar with sympathetic strings; and a small-bodied 12-string Teardrop-shaped acoustic with a cutaway.

ESSENTIAL ALBUM:

Led Zep III is regarded as the band's most 'acoustic' album - check out 'Friends' (weird and Indian) 'Tangerine' (strummy 12-string), and 'Going To California' (multi-layered acoustics).

FINEST MOMENT:

It has to be 'The Rain Song' - loads of jazz voicings in DGCGCD tuning, using plectrum and some flatpicking. It's such an unusual guitar part that it even works if you try it without the vocal line.

KNOWLEDGEABLE FACT:

The solo album *Outrider* (1988) was originally written and partly recorded as an acoustic project, but the master tapes were stolen, so he had to start again, and the second version was predominantly electric. This 'lost album' has, of course, since become surrounded in rune-clad mystery and myth among fans.

INSTANT OPINION:

Kula Shaker would never have existed without Jimmy Page.

ACCEPTABLE CRITICISM:

Robert Plant's voice isn't what it was, and recent albums lack some of the energy that early Led Zep stuff had.

Django Reinhardt

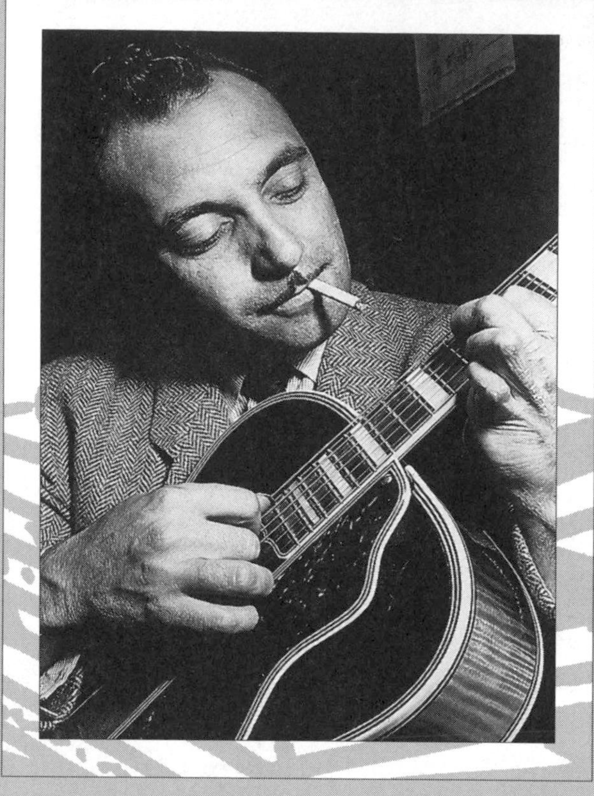

HISTORY AND BACKGROUND:

Django was born into a gypsy family – his father worked as a travelling show entertainer. Originally learned banjo and violin. A caravan fire in 1928 damaged his hand, and while he recovered his gypsy friends loaned him a guitar. His third and fourth fingers were locked at the first joint due to the fire, so he could use them for basic chord shapes only – he then developed the two-finger lead style which was his trademark. The famous Quintet du Hot Club de France was formed in 1934 and featured Django and violinist **Stephane Grapelli** as part of a line-up of three guitars, bass and fiddle. The Quintet had international success until 1939. Django travelled Europe and the USA throughout the war, settling down in the late 1940s to record his biggest hit 'Nuages'. Died in 1953, having suffered a brain haemorrhage.

PLAYING STYLE:

High-speed (acoustic) single-note runs and arpeggios (with or without bends), punctuated with partial chord stabs.

TECHNIQUES TO STEAL:

Set up a swing groove at a high tempo (200 BPM+) and play arpeggiated swung quavers over it – if you can!

GEAR:

Selmer-Maccaferri acoustic with characteristic 'D' shaped soundhole, although he also played a borrowed archtop f-hole acoustic for one post-war tour. Added a pickup to the Maccaferri later, and went fully electric in 1950.

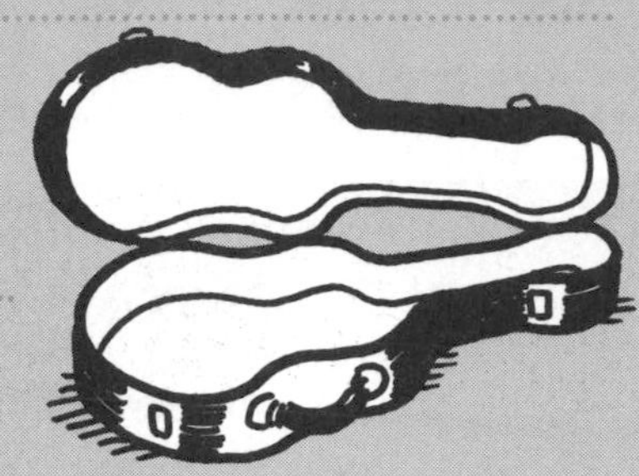

ESSENTIAL ALBUM:

Any *Quintet du Hot Club de France* compilation is essential listening. For maximum cred, try some of his really late recordings (early 1950s) – he's just starting to get into bop.

FINEST MOMENT:

You should learn 'Nuages' note-for-note anyway because it's such a technique-fest. Many players feel he's at his best when performing standards, adding fun and astonishing ideas to established classics. Check out his versions of 'Sweet Georgia Brown' and 'Ain't Misbehavin'.

KNOWLEDGEABLE FACT:

Although he's best-known for the European Hot Club material, Django also worked with big American names such as **Duke Ellington**, **Glenn Miller** and **Dizzy Gillespie** during the 1940s.

INSTANT OPINION:

"Reinvented jazz for Europe".

ACCEPTABLE CRITICISM:

Bien sûr, you are joking, n'est pas?

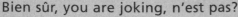

Emergency backup bluffs

Here are some condensed catalogues on a further eight players, just in case you need additional reference to prove your depth of knowledge.

1. Lonnie Johnson

New Orleans acoustic jazz-blues artist. First recorded under his own name as a guitarist as early as 1925 ('Mr Johnson's Blues'). Duetted with **Eddie Lang**, who used the pseudonym **Blind Willie Dunn**. Pioneered acoustic 12-string as a solo jazz instrument (while Leadbelly did the same for the instrument in Country-Blues). Very firm, tough flatpicking style, on a Grunewald 12-string and Gibson J100. Practically invented the acoustic jazz guitar solo.

2. Robert Johnson

Seminal 1930s bluesman. Extensive use of open tunings, including open G and open A with or without capo. Slide and fingerstyle player. Played slide with bottleneck or knife. Guitars included Gibson L1, Stella and Kalamazoo models. Died in 1938, almost certainly murdered. Influenced dozens of acoustic and electric blues players.

3. Martin Carthy MBE

Legendary folkie, with one of the longest careers of any acoustic guitarist (first album 1965, and still recording). Inspired **Paul Simon** and **Bob Dylan** in the mid-'60s. As well as 22 solo albums, has played in **Steeleye Span**, **The Albion Band**, **The Watersons** and **Brass Monkey**.

Has done more to bring traditional folk music to the fore than any other British player. Plays a Martin - well, he would, wouldn't he?

4. James Taylor

US singer/songwriter and guitarist - author of many a singalong classic including 'Fire and Rain' and 'Sweet Baby James', and also recorded successful cover of **Carole King**'s 'You've Got a Friend'. Plays fingerstyle in normal tuning or occasionally dropped D, usually with capo. Uses single open chord shapes but complex picking parts.

Notoriously melancholic voice - it's been said that he could sing the phone book and make it sound mournful.

5. Nick Drake

British singer-songwriter and acoustic martyr. Recorded only three albums before he died of an overdose aged 26. Untutored guitarist - made up tunings specifically for songs, used unorthodox fingerpicking techniques. Last album 'Pink Moon' was purely acoustic guitar and voice - the tapes were sent to the record company by post.

It's extremely fashionable to like Nick Drake these days, so do get hold of some of his stuff.

6. Michael Hedges

American acoustic guitar virtuoso. Used many unusual tunings, including BADEAB and DAEEAA, and applied advanced techniques such as two-handed tapping, hitting the instrument with palms and knuckles, fretted and open harmonics.

Recorded with a regular acoustic, but also with 11- and 17-string harp guitars. Died in a car accident in 1997, aged 43.

7. Suzanne Vega

US singer/songwriter and guitarist, partly responsible for 1980s revival of interest in female acoustic singer-songwriters - since then we've had **Shawn Colvin**, **Beth Orton** and **Jewel**, among others.

These are really now the only artists keeping acoustic guitar songwriting in the album charts, apart from the old guard of ex-rockblokes on the MTV circuit. Uses a thumbpick and fingers, generally in normal tuning, with capo. Favours sus2 chords which gives much of her early material a spaced-out, ethereal sound.

8. Nick Harper

British singer/songwriter and player. Son of **Roy Harper**. Plays a Lowden fitted with banjo pegs which allows him to incorporate bizarre tuning changes and bent harmonics into a song. First full-length album *Seed* was primarily acoustic. Follow-up *Smithereens* half-electric, half-acoustic, but used the same banjo peg fingerstyle techniques.

Uses tunings such as open G and DADGAD, but dropped by up to four whole steps into 'baritone' guitar range. Heavily influenced by **Jimmy Page**.

Bluffer's Chords or
Easy chord shapes with really complex names

In this section you'll find some of the acoustic bluffer's most essential chords. You know the ones - those ringing, heavenly chords that sound great on intros or as picked accompaniment through loads of reverb.

Most of the time they're achieved simply by placing a simple shape somewhere on the fingerboard and letting some open strings ring on. Not only do they all sound great, they're particularly good for impressing other players, when you casually say something like "oh, that? It's just a D♭maj13♯9♭5".

And remember that however strange a chord sounds, there's always a name for it: strum all the open strings in normal tuning and you get A dominant 9th (no 3rd) in second inversion, or E minor 11th (no 9th) in root position.

'Star Man'

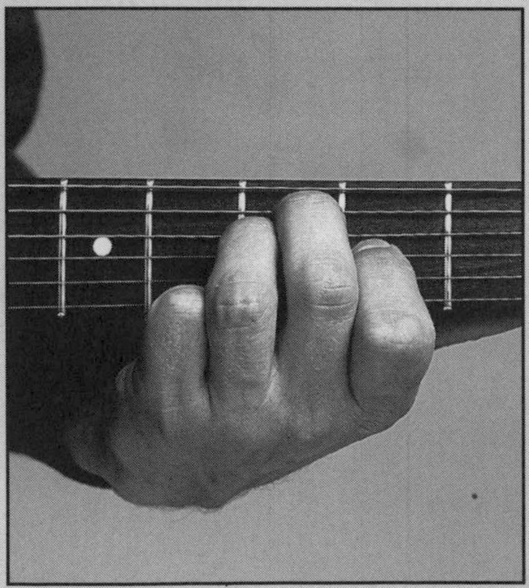

Fmaj7♯11(third inversion)

This is the chord that **David Bowie** strums in the fade-in intro to 'Star Man'. Some players put the first finger on the first fret of the sixth string to make a 'normal' Fmaj7♯11.

David Bowie probably didn't use the words "Fmaj7♯11 third inversion" when he wrote the classic 'Star Man' - more likely he said "play an E, but move it up a bit".

'Thunder and Lightning'

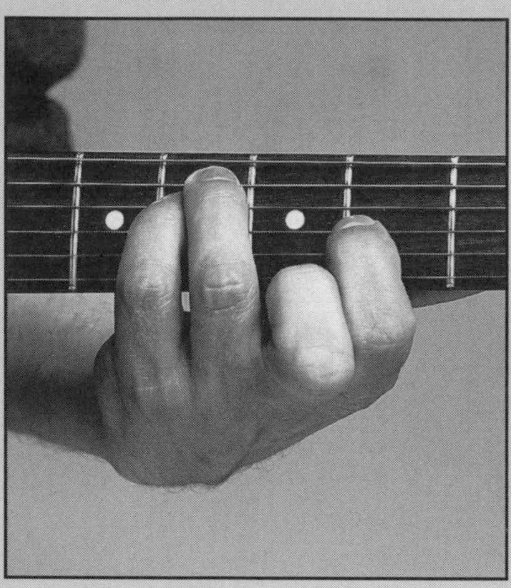

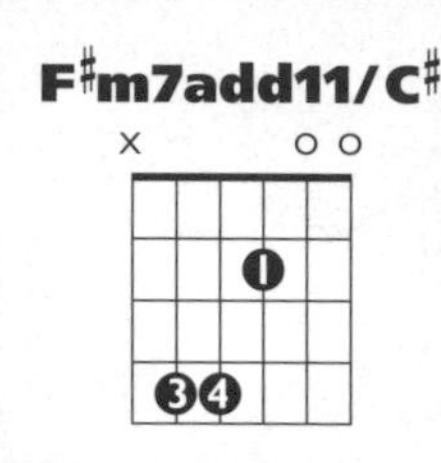

F♯m7add11/C♯
It's probably not what **Noel Gallagher**, and **Paul Weller** would call it, but this F♯m substitute sounds great on acoustic. It most famously appears in **Thunderclap Newman**'s rock classic 'Something In The Air'.

'Luka'

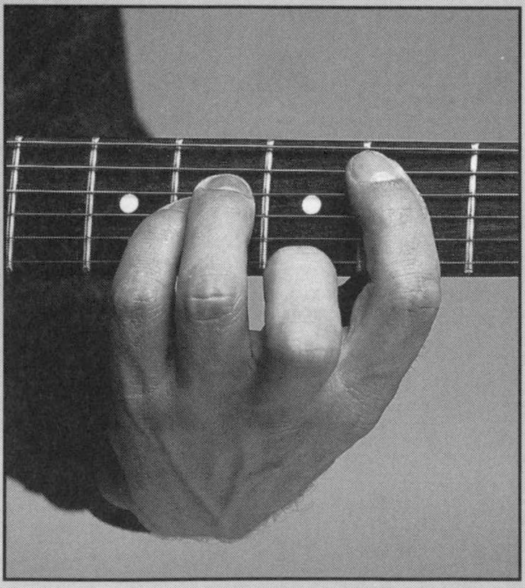

Bsus4
This is the second in the four-chord sequence which makes up the verse of this **Suzanne Vega** song. The doubled fretted/open B note creates a 12-string effect.

'Wild Wood'

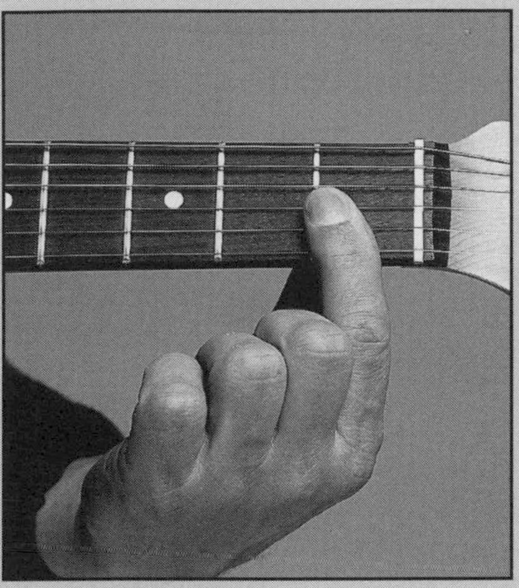

Dm7♭5

Paul Weller strums this chord with a capo at the 2nd fret in the title track of his album 'Wild Wood'. The whole song just loops open chord shapes of Am, Em (with A in the bass), Dm, then Dm7♭5, before returning to the Am.

'Dream On'

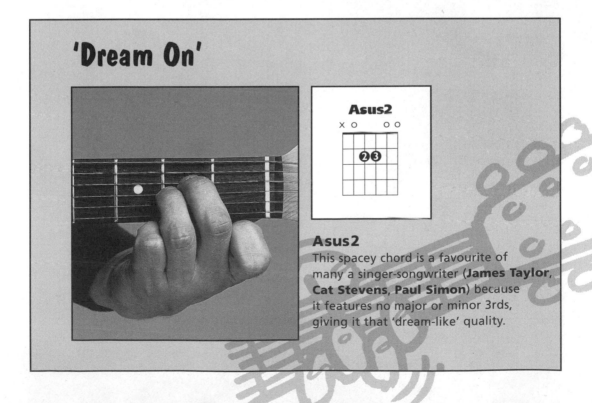

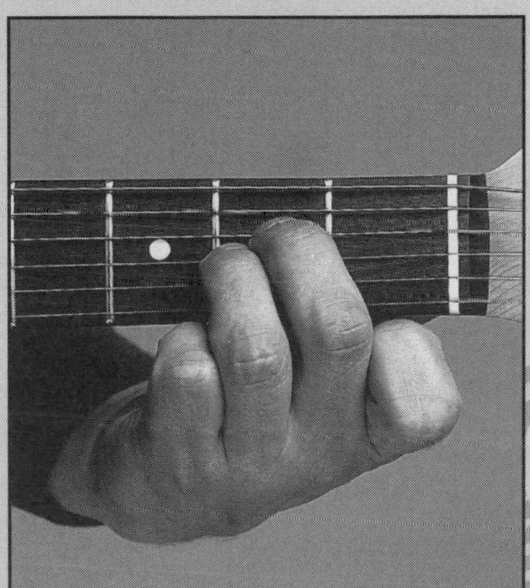

Asus2

This spacey chord is a favourite of many a singer-songwriter (**James Taylor**, **Cat Stevens**, **Paul Simon**) because it features no major or minor 3rds, giving it that 'dream-like' quality.

In the 1970s, folk-rockers such as **James Taylor** kept open chords alive - with a capo!

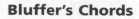

'Fire and Rain'

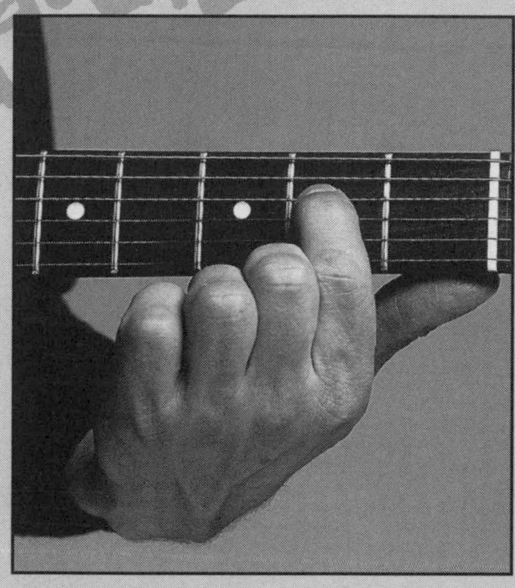

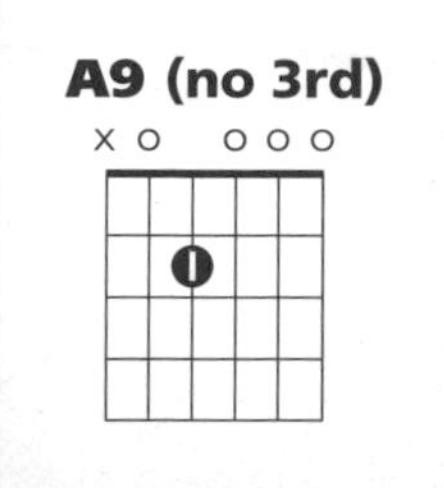

A9 (no 3rd)

Sounds great after a straight A7 chord, as used by **James Taylor** at the end of each chorus of 'Fire & Rain'.

'The Pretenders'

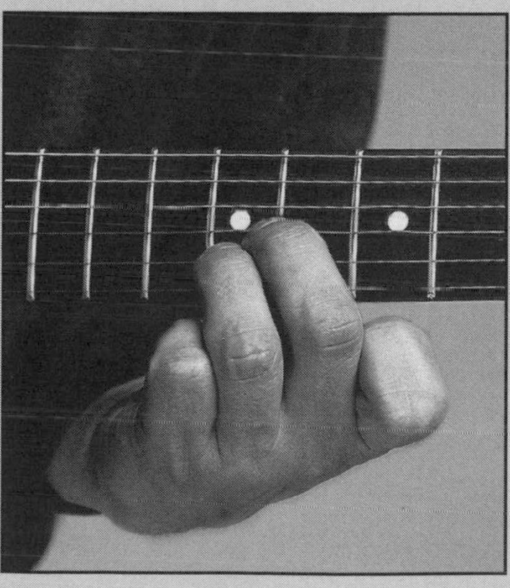

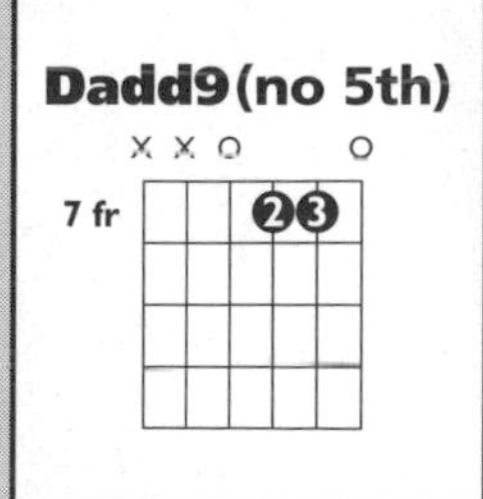

Dadd9 (no 5th)

Although this was played on an electric guitar in **The Pretenders'** song 'Back On The Chain Gang', it's a big favourite with acoustic players too. It works equally well whether strummed or picked.

Bert Jansch - responsible for some of the most fiendish folk picking parts of the 1960s.

Rhythm and Picking Patterns or 'Flash don't make cash'

If you have to bluff your way through a whole acoustic gig, you'll need to convince everyone in the band that you know your 'rhythm chops', so it's vital that you can play some basic accompaniment styles. In this section you'll find a selection of rhythm parts and picking patterns, in progressive order of difficulty, which guitarists use when accompanying vocalists or other soloists.

Foolproof Acoustic Rhythm

- When you're playing strummed chord parts, keep the hand moving up and down in an even 8- or 16-to-the-bar pattern, and don't hit the strings at certain points simply to create rhythmic gaps in the part. If you try to stop your hand moving to create gaps, the part won't flow evenly.
- **For subtle, precise rhythm playing, strums should pivot from the wrist. For big, ringing open chord parts, try pivoting from the elbow.**
- Most of the time, you'll get the fullest sound by strumming directly over the soundhole.
- **If you're not using a pick, strum with the backs of the nails on the downstrokes, and with the thumbnail on the upstrokes.**
- If you find that you're using lots of barre chords on a simple acoustic part, try using a capo where the barre would be - it sounds more musical.

Foolproof Acoustic Picking

- The most common mistake people make when they start to learn fingerstyle is to miss the strings with the picking hand. Try anchoring your hand, either by resting the palm on the bridge, or putting your little finger on the body next to the soundhole.
- **Generally, use your thumb on the three bass strings and the first, second and third fingers on the three treble strings.**
- There are three methods of picking - fingers only, pick and fingers ('hybrid picking') or thumbpick and fingers. Bear in mind that if you use hybrid picking, you can't use your first finger on the treble strings.
- **When learning a new fingerstyle part, practise it over and over using just one chord until your fingers 'learn' the rhythm and can do it automatically.**
- Develop the ability to play every thumb-picked and finger-picked note at the same volume - don't let stronger fingers dominate the picking part.

'Wrist And Shout'

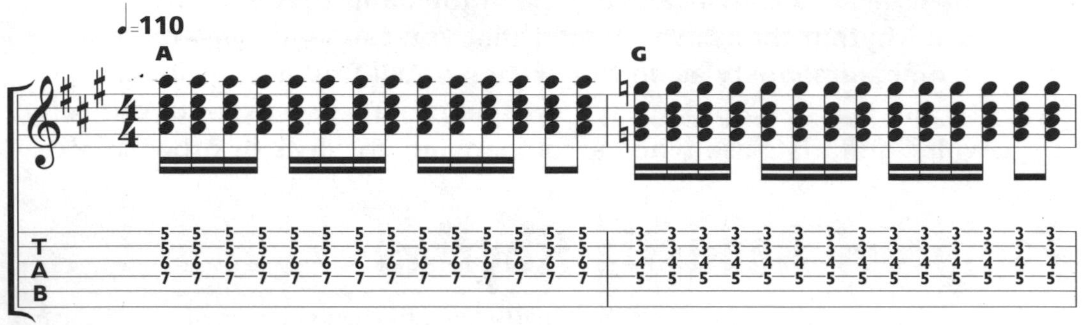

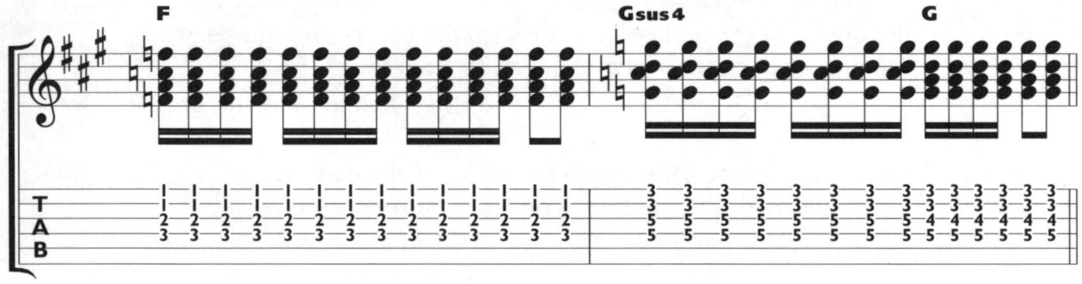

Here's a busy, heavily strummed pattern consisting almost entirely of semiquavers. To avoid sounding 'wooden', try varying the strumming attack and accent throughout. Whack the last two beats with wild abandon!

For more ideas, check out **Pete Townshend**'s acoustic on the Who's 'Pinball Wizard', or **Justin Hayward**'s open C-tuned 12-string on The Moody Blues' 'Question'.

'Party 16'

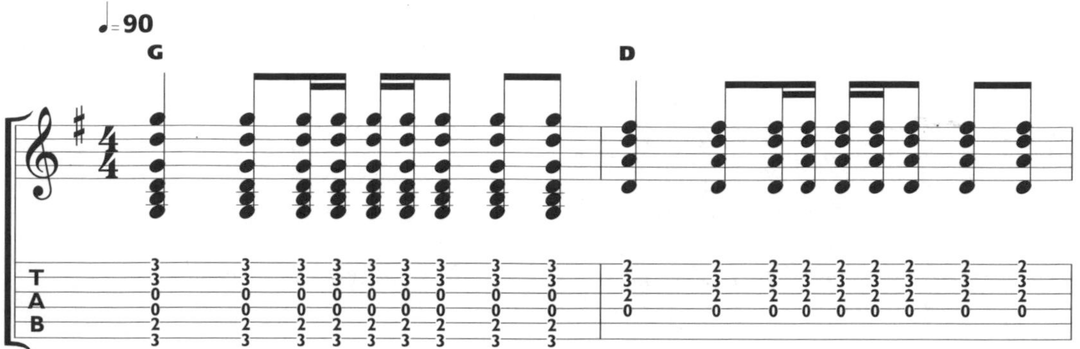

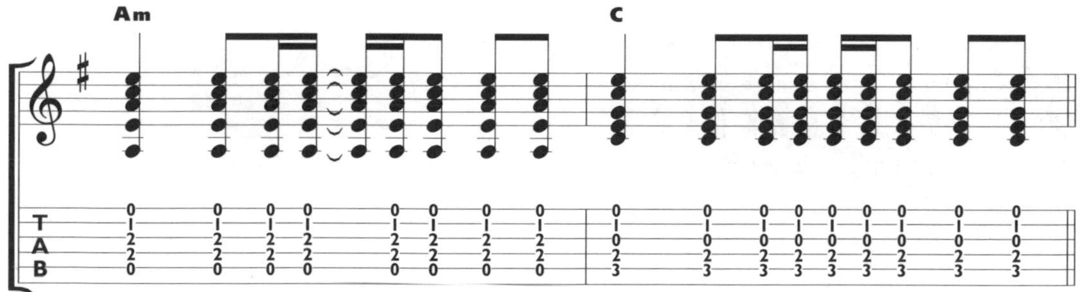

This '90s-style accompaniment rhythm is used by dozens of pop artists, from **Sheryl Crow** to **Oasis**. For a more 'Manchester' type sound, add a little swing to the semiquaver beats.

This style could prove very useful at parties, especially if anyone has the audacity to claim they don't want to sing 'American Pie'!

'Feeling All White'

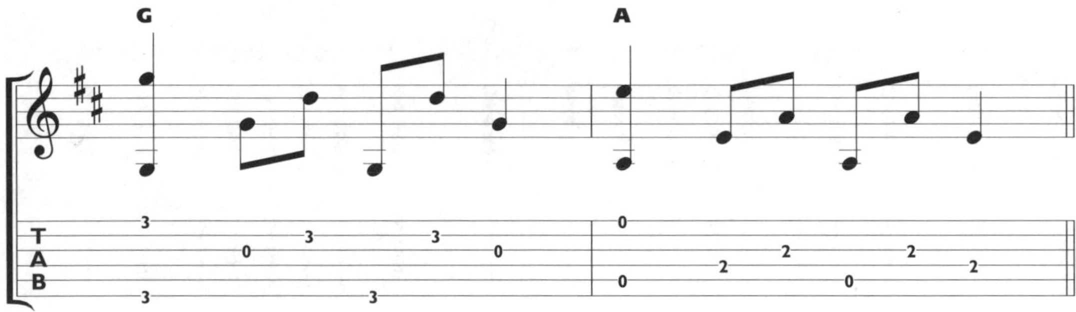

Apparently, **Donovan** showed **The Beatles** this technique in India around 1967. Consequently you'll find the basic pattern all over the *White Album* - take a listen to 'Julia', 'Happiness is a Warm Gun', and 'Dear Prudence' for examples.

Due to the simultaneous root/top notes at the beginning of each bar, this example is best played fingerstyle, with or without a thumbpick.

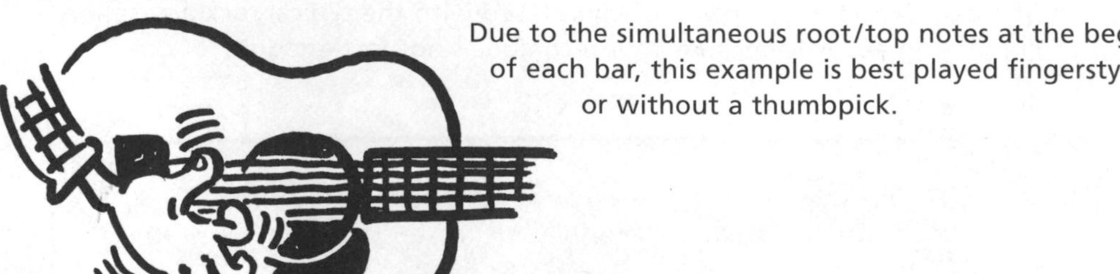

'Showing Off For No Apparent Reason'

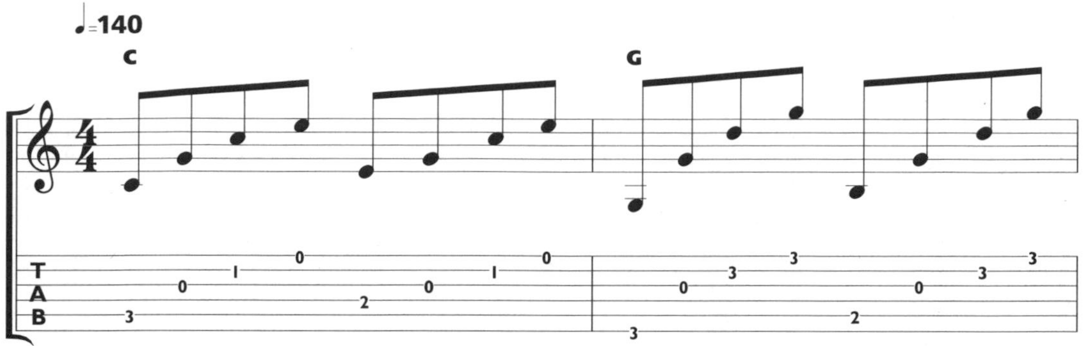

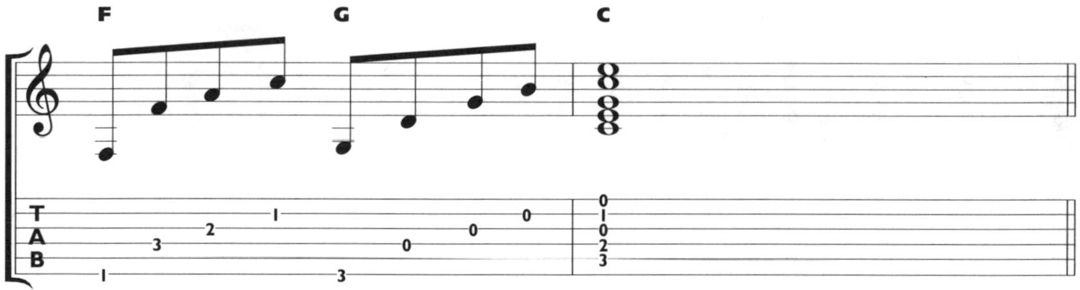

This ascending pattern can be played very quickly indeed once you know the thumb part.

As such, it makes for an excellent bluff when faced with the typical rock accusation that you're playing acoustic because your technique's not fast enough!

'Trumpley Chigwick'

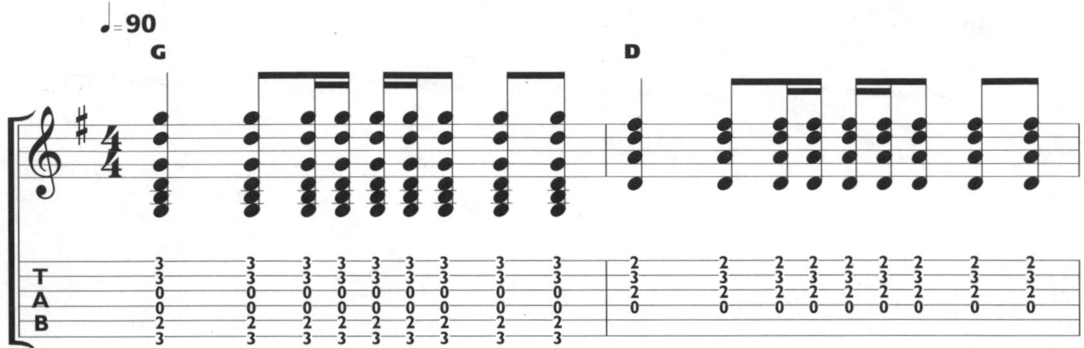

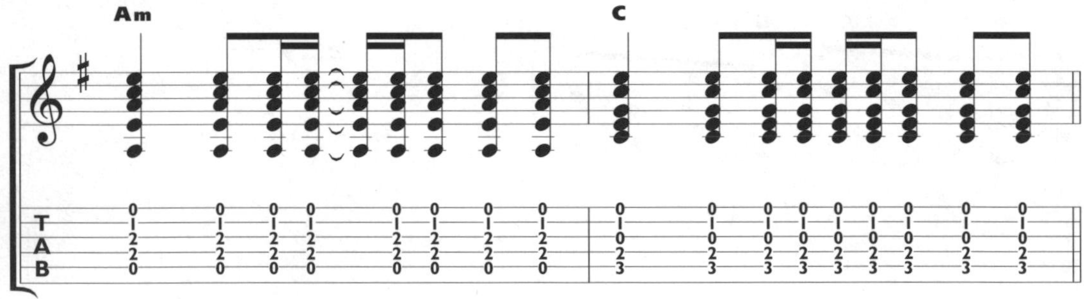

As with most of these patterns, this example is based around the principle of thumb for the three bass strings, with the index, middle and ring finger covering the top three.

Again, this is a standard technique, but you might perhaps recognise a little of the 'Clock' theme from 'Trumpton' there somewhere.

'The Hidden Claw'

One essential skill to develop is your fingers' ability to pluck three strings at once.

After the initial plucked chord, the same notes are arpeggiated - i.e. played one by one. Bar 3 shows the chord changes in half time (for a hint of **Ralph McTell**), followed by the simplest of endings.

Noel Gallagher's four-chord strum-fest 'Wonderwall' became an immediate acoustic favourite.

Musical Examples or 'Don't let them see your fingers or they'll find out how easy it is...'

In this section you'll find 16 musical phrases in progressive order of difficulty, giving an overview of all the common techniques used by acoustic players. Some of them feature a capo, but can be played without if you don't own one.

The one thing that all of these examples have in common is that they sound more difficult than they really are. And let's face it, if you're trying to impress them at your local acoustic jam session, that's what really counts...

Make It Look Difficult

Five easy tricks to make people think you're better than you really are.

- Use a capo really high up (6th-11th fret). The simplest picked chord part sounds more difficult because people are less used to hearing the higher-sounding chords.
- **Remember, any simple picking part played on a 12-string sounds more complicated because of the octave strings. Yes, I know it hurts!**
- Learn two or three syncopated fingerstyle patterns at really high speed. You'll be surprised at how relatively little effort is needed to play a comfortable fingerstyle pattern at a fast tempo.
- **Use a combination of fingerpicking and hammer-ons (with the fretting hand). Never fails.**
- Try to figure out chord shapes which use open strings combined with really high fretted notes. Then try fingerpicking them.

'Alternative Country?'

The country feel of this one is influenced by **Chet Atkins** and **Merle Travis**. This is an 'alternating' bass pattern and can be played with or without a plectrum.

Bluffer's Tip

If you want to flat pick this riff use only down strokes and keep the attack nice and even. If you are fingerpicking, use your thumb for the bass notes, with index middle and ring fingers chiming out the top line.

'Plectrum Fingerstyle?!'

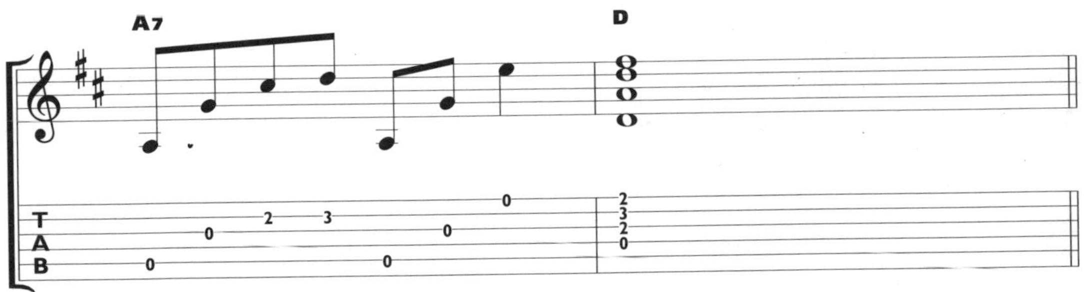

Once you enter the realms of fingerstyle/flatpicking, the acoustic guitar has infinite possibilities. This riff will project better with a plectrum. Think of **George Harrison**'s playing on 'Here Comes The Sun', where the acoustic guitar could carry the whole track - including the vocal melody - with no accompaniment whatsoever!

This is a great way to impress other players with a minimum of effort.

'Babe I'm Gonna Pick You'

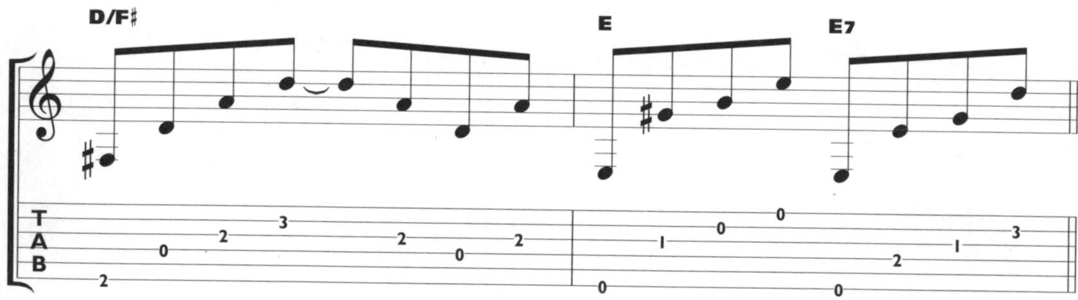

Most suitable for fingerstyle or fingers with a thumbpick, this riff features a pattern similar to 'Babe I'm Gonna Leave You', from the first **Led Zeppelin** album. With the exception of bar three, the arpeggiated chords are arranged in an ascending pattern throughout.

'All The Wrong Chords'

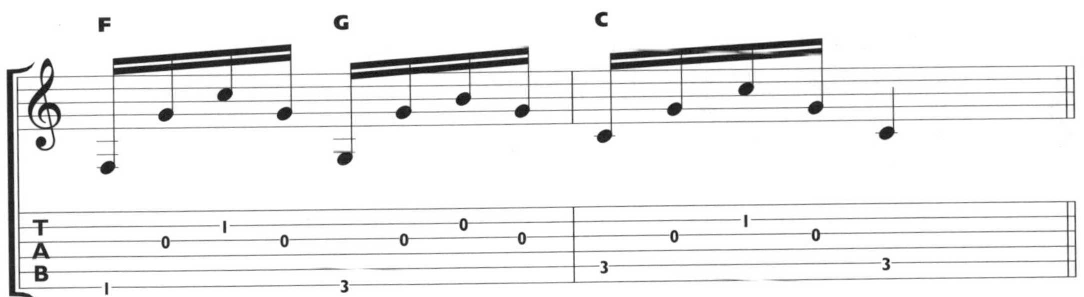

This brisk two-to-the-bar pattern demonstrates the freedom fingerstyle playing can provide from traditional chord voicings/fingerings.

The first fret of the second string is held throughout, while the bass note moves to imply different harmonies every beat. Though taking its origins from the classical guitar, this is a must in every acoustic bluffer's arsenal.

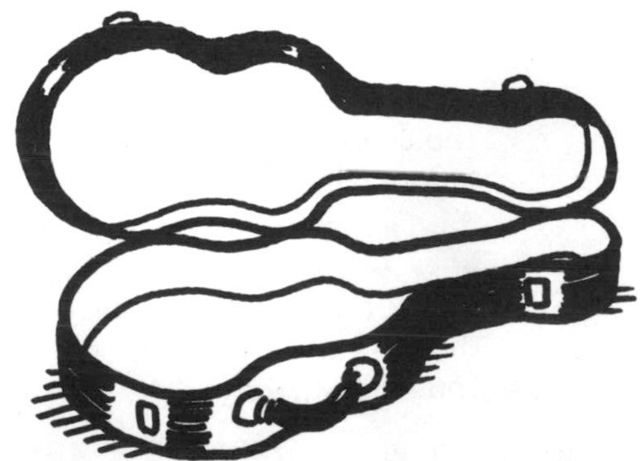

'Bob's Clawhammer'

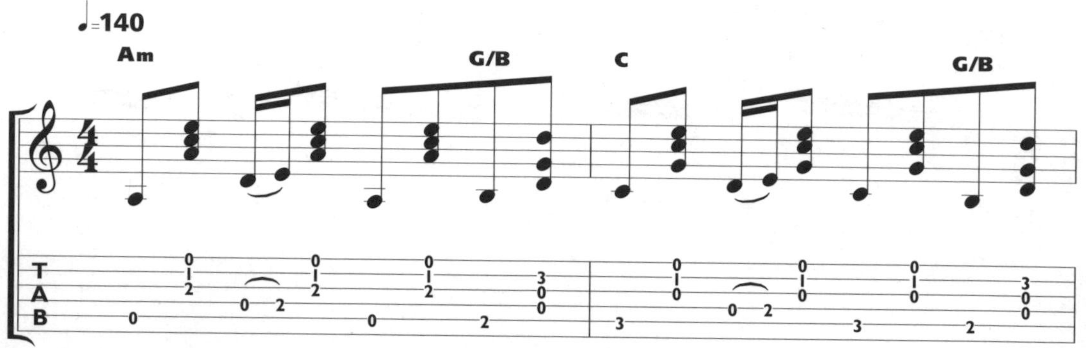

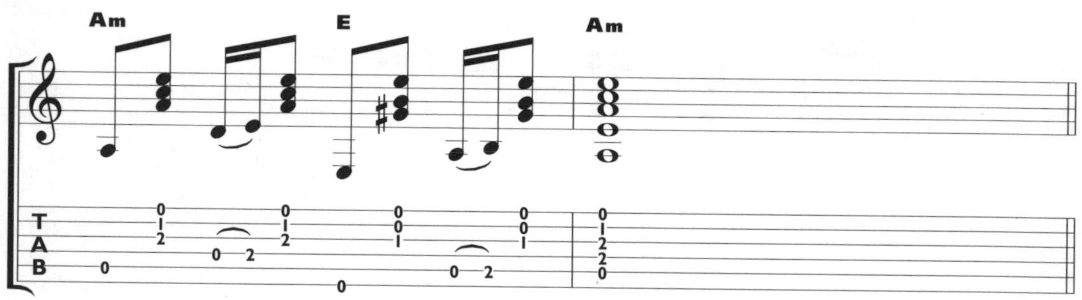

If you incorporate hammer-ons into a pattern which uses a finger 'claw' technique, it's called - you guessed it - clawhammer technique. This example is influenced by early Country and American folk-blues, which was later taken on board by **Donovan** and **Bob Dylan**.

The chord changes in this style of music don't need to follow the same 'rules' as far as timing goes. Bob would often hold on to a chord for an extra beat, or change earlier in the bar than you may expect.

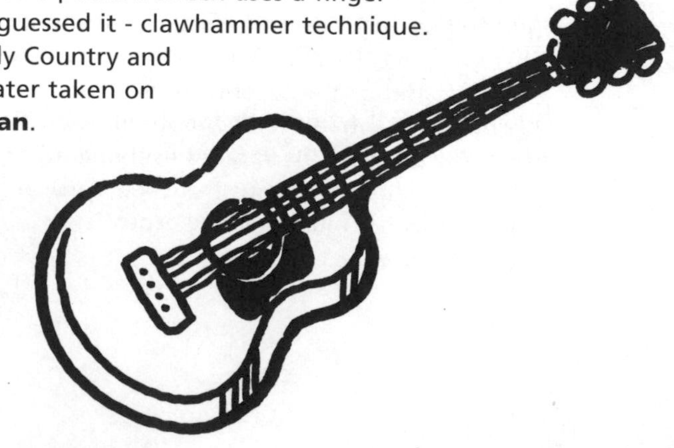

'Protest Too Much'

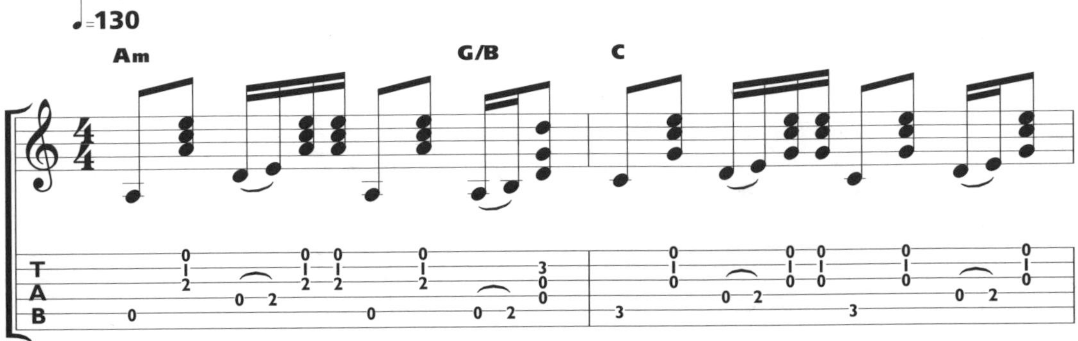

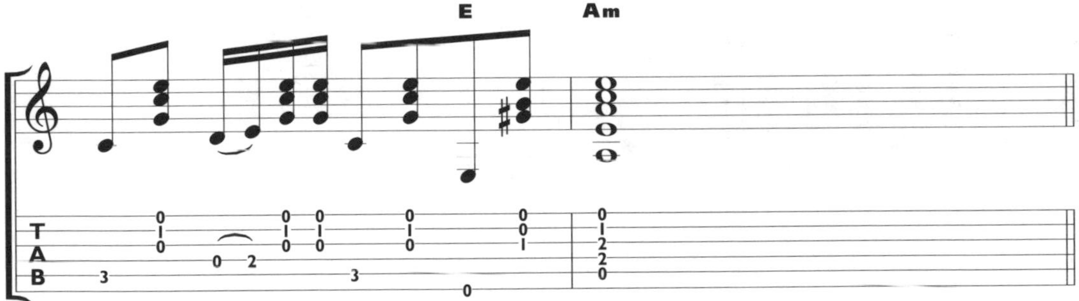

Moving forward a few decades, here is a clearer example of the **Dylan**/protest song style. Usually played with a plectrum, Bob would usually stick with open chords and use a capo to change key for different songs.

Again, watch the third bar for a demonstration of the 'freetime' approach, which will endear you to dyed-in-the-wool folkies and blues dudes alike.

'Carter Picking'

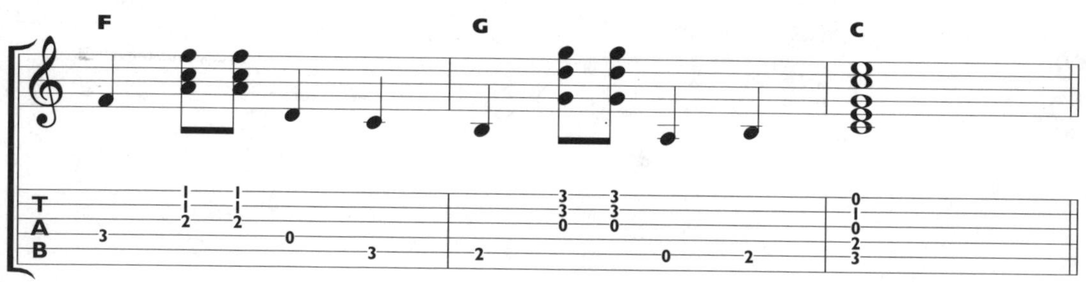

This example demonstrates how you can create the illusion of two guitars playing at once by playing the tune in the bass and strumming the top few strings in the gaps between notes, as popularised by 1930s Country band **The Carter Family**.

Using a capo at a higher register can give a banjo-like effect.

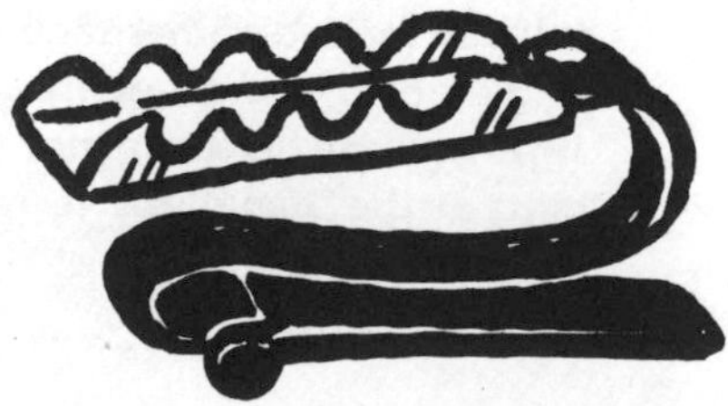

'Droning On And On About India'

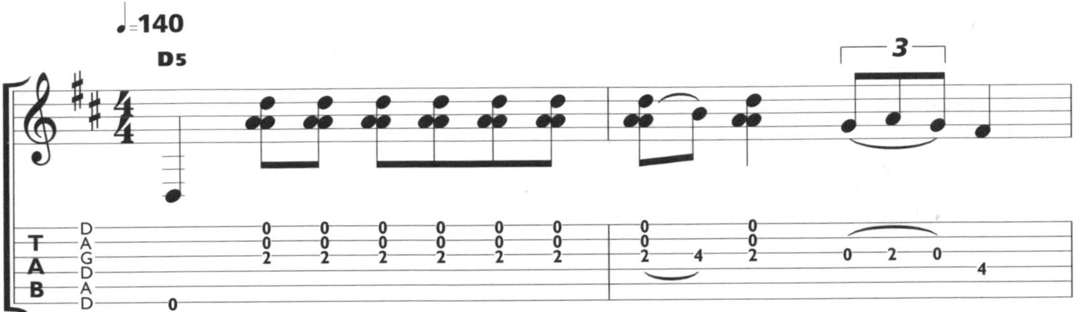

Here's our first example in a tuning (see page 237) - this one uses DADGAD. The riff itself keeps things moving, while the open strings act as a drone, or pedal note.

Apparently based on a sitar tuning, it's easy to hear the Indian heritage if you try sliding single notes or octaves around the neck, **Jimmy Page/Nick Harper** style. The last bar hints at the 'banjo roll' technique favoured by country players.

'Sliding A Broom'

This typical bottleneck/slide pattern uses open D tuning (as in **Elmore James**' version of the blues standard 'Dust My Broom'). Open tunings are probably the biggest secret of slide playing, as they allow whole or partial chords to be played using only the slide.

Style Tip

Mute behind the bottleneck with your fretting hand for a cleaner, more defined sound.

'Little Ben'

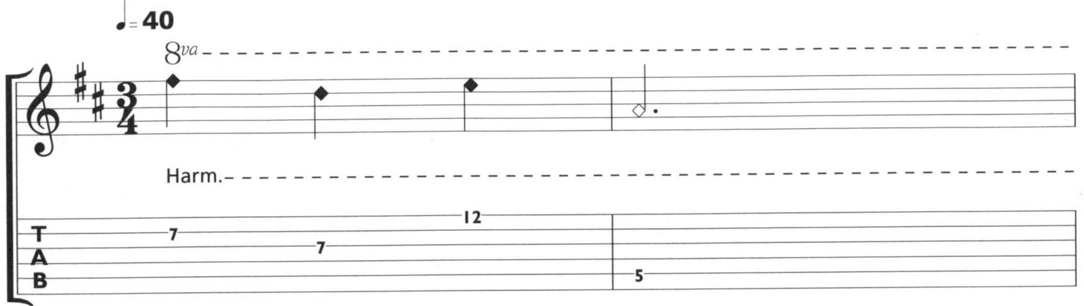

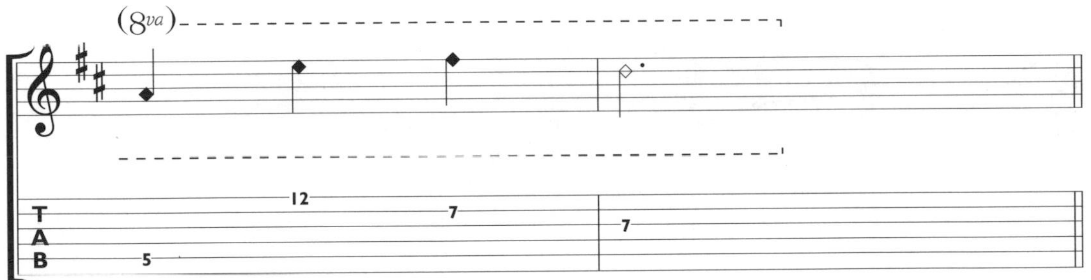

Okay, so this one isn't all that difficult, but it does demonstrate how melodies can be played using harmonics exclusively. This 'Big Ben Chimes' example is only the beginning.

To hear this technique being taken further, check out 'Horizons' from **Steve Hackett**'s acoustic album *Bay Of Kings*.

'Hedgerow Of Harmonics'

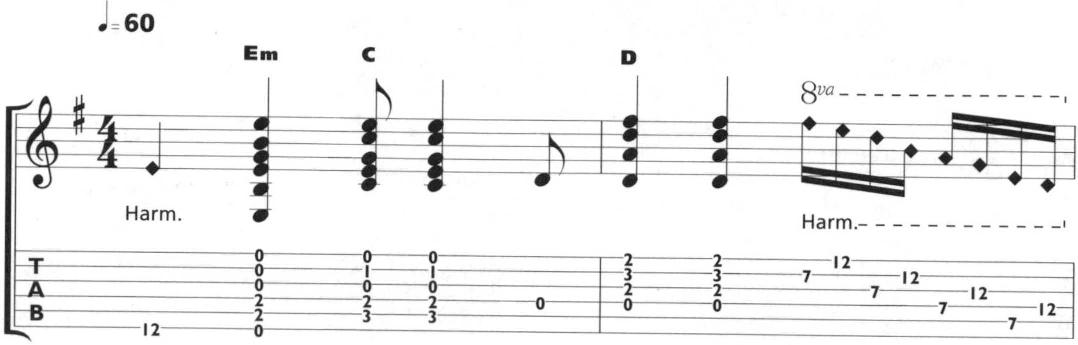

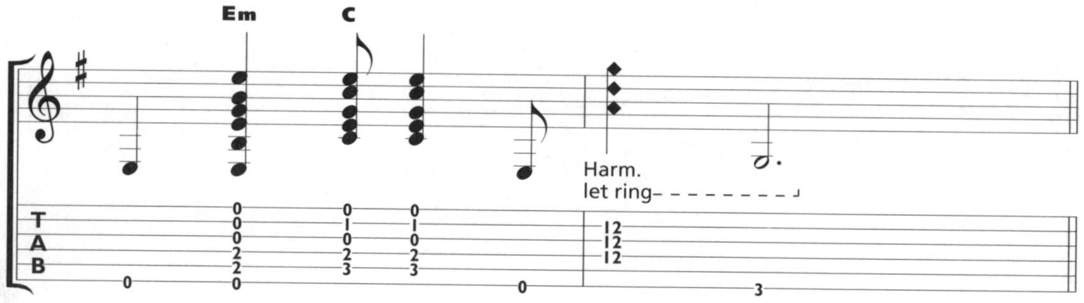

Incorporating natural harmonics into a riff gives an impressive effect, without having to make a supreme amount of effort.

During the second bar, ripple out these **Michael Hedges**-style harmonics at the 7th and 12th frets, jumping seamlessly back into the main riff. To finish, the 12th fret harmonics are superimposed over a low E, then G, to give your listeners an extra surprise!

'Rollin' Banjos'

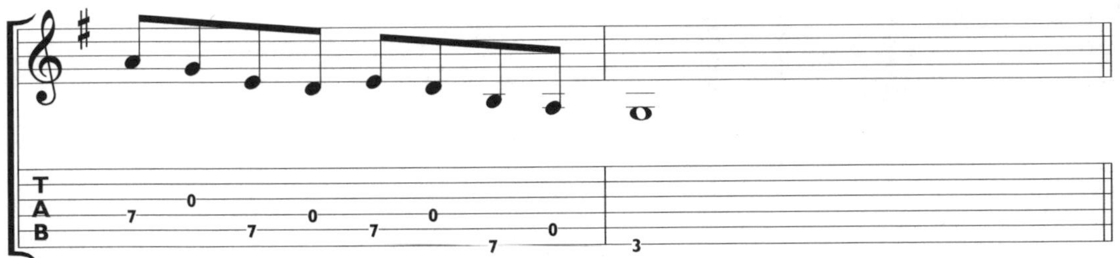

This example of a banjo roll technique combines open and fretted notes to produce ringing scalic lines. Famously associated with **Chet Atkins**, the sky is the limit as far as tempo is concerned!

There are lots of opportunities for this kind of playing all over the fingerboard - if you can find them! Try this approach using open tunings and you'll really flummox the tab transcribers in your audience.

'Byrds In The Hand'

This bluegrass style lick is based around the style of **Clarence White**.

Entirely in open position, it features two different parts. It starts with a descending scale pattern with repeated open string pedal tones, followed by a chromatic alternate-picked line in the last two bars.

This will take some practice, but will earn you the respect of even the most cynical acoustic expert.

The legendary **Clarence White** - the grand-daddy of open-position plectrum flatpicking.

'Harping On'

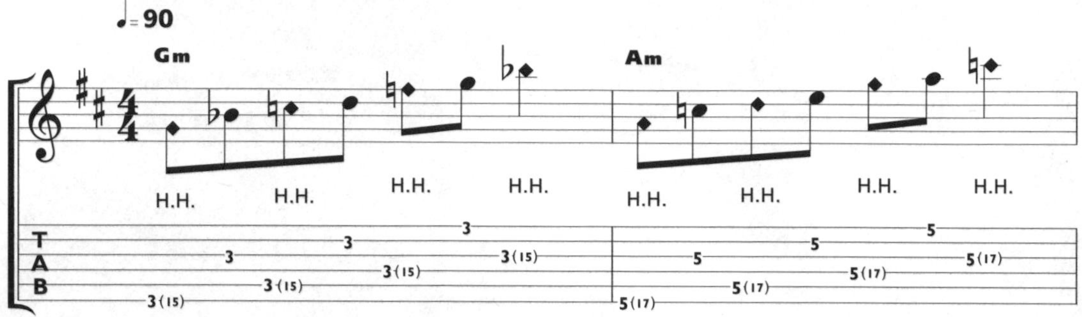

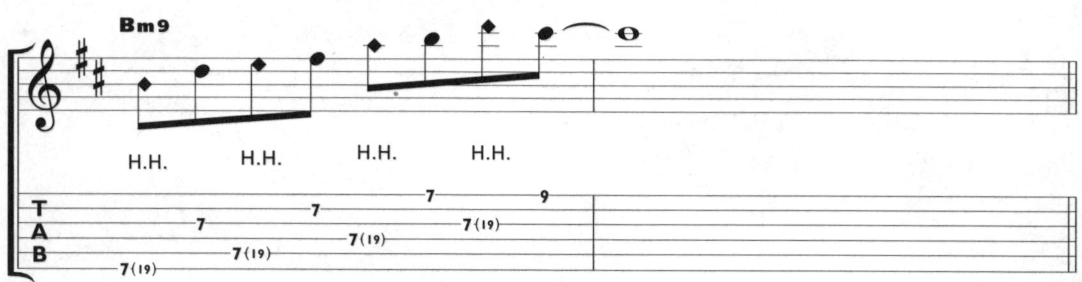

Once you've mastered the technique required to fret and pluck the harmonic simultaneously, be prepared to receive surreptitious admiring glances from other players, who will wonder exactly how you are doing it.

You should keep your back to these people, naturally. Unless they've got a copy of this book too...

'Acousto-Electric'

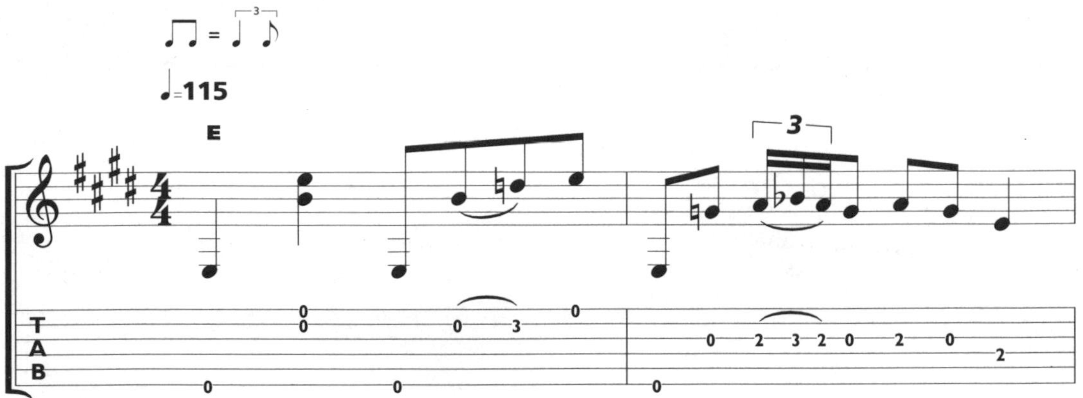

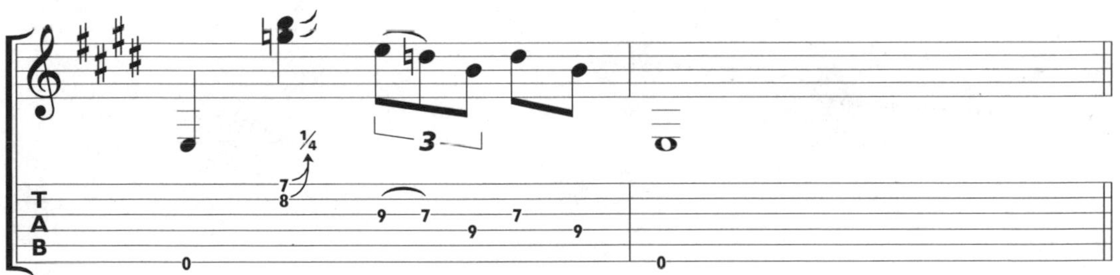

This example shows how acoustic players can borrow electric guitar techniques and adapt them for their own ends.

Here, the bluesy quarter-tone bends should work even with heavy strings, and the hammer-ons are really just there as an aid to speed.

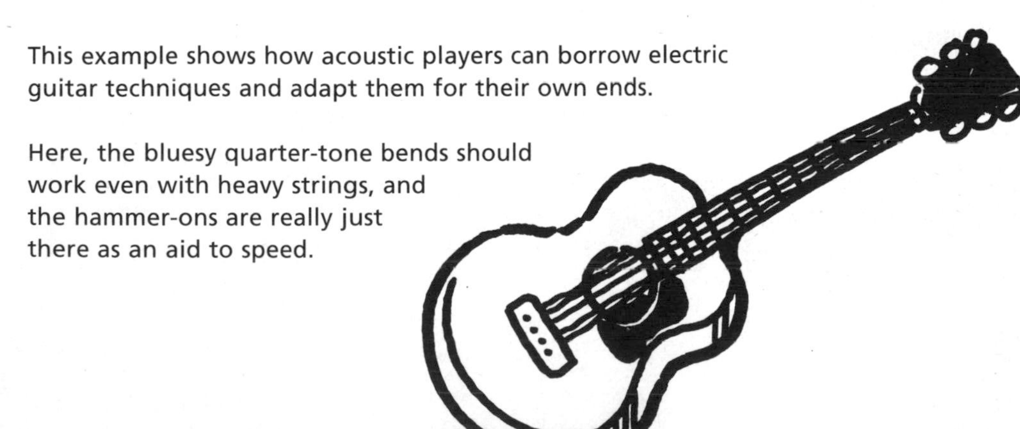

The late **Michael Hedges** - a modern-day virtuoso of the acoustic guitar.

'Easy And Mellow'

Based in the key of G, this fingerstyle workout spends the first four bars using a **Beatles/Donovan** picking style, which shifts up a gear for a descending sequence in bars 7 and 8. This is a classic **Beatles** songwriting device. The Gsus4 chord in the second half of bar 7 is pure **Eagles**, as in the intro to 'Take It Easy'.

Chord Sequences or "Why does everything I play sound like country?"

When acoustic players try to write songs, their musical ideas are often very 'samey'. This is due to the fact that the open chords we all know and love - G, C, D, Am etc - have been used thousands of times by other songwriters.

In this section, the five chord sequences supplied are designed to break your playing out of such ruts by giving you harmonic ideas from a variety of styles. And if someone does accuse your playing of being predictable, you can always tell them that **Bob Dylan**'s a big influence...

Songwriting Cliché Hell

We all do it - write a new song and it just goes G, Em, C etc... and then we realise we've heard it all before. So just how do you avoid all your own clichés?

- Try a new tuning. Even simple dropped D will give you new ideas for chords.
- **Try a different strumming pattern. Do you *really* need to use the right hand part from 'Wonderwall' on everything?**
- Play it slower, or faster. A simple change of tempo will alter the feel of the changes and inspire you differently.
- **Learn a new chord! Do your songs always avoid E♭6 because you don't like the sound of it? Or is it really because you can't play it?**
- If it's strummed, play it fingerstyle. And vice versa.

'Loopy Chords'

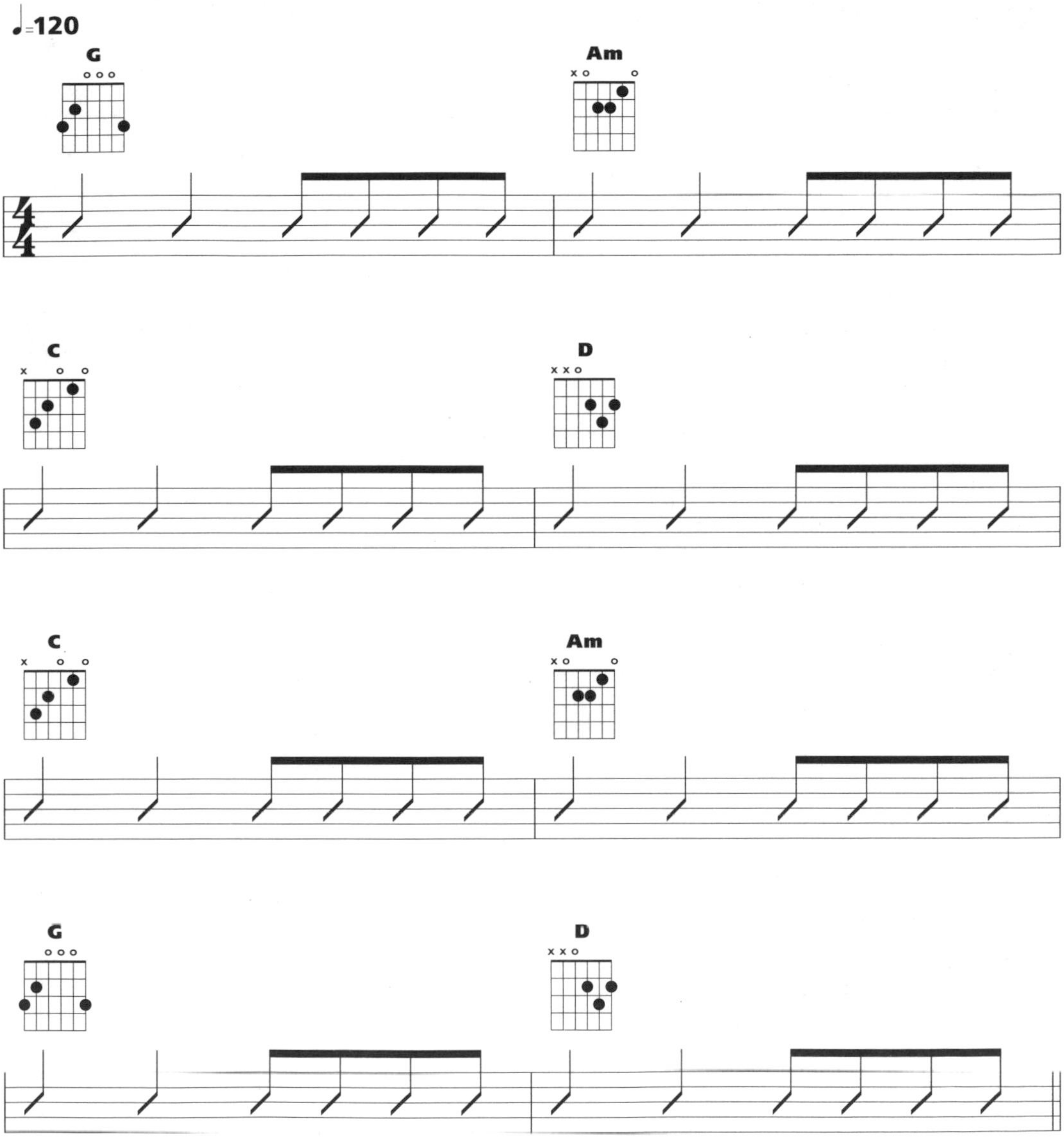

♩=120

G | Am | C | D | C | Am | G | D

This kind of sequence works played over and over, i.e. the final D chord is the ideal vehicle for leading back to the G chord, where you would begin again. The rhythm notation is here for guidance only - depending on the strumming pattern you chose, this could be effective as straight country, blues, R&B or even reggae!

'Jazz At Five'

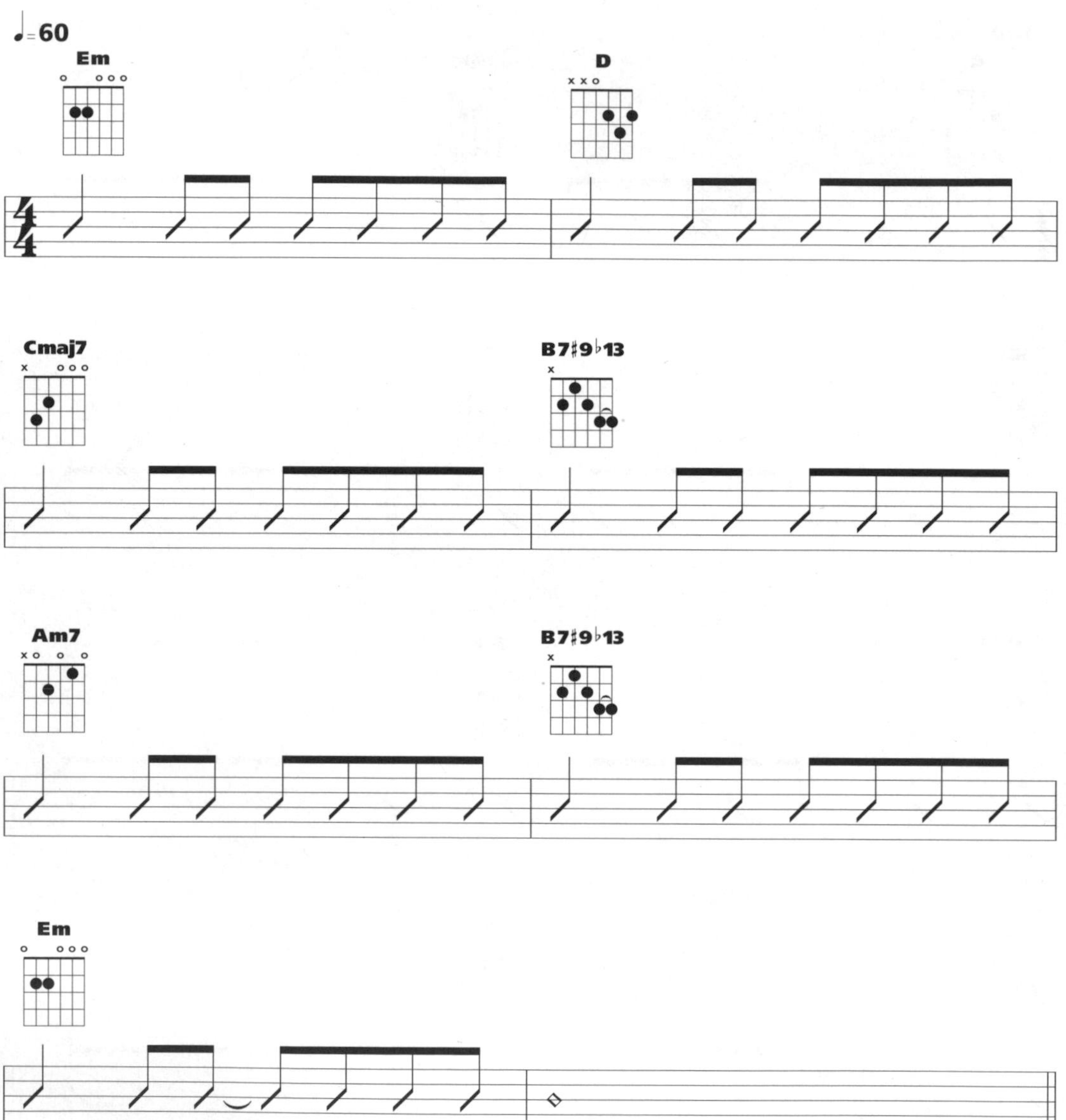

More moody in feel, this E minor based example features a jazzy B7♯9♭13 chord, giving a sound reminiscent of songwriter **John Martyn**. The Am7 adds extra detail to the picture, though the temptation to use these jazzy 7ths all the time is a little like leaving a chorus pedal constantly switched on - you can have too much of a good thing!

'Jingle Jangle Morning'

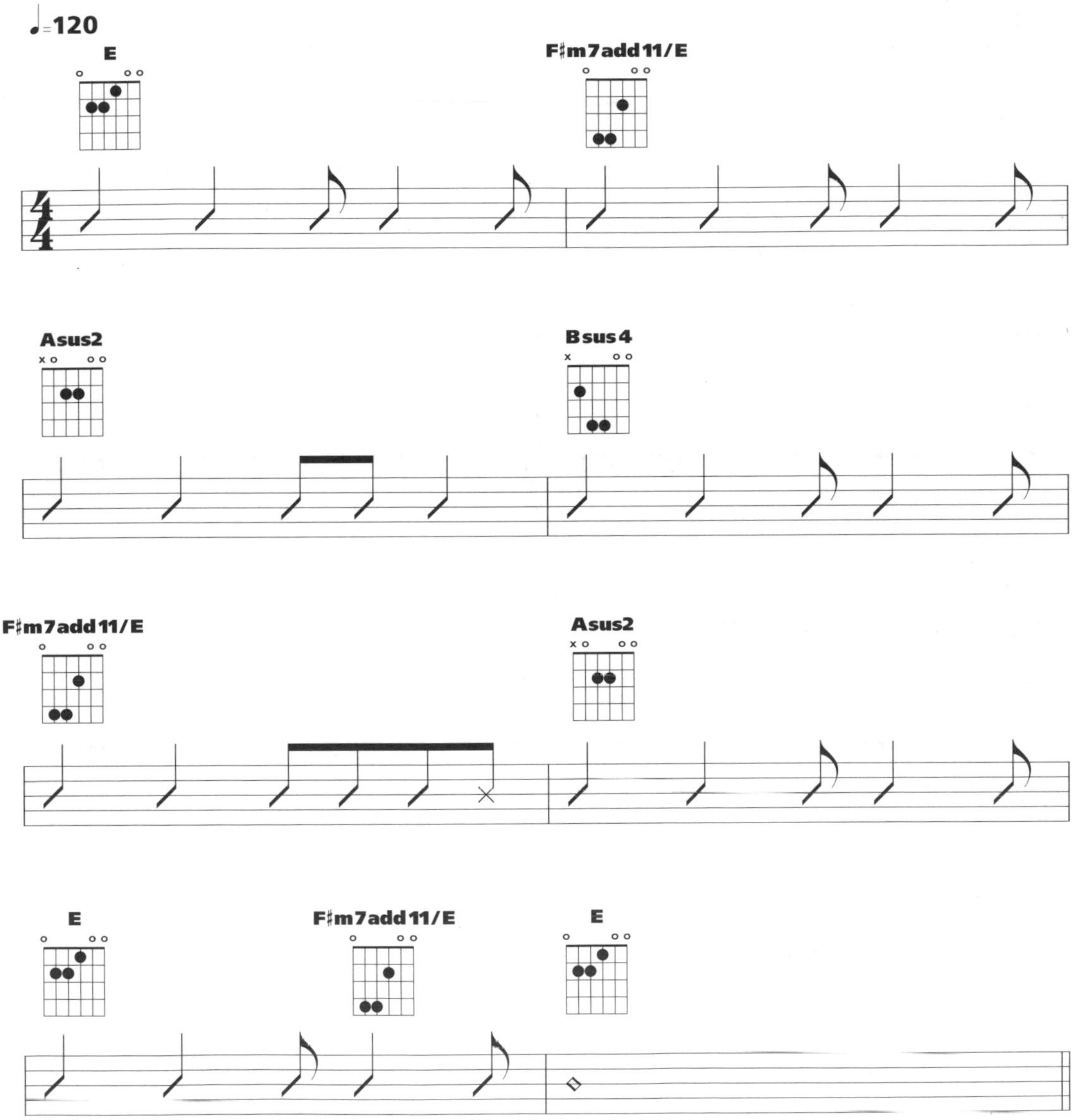

♩=120

E | F♯m7add11/E

Asus2 | Bsus4

F♯m7add11/E | Asus2

E F♯m7add11/E | E

The key to this example is the big-sounding open E voicing – the progression features the first and second strings ringing openly throughout. There are a few rhythmic details added as suggestions, but if you regard this as the big acoustic backing for a country rock song (especially on a 12 string), just sit back and let your strumming arm do the work.

'Acoustic Attitude'

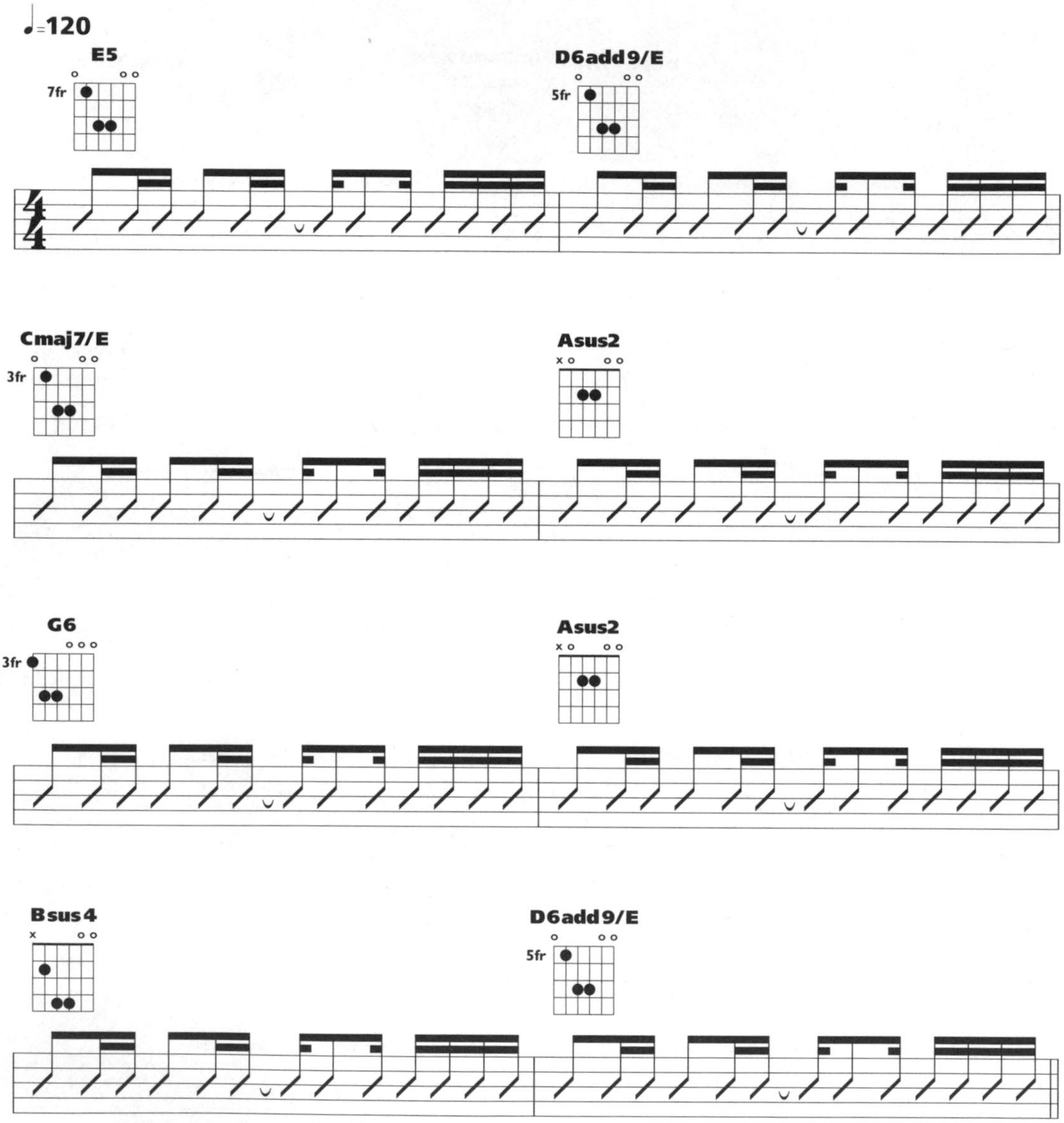

♩=120

E5 (7fr) | D6add9/E (5fr)

Cmaj7/E (3fr) | Asus2

G6 (3fr) | Asus2

Bsus4 | D6add9/E (5fr)

This example has a more dramatic feel, due to the dissonant voicings and frantic strumming pattern. Even raking across the chords slowly, you can feel the tension building, ready to kick back into an acoustic rock feel. This proves acoustic guitars are about more than just real ale and pullovers!

'Cambric Shirt'

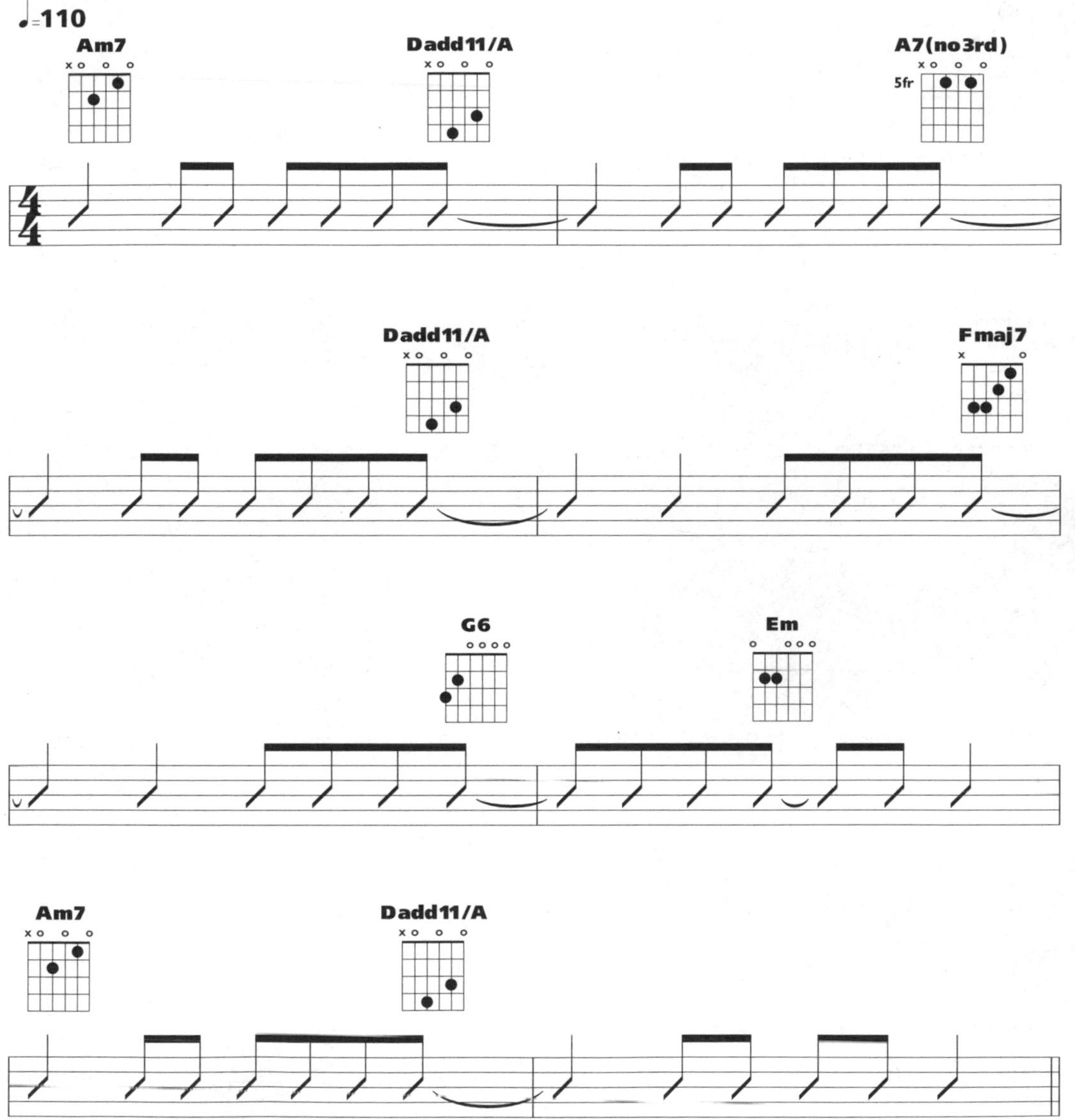

These are actually quite traditional folk chords, especially the ethereal Dadd11/A, which recurs throughout. This sort of voicing features prominently in **Paul Simon**'s arrangement of 'Scarborough Fair' - note that the chords work far better as a picked pattern than as complete strums.

Martin player **Stephen Stills** was a big fan of the EBEEBE tuning - check out his fingerpicked recording '4+20'.

Altered Tunings or "I just don't understand - it was in tune when I got it back from the shop."

One way of avoiding the more obvious clichés of the acoustic guitar is to tune it differently. This can be as simple as altering the bass string to create a low bottom note (The Beatles, Chet Atkins, Stephen Stills) or making up a completely new tuning specifically for the song (Gordon Giltrap, Nick Drake, Paul Simon).

Either way, tunings are a really useful way of coming up with exciting new sounds on the acoustic guitar. In this chapter you'll find five tab examples, each showing a typical usage of that tuning. Tip - the more obscure the tuning, the more you can gleefully annoy other guitarists in the audience who try to figure out what you're playing. And if you use a capo as well you'll probably not make it out of the gig alive...

All The Tunings

Here, I've listed all the other commonly-used alternate tunings for you to try. Don't blame me if you break a string, though!

- **"DOUBLE DROPPED D" DADGBD** Same as open G but without the A string altered.
- **"DROPPED C" CADGBE** Just drop the bottom string two semitones lower and play a big C major chord.
- **"OPEN D MINOR" DADFAD** Good for English folk, this one.
- **"ALL THE 4THS" EADGCF** Only used by a few jazzers and some 6-string bass players. Difficult.
- **"DADGAE"** A variation on DADGAD, as used by Joni Mitchell.
- **"NASHVILLE" EADGBE** The three bass strings are tuned an octave higher (so you need thinner strings!). Popular in Country, y'all.
- **"LAZY BOTTLENECK" EADGBD** A quick way of tuning your guitar to open G which works for bottleneck lead parts, as long as you don't play the two bass strings.
- **"E♭ TUNING" E♭A♭D♭G♭B♭E♭** The whole guitar, dropped a semitone in tuning.
- **BARITONE TUNING** Any tuning (usually regular, dropped D or open G) with all the strings dropped a fourth or a fifth (e.g. regular tuning would become BEADF♯B).

'Dropped D' - DADGBE

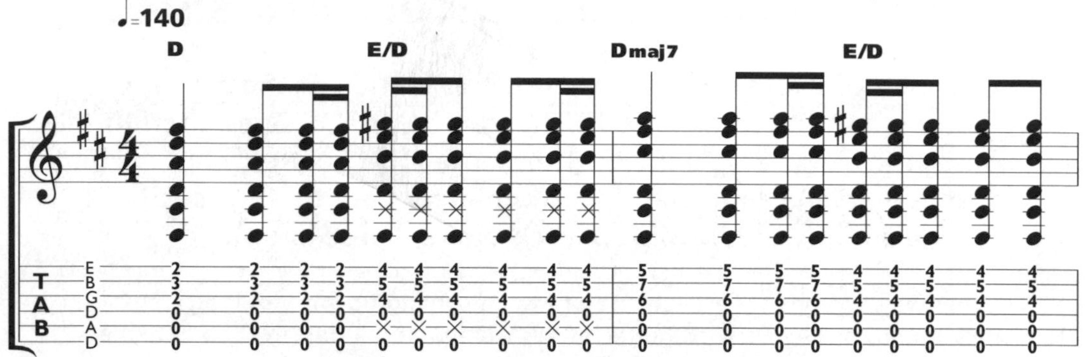

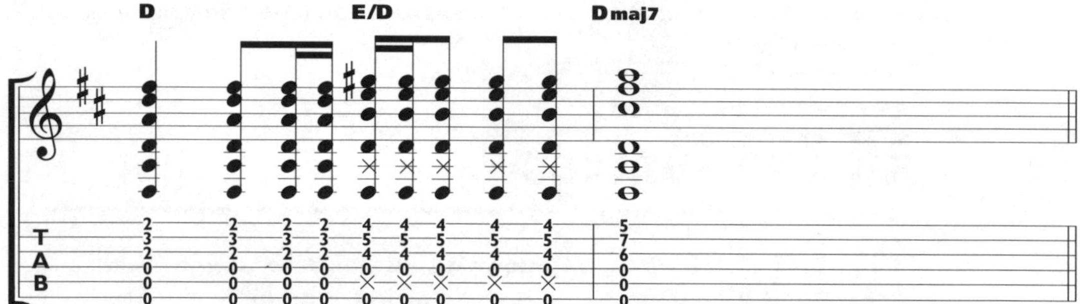

Taking the 6th string down to D gives you lots of freedom with moveable D major/minor chord shapes, as you can leave all six strings ringing all the time.

Of course you may want to save the impact of this low D for a critical moment, as in **Fleetwood Mac**'s 'Oh Daddy'. Using it as a pedal tone under other chords (like A7) can also give pleasant results.

'Open G' - DGDGBD

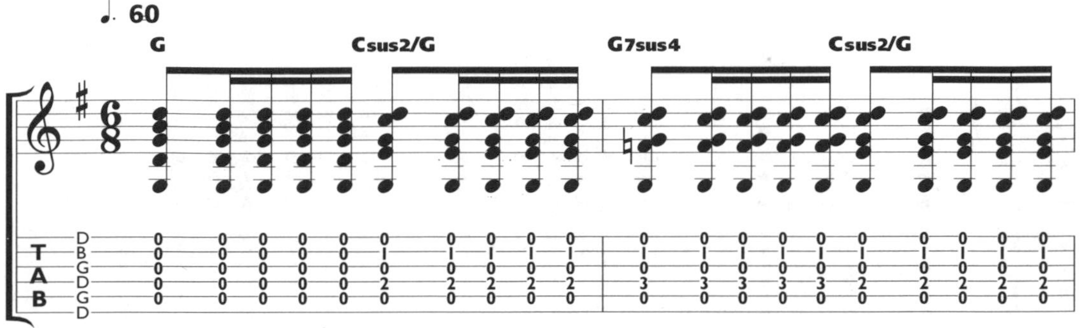

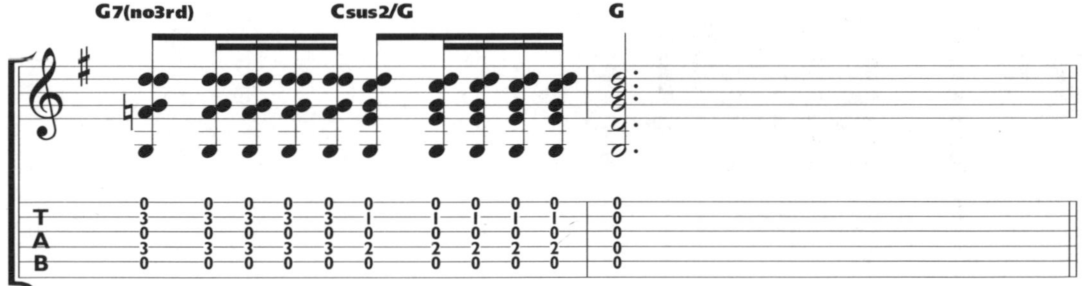

This open G tuning is one of the most popular, and can be heard on recordings by artists as diverse as **The Rolling Stones** and **Gordon Giltrap**, whose smash hit 'Heartsong' (known to many as the theme for TV show 'Holiday') uses this tuning in a similar pattern. The sixth string - detuned to D - is not often used.

'Open D' - DADF♯AD

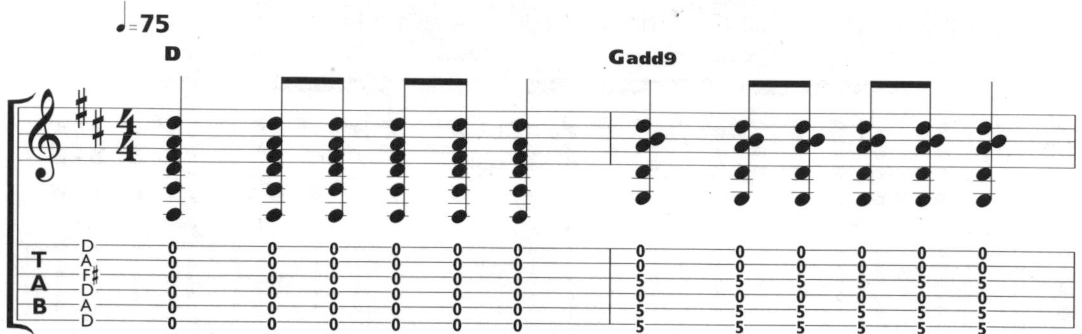

Another popular folk tuning, this open D is along similar lines to the open E used by **Joni Mitchell** in 'Big Yellow Taxi'.

It lends itself to big, full-sounding strummed chords. Most patterns which work in open G can be transferred across a string for a deeper, more resonant sound.

This tuning can also be heard in action during the acoustic intro of the **Stones**' 'You Can't Always Get What You Want'.

'Open C' - CGCGCE

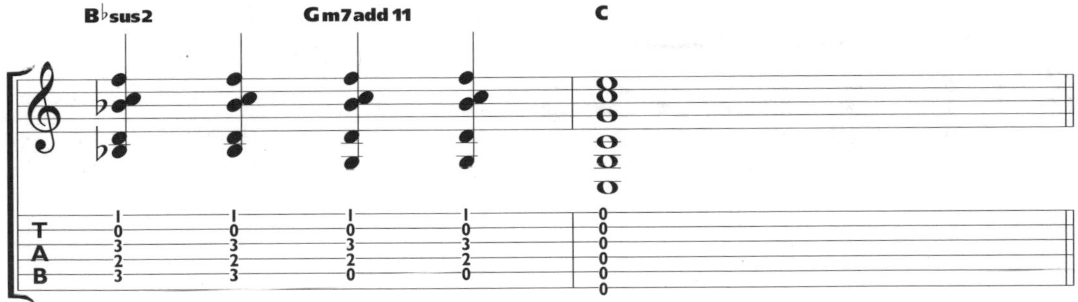

This tuning is great for meandering Indian influenced lines, using the open strings as a sitar-like drone (remember **Jimmy Page**'s 'CIA' connection?).

This example demonstrates a moving octave shape over the C drone, changing to some open position chords which would be totally unplayable in standard tuning. Let it be our secret...

'Dad-Gad' - DADGAD

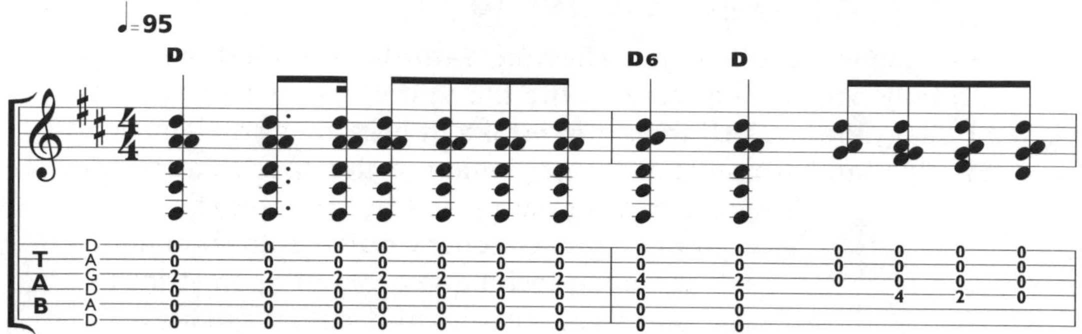

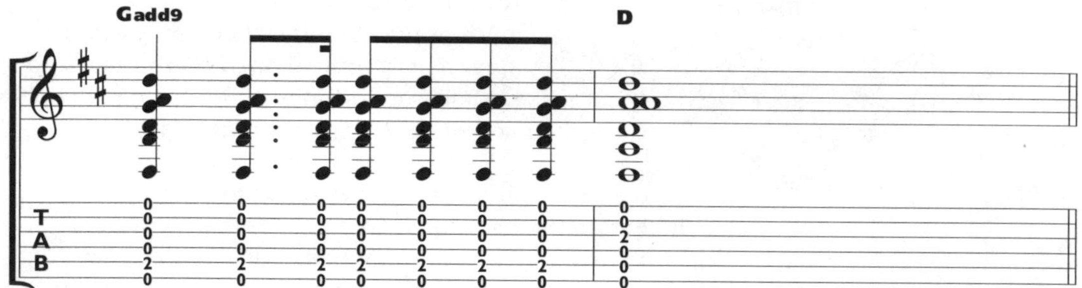

If you're a **Zeppelin** fan, this tuning suggests 'Black Mountain Side' and 'Kashmir'. If you prefer the older school of folk guitar playing, think of **Davey Graham** and **John Renbourn**.

Whichever way you look at it, this tuning is as authentically 'folk' as a flagon of cider with a plate of kippers, under the olde (f)oak tree.

Music Shop Classic or 'How do I fit everything in this book into 24 bars of showing off?'

Even the most sullen, gum chewing Saturday assistant breaks into a grimly patronising scowl at the thought of yet another version of 'Blackbird'. Watch the sharp intake of breath as you launch into the rippling harmonics at the beginning of this specially-designed showcase of your ample ability. This piece has everything a great acoustic guitar solo should – flash-sounding techniques, lots of open strings, and that somehow-heard-it-before quality.

The opening run consists entirely of harmonics, which should be allowed to ring together as much as possible. The chord progression stays mostly around open chord shapes, to maximise opportunites for soloing high up the neck while the open strings ring out.

For the last section, we're moving our fretting hand higher up the neck for some single-note lead playing, with a bluesy quarter-tone bend added in for good measure. The dramatic harmonic ending is played in 'free time', giving you a chance to think up clever answers to all the questions the admiring throng around you are bound to ask!

'Influences'

Just so you know who to name-drop when you're describing your 'influences' to the shop assistant, the Music Shop Classic features techniques and ideas taken from:

Adrian Legg, Michael Hedges, Pink Floyd, Neil Young, Nick Harper, Pete Townshend, Mark Knopfler, Jimmy Page.

Hope it gets you a discount!

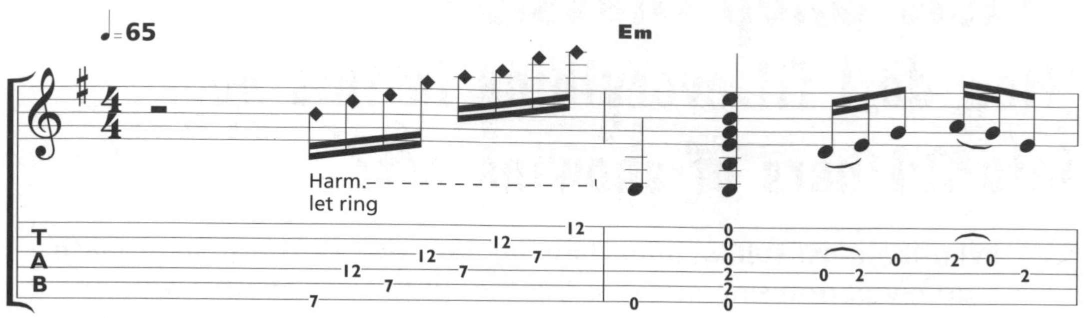
♩= 65
Em
Harm.
let ring
T
A
B

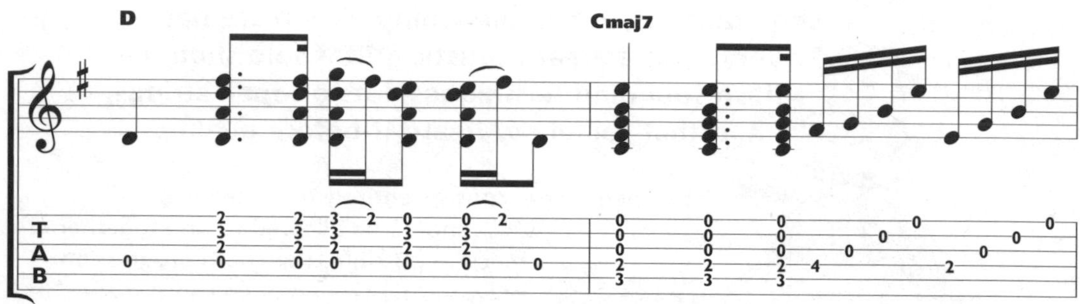
D
Cmaj7
T
A
B

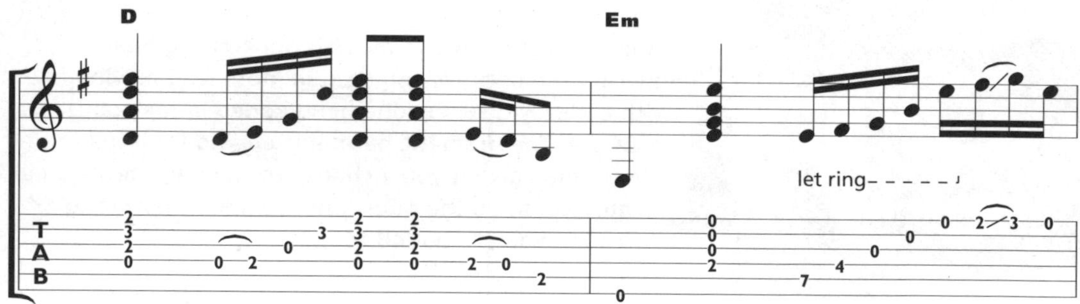
D
Em
let ring
T
A
B

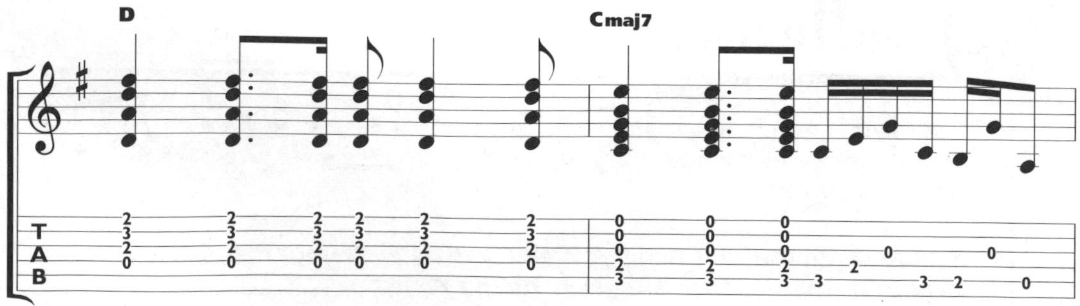
D
Cmaj7
T
A
B

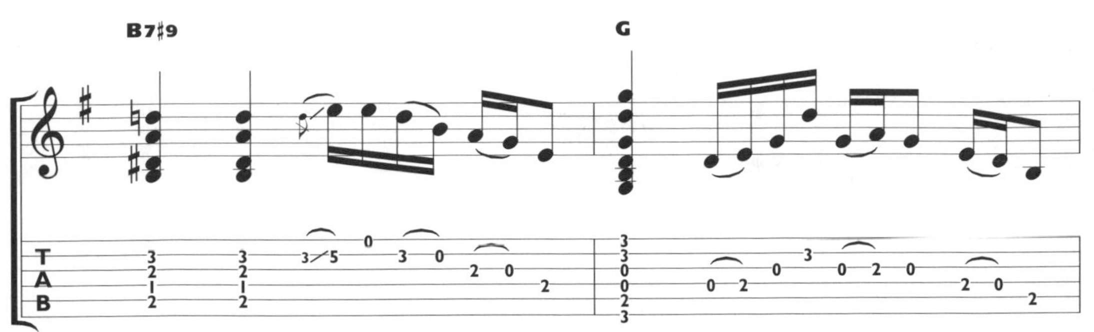
B7♯9
G

D
Am7

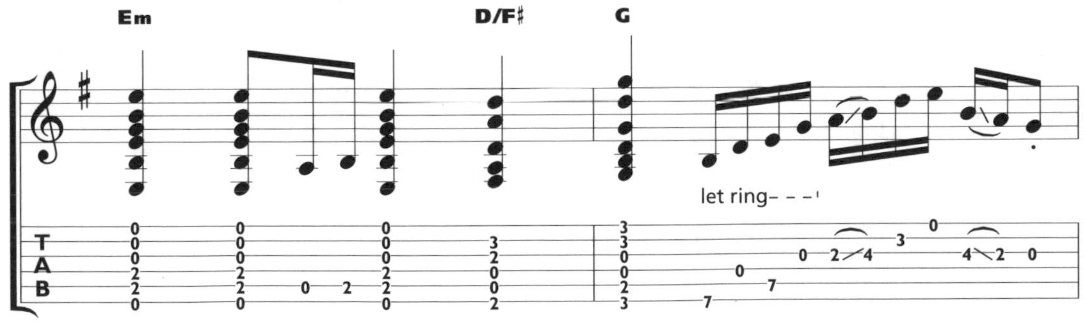
Em
D/F♯
G
let ring

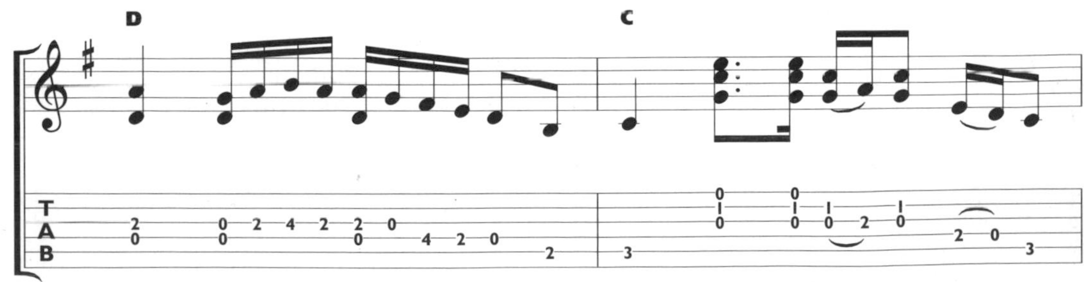
D
C

B7♯9
Em
T
A
B

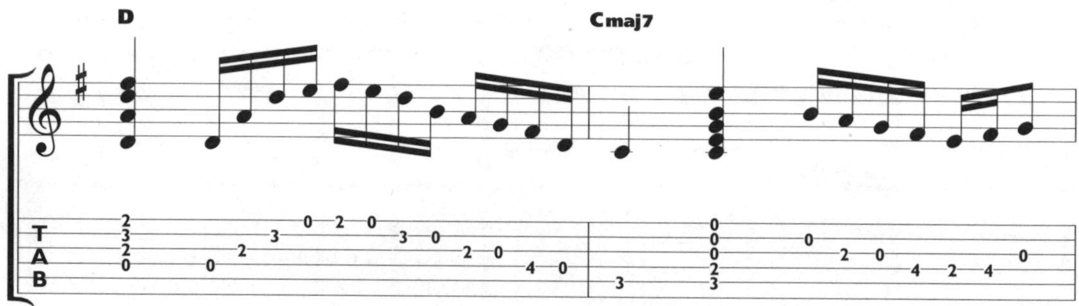
D
Cmaj7
T
A
B

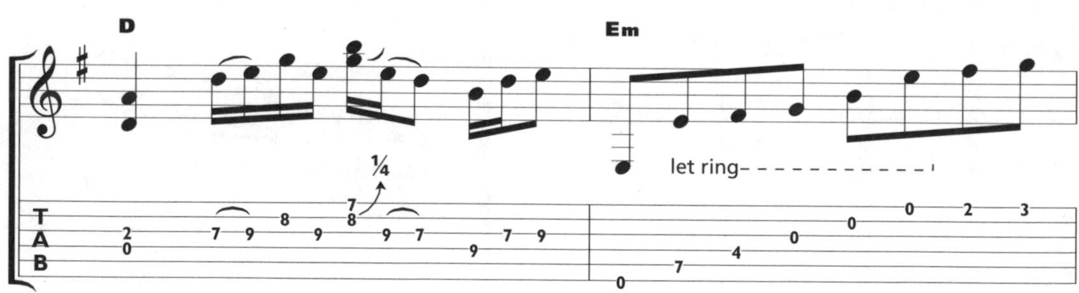
D
Em
¼
let ring
T
A
B

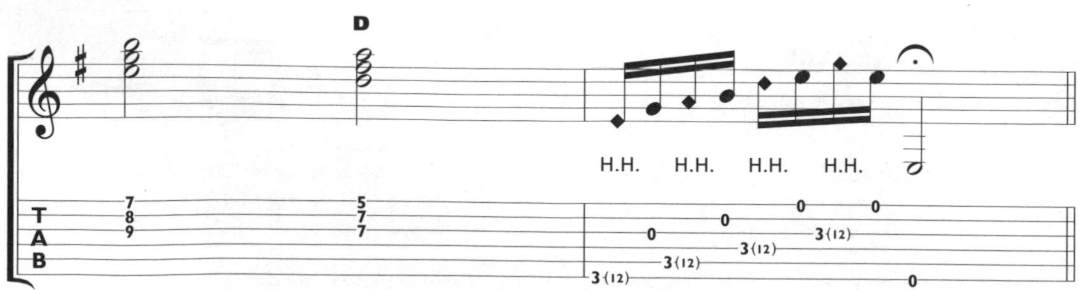
D
H.H.
H.H.
H.H.
H.H.
T
A
B

Music Shop Riffs - the dos and don'ts

If you *have* to play party pieces in a music shop, you might as well choose one of the 'standards'. On this page, I've listed some of the most popular acoustic pieces currently being played in UK music shops.

You can get away with some of them yourself - indeed, several are expected of you - but others will result in laughs of scorn from those in the know. Next to each riff is listed an advisability rating (10 means it's essential repertoire, 1 means you'll be lucky to leave the shop with your nose still attached to your face) and tips on which bit to play.

Title	Artist	**Rating**	Tips
Anji (aka 'Angie')	Davey Graham	**9**	You need your fretting hand thumb over the top of the neck to play this tune, but if you can cope with the speed, it's an excellent showpiece. Most people only learn the first two bars and play them endlessly.
St James' Infirmary	Various	**8**	Great for cementing your Delta Blues credentials. This well-loved minor blues is instant cred.
Alice's Restaurant	Arlo Guthrie	**6**	The guitar part for this classic '60s talking blues is only 16 bars long (even though the song itself lasts for 18 minutes!). Even so, it's a great fingerstyle part with a nice swing to it.
Wonderwall	Oasis	**5**	Has the advantage of being (fairly) contemporary, and dead easy to play, but has worn a bit thin with most retailers now. Capo 2nd fret, in case you didn't know.
Hotel California	The Eagles	**5**	Well-known, but not as clichéd as 'Stairway...'. Go for the fingerstyle intro, but bear in mind that the thumb part isn't a simple alternating 4-to-the-bar.
Streets Of London	Ralph McTell	**2**	A great song in its time, but forced into cliché hell by too many bad folk club versions. Avoid.
Stairway To Heaven	Led Zeppelin	**0**	One of only two intros to be banned absolutely by international treaty. (the other being 'Smoke On The Water'). Never, EVER play this song.

Guitars! or 'Surely it's more important to be a good player?'

More important than technique, waistcoat colour, even beard length, is the type of guitar you're seen with. A player can get away with horrendous musicianship if they own an envy-inducing instrument.

The reasoning goes something like this; if you see someone with a guitar which cost more than your house, you get to thinking that they wouldn't have spent all that money unless they could really get the best out of it. All too often, of course, it just means that they've got more cash than you. But admit it, for a second, when you saw that guitar in its case, you thought the owner was a better player, didn't you?

Here, then, is a selection of the guitars to know if you want to command maximum respect amongst the acoustic community. All usage of jargon has, of course, been maximised for your convenience.

If you're a good player, you can even get away with one of these!

National/Dobro

ANORAK DATA:

In modern times, famously appeared on the cover of the 1985 Dire Straits album *Brothers In Arms*. These all-metal or metal-and-wood guitars had a convex bowl at the front to reflect the sound. They came about because of the need to make the acoustic guitar louder (which is why sales dipped when the electric guitar was invented). The National and Dobro brands were basically the same company, but various corporate arguments, law suits and shareholder buyouts led to great confusion about which was which. Nowadays, either word can be used to describe this type of guitar.

FAMOUS NAMES:

Mark Knopfler, Sol Hoopii (famous 1930s Hawaiian player), various bluesmen (Son House, Bukka White, Blind Boy Fuller).

DESIGN:

The bridge is mounted onto a bowl-like aluminium cone, and it's the cone, rather than the whole guitar body, which vibrates. Even though the bowl appears to be directing the sound towards the back of the guitar, the system does seem to work. More expensive models had a complex three-cone arrangement.

SOUND:

Very loud, allegedly 7 times louder than normal acoustic, and on a par with the banjo. Metal cone reflectors give an upper-midrange emphasis that adds to apparent volume.

KNOWLEDGEABLE FACT:

Some models had a squared-off hollow neck, making them suitable for Hawaiian lap slide techniques, but impossible for regular guitar playing.

INSTANT OPINION:

The classic sound for acoustic bottleneck lead playing. And they look soooo cool...

ACCEPTABLE CRITICISM:

Not very versatile outside of blues and Hawaiian styles.

1935 (Dobro) Regal 16M Artist.

Martin D-28

ANORAK DATA:
This is the original 'Dreadnought' guitar shape, and almost every manufacturer in the world has come up with a similar-looking instrument. (The name, incidentally, comes from the huge 1906 battleship HMS Dreadnought, and refers to the fact that it was the largest Martin guitar). Production model introduced 1931, and still being made today. A vintage D-28 from the early 1930s in good condition can fetch as much as £25,000.

FAMOUS NAMES:
Joni Mitchell, Jimmy Page, Paul Simon, Bob Dylan.

DESIGN:
Spruce top, round soundhole, black pickguard, bound body, ebony fingerboard (old models), rosewood fingerboard (new models). Basic and uncomplicated.

SOUND:
Due to its large body size, a D-28 gives a rich, deep bass end and a warm midrange. Beware - although a cheap copy may look the same, it will always sound different due to different construction materials.

KNOWLEDGEABLE FACT:
In 1959 Martin brought out an electric version, the D-28E. This curious-looking beast had two pickups, two volume and two tone knobs, and a three-position slider switch. Not popular with the purists!

INSTANT OPINION:
Worth selling your house for. If it's a vintage one, throw your soul into the bargain.

ACCEPTABLE CRITICISM:
No-one's soul is worth that much cash.

1940 Martin D-28 with Herringbone Trim.

Ovation

ANORAK DATA:
Ovation guitars are best-known for their synthetic round backs. Founder Charles H. Kaman initially approached Martin with his revolutionary guitar design ideas, before deciding to start out on his own. First model was the 1967 Balladeer. Still best-sellers, although the synthetic design still worries some traditionalists. Kaman music also owns Takamine guitars.

FAMOUS NAMES:
Glen Campbell, Jimmy Page and Richie Sambora (both twin-neck 6/12 strings), John Williams and Kevin Peak (roundbacked classicals with '70s supergroup Skye), Adrian Legg, Al Di Meola.

DESIGN:
Apart from a flat wood top (it's actually laminate of wood and carbon graphite), the rest of the body is all synthetic. Most models are active electro-acoustic, with a piezo pickup, 3-band EQ and volume control. Distinctive bevelled headstock.

SOUND:
The bowl back reflects a lot of mid and treble, and when plugged in the pickup adds yet more top end. There's not a lot of bass to be had but this can be partly fixed with the tone controls.

KNOWLEDGEABLE FACT:
Charles H. Kaman had a background in helicopter design, forming the Kaman Aircraft Corporation in 1945. The original Ovation prototypes were built by aerospace engineers.

INSTANT OPINION:
The most revolutionary acoustic guitar design this century.

ACCEPTABLE CRITICISM:
When unamplified, the guitars don't have the same rounded warmth as large-bodied wooden acoustics.

1978 Ovation Adamas with fibreglass 'bowl' back.

Unplugged? or 'How loud should I have the amplifier?'

Have you ever watched an 'acoustic set' by any guitar-based artist? Chances are, they're using more technology than the space shuttle program to create their sound. If the acoustic guitar is going to be recorded or amplified, you need to get its sound into a combo or mixing desk in some way.

On this page I've shown some tips on amplifying the acoustic guitar, based on the pitfalls that many players experience when they try to play a live acoustic set for the first time.

There are two basic methods - mike up an acoustic guitar, or use one with an on-board pickup. If you want a convenient, consistent sound, I'd strongly recommend the latter. Apart from the fact that microphones are more prone to feedback, peripheral noise, stands falling over etc, they have the added disadvantage that they pick up the sound of your swearing when you hit a bum note...

Strings

- **Use new strings if you can afford to - they have more treble and will stay in tune better (once you've stretched them, that is). If you can't afford a new set, clean the existing ones with string cleaner.**
- Don't put nickel electric strings on an acoustic guitars. Use bronze or phosphor bronze types.
- **Don't be a strings wimp! If your guitar is set up properly, you should be able to play with .012 gauge strings quite comfortably. Some acoustic guitar manufacturers recommend you don't use anything less than a .013 set on their instruments. If your style doesn't involve bending notes, you should be able to go to .014 or even higher. Generally, use the highest gauge you can stand - the guitar will always sound the better for it.**
- Have your guitar set up to make sure the nut is cut properly. If it's not, you'll have tuning problems, not to mention some pain on the open chord shapes.

Unplugged tips:

Miking up

- Try to use a guitar with a naturally loud sound - this gives the mic more to work with and will ultimately sound less apologetic. Similarly, thicker strings (0.12 and beyond) will make the body vibrate more, giving you a better/louder tone, and therefore a clearer mic signal.
- If you're using PA, don't place the mic directly in front of the soundhole! The guitar body will act as an air chamber (as it's designed to) and create bass-end feedback.
- Place the microphone in front of the top few frets instead - close to the soundhole but not so close that you get feedback.

Guitars with pickups

- The most common type of pickup is the 'piezo' - a crystal-based pickup which lives in the bridge of the instrument. These are sometimes too bright-sounding, so you may have to turn down the treble to get the most natural sound.
- Just because it's got a jack lead, it doesn't necessarily follow that you have to use effects pedals. Reverb perhaps, chorus if you must, but really, do you need that multi-tapped flange ring modulation distortion filter?
- Don't plug it into a regular guitar amp - use a PA, keyboard amp or dedicated acoustic combo. Guitar amps have speaker systems which are designed to emphasise the midrange frequencies of the electric guitar. Acoustic guitars benefit from a more natural, pure sound.

Many gigging acoustic guitarists use electro-acoustics such as this Gibson. They don't sound *exactly* like a mic-ed up acoustic, but they sure beat bumping into the mic stand.

Above: 1990 Gibson 'Chet Atkins' SST (steel string) electro-acoustic.

Acoustic light-bulb jokes

Q: How many bluegrass guitarists does it take to change a light bulb?
A: What, you mean this sucker's electric?

Q: How many folk guitarists does it take to change a light bulb?
A: Five - one to change the bulb, and four to sing about how great the old one was.

Q: How many blues guitarists does it take to change a light bulb?
A: You mean the light bulb's gone and left me too?

Q: How many keyboard players who try to imitate acoustic guitar sounds does it take to change a light bulb?
A: Two - one to use a sampler to record the original bulb's light, then another one to paint a picture of a candle and say 'hey, that's just like a real light bulb!'

Q: How many fingerstyle players does it take to change a light bulb?
A: Only one - if you can't do the whole thing on your own, your technique's obviously not up to the job.

Q: How many acoustic jazz guitarists does it take to change a light bulb?
A: Man, I only change my bulbs once every ten years, however dead they get.

Q: How many 12-string guitarists does it take to change a light bulb?
A: Only one, but he needs a couple of hours to get ready.

Q: How many capo-equipped acoustic guitarists does it take to change a light bulb?
A: None. Just move the window up a bit, then you won't be needing any other bulbs.

Q: How many guitar makers does it take to change a light bulb?
A: Ten. **One** to scour the Brazilian rainforest for the perfect piece of glass; a **second** to let the glass dry out for 100 years in oak-aged casks; a **third** to treat it with a special secret resin which can only be obtained by distilling the milk of an Austrian mountain yak; a **fourth** to ensure that the bulb and its holder are perfectly bookmatched so that you can't see any difference between the two; a **fifth** to visit the glaziers to insist on laminated glass rather than that cheap bonded rubbish; a **sixth** to put the glass into a mould of his own design which bears no relation to the design of any other well-known light-bulb manufacturers; a **seventh** to apply decorative edging to the socket; an **eighth** to cut his own socket from animal bone; a **ninth** to make sure the bulb is glued, NOT screwed into the socket; and a **tenth** to line the bulb's box with the finest ermine so that its light-giving subtleties will last well into the next century.

Oh, and we have to keep our guitars in low-light conditions at all times to avoid damaging the perfection of the grain, so we won't be needing that bulb.

Campfire Hell

I'm sure that after reading this book you'll have everything you need to build a successful career as an acoustic musician, but even if you do, at some point in your life you'll experience Campfire Hell.

This is where a bunch of players and singers get together late at night and challenge those autocratic and oppressive musical concepts like tuning accuracy, knowing how the song goes and playing the same chords as each other.

If you do get caught in such a situation, it helps to have done some preparation:

Firstly

Learn the entire Beatles back catalogue. That's just under 140 songs, so start with crowd-pleasers like 'Hey Jude' and 'Let It Be' and work your way up to 'The Continuing Story of Bungalow Bill' and 'Revolution #9'. I guarantee you'll be asked to play every Beatles tune at least once in your life.

Secondly

Have at least one classic diddly-dee folk tune at your fingertips (Scarborough Fair, unfortunately, doesn't count because someone's had a hit with it). If you can't start an obscure 'traditional' tune on your own you'll be considered a phoney by the diehards. Don't worry if you don't know one - just improvise a melody in open C and call it 'The Hangman's Gypsy Shanty Mineshaft Disaster' or something. Should fool 'em OK.

Finally

Bring along a capo. It's a dead cert that someone else in the group will have one, so if you're frantically trying to follow their chords, the last thing you need is to be instantly transposing the song as you play. Plus, of course, there's always some dreadful warbling female singer or grunting Johnny Cash impersonator who can't do 'Blackbird' in the original key. Unless you'd rather try and figure it out using barre chords? Thought not.

If you've enjoyed this book, why not check out the other books in this great new series, available from all good music and book retailers, or in case of difficulty, direct from Music Sales (see page 2).

It's Easy To Bluff...

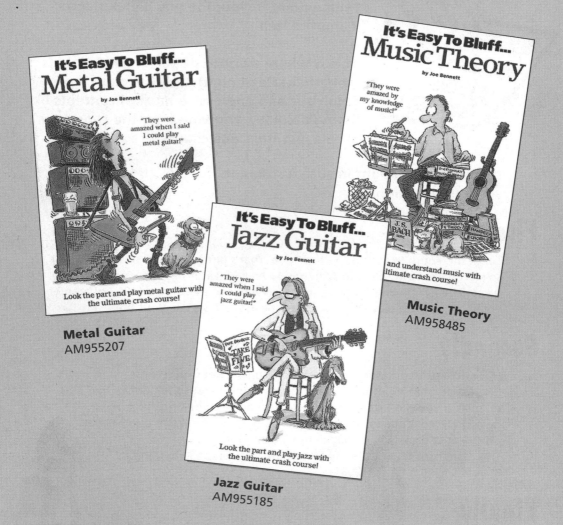

Metal Guitar
AM955207

Jazz Guitar
AM955185

Music Theory
AM958485

JOE BENNETT has been teaching guitar since 1983, and works as a guitarist and lecturer in Bath, UK. He is a senior examiner in electric guitar for the London College of Music, head of Commercial Music at Bath Spa University College, and guitar technology specialist for the International Guitar Festival. Joe's publications include the It's Easy to Bluff and Really Easy Guitar series, The Little Book of Scales and Guitar on Tap, plus tracks and articles for Future Music, PowerOn and Total Guitar magazines.